PRAISE FOR CONSCIOUS CLASSROOM MANAGEMENT

"Every chapter of Conscious Classroom Management, 2nd edition, is filled with practical, take-away strategies on effective teaching that are innovative yet easy to implement. Use this book to learn to teach with compassion, confidence, and clarity as you create a safe and structured learning environment, prevent off-task behaviors before they begin, and intervene appropriately to avoid confrontations with students."

Cindy Douglas
Director of Instruction and Professional Development
Grossmont Union High School District, San Diego, CA

"This is a book for everyone — for classroom teachers and beginning teachers; for principals who wish to coach their teachers to more effective ways of facilitating learning; and for teacher preparation instructors who can use the text to spark meaningful dialogue about teaching, students, and the management of learning. Rick and Grace are exceptional teachers to all of us. Their common sense and creative solutions for student instructional and management issues are invaluable to everyone who loves working with young learners. Written in a wonderfully conversational style, reading this book is almost like Rick or Grace is having that one-on-one talk with you about your work. It's simply that good!"

Michael Murphy
National Education Leadership Consultant
Co-Author, *Leading for Differentiation: Growing Teachers Who Grow Kids*
Author, *Tools and Talk: Data, Conversation, and Action for Classroom and School Improvement*

"I have been using Conscious Classroom Management to teach graduate and undergraduate students at the university level for the past six years. It is an amazing resource that guides my students' learning. It strongly connects to the hearts and minds of veteran, novice, and pre-service teachers, shaping teaching practice and teacher dispositions in ways that have tremendously positive outcomes for students."

> Gail Jessett
> Adjunct Professor
> Gonzaga University, Spokane, WA

"Conscious Classroom Management has continually remained my bible of classroom reference throughout ten years of teaching in both public and private school settings."

> Naomi Elphick
> Veteran HS English Teacher
> Kenmore, WA

"Conscious Classroom Management, 2nd edition, is bound to make Rick Smith and Grace Dearborn household names in the field of education. I discovered Conscious Classroom Management on my Fullbright assignment in the US. Since then, it was not only a lifesaver, but has also been a constant companion for me and most of the teachers of my school in India."

> Anupama Ramachandra
> Principal
> Delhi Public School
> Bangalore, India

"Conscious Classroom Management is like Harry Wong 2.0. Our teachers rave about the immediate impact it has on their classroom management and student engagement! The clickable online calendar by itself is an amazing resource for brand new teachers! If you are a professor, staff developer, or mentor teacher, and can use only one book to train teachers for starting off, this is the one for you."

Claudette McCann
Consultant, Former Staff Development Coordinator
Leon County Schools, Tallahassee, FL

"The Great Beginnings program has more than one thousand new teachers every year, and has been using Conscious Classroom Management as a resource tool for each of the last ten years. Our new teachers find it to be extremely valuable in helping them to establish critical routines and procedures at the beginning of the year, and the quick, easy-to-read format of the book helps them to put the suggestions into place with minimal effort. Our teachers and our mentors continue to find Conscious Classroom Management to be an invaluable resource."

Richard Culp
Educational Specialist
Office of Professional Learning and School Support
Fairfax County Public Schools, Fairfax County, VA

Conscious Classroom Management:
Unlocking the Secrets of Great Teaching, Second Edition
By Rick Smith and Grace Dearborn

Published by Conscious Teaching, LLC
21 Crest Road
Fairfax, CA 94930
Phone: 800.667.6062
Email: mail@consciousteaching.com
Website: www.consciousteaching.com

I.S.B.N. 978-0-9796355-9-5   Library of Congress card number pending

Cover Design: George Foster
Cartoons: Tom Hermansen
Book Design: Mary Lambert, Alexis Clark
Copy Editing: Kristin Donnan
Printed in the United States of America

Conscious Classroom Management:

Unlocking the Secrets of Great Teaching

SECOND EDITION

RICK SMITH

GRACE DEARBORN

TABLE OF CONTENTS

Intervention — What We Do in Response... 199

PREFACE

WHEN *Conscious Classroom Management* came out twelve years ago, it created quite a stir in the education community. Michael Kelley, book exhibitor at the National Symposium on Teacher Induction in San Jose, California, said, "Not only did *Conscious Classroom Management* outsell any other book at the conference, but also there was a 'Harry Potter-like' frenzy, with people lined up three and four deep to purchase copies before they were all gone."

Chuck Korkegian, book exhibitor at the National Dropout Prevention Conference said, "[it] outsold any book I've ever sold in all my years' working exhibits. Teachers were lined up at my booth to get their hands on it."

What made *Conscious Classroom Management* so in demand is its mixture of easy-to-use, practical strategies and simple, yet compelling, positive approaches and assumptions. For more than ten years, this combination has helped classrooms and schools become affirming environments where referrals and suspensions are down and student engagement and teacher satisfaction are up. Repeatedly, the feedback we have received is that *Conscious Classroom Management* is practical, easy to use, and makes an immediate difference.

Why, then, write a second edition?

While *Conscious Classroom Management* is still just as relevant and powerful today as it was twelve years ago, a lot has happened in education since then. Technological advances have brought tablets and smart phones into the classrooms. Brain research has blossomed and deeply informed teaching practice. Schools have grown increasingly diverse; now, for example, the California Department of Education reports twice as many Latino students as Caucasian students in California public schools.[1] This reality heightens the need for teachers to be more culturally proficient as they create inclusive and safe spaces for all students to learn. In addition, with various new statewide standards, curricula must likewise reflect an increased focus on student-centered learning and independent inquiry.

These shifts have led to a rapid change in whom we teach, what we teach, how we teach it, and how students learn. Teacher and student

comfort zones are challenged, often resulting in behavior issues and conflicts in the classroom. In other words, there is an even greater need today for a focus on classroom management to help teachers find their "sea legs" and adjust to the new challenges in their classrooms.

Conscious Classroom Management II addresses these challenges, offering practical and kind approaches and strategies. The focus is not simply about getting students quiet; it's about empowering them to become agents of their own learning and for each to find his own internal locus of motivation. In addition, *Conscious Classroom Management II* is designed to help teachers learn new ways to support, engage, and motivate all their students with dignity and kindness, thereby keeping students in the classroom, engaged, contributing, and learning.

While classroom management is rarely at the top of lists about education reform, it remains the essential glue that allows teaching and learning to happen, increasing growth and wonder for both student and teacher.

If you've read the first edition of *Conscious Classroom Management*, you'll see that much of it remains in the second edition. However, you'll also find brand new, additional material that solidifies and extends the strategies from the first edition, thus addressing the changes in education outlined above. Woven throughout this book is an even deeper and more abiding focus on teacher wellness, positive connection with students, de-escalation of conflict, and student-centered learning.

New Chapters

We've added three innovative chapters. The first is called "**Strategies for School Administrators and Teacher Leaders**," and is designed to help education leaders support their teachers and students. The second is called "**The First Week of School**," and offers detailed road maps for teachers to thrive in their first week. The third new chapter is called "**Making Changes.**" It provides practical, step-by-step approaches for implementing new policies and procedures in the classroom, thus minimizing the stress involved and maximizing the likelihood of real and lasting positive change.

Online Toolbox — A Treasure of User-Friendly Support for New Teachers

Each copy of the book comes with a unique password that allows you online access to a wealth of supporting material, including lesson plans, samples, checklists, and videos.

In particular, the online component of the new chapter "The First Week of School" includes a large cache of teacher-created lesson plans — organized as a clickable calendar — to help teachers help their students in the first five days of the school year.

This book is designed to help teachers excel in managing their classes, motivating and empowering their students, and bringing wonder into the classroom. It's for beginning teachers, veteran teachers, struggling teachers, and successful teachers, who want to take their craft to the next level. It's also for administrators, professors, mentors, and staff developers who want to help their teachers get there.

Research-based, aligned with best teaching practices, and exceedingly practical, the strategies and approaches in *Conscious Classroom Management II* will work for any and all teachers pre-K through 12. *Conscious Classroom Management II* can work on its own as the central resource for classroom management at your school or district. Or it can be used to support and enhance any classroom management program that's already in place. It shines a light on key underlying principles of management, and provides specific and easy-to-use road maps for teachers to follow.

We invite you to dive into the second edition of *Conscious Classroom Management*. You'll find all the practical strategies that made the first book a must-have resource, plus much more to support you to survive and thrive in today's classroom, all the while empowering your students to be their best. In this new edition, the keys to unlocking the secrets of great teaching are placed even more firmly in your hands.

1

INTRODUCTION

> *"I'm a teacher. A teacher is someone who leads. There is no magic here. I do not walk on water. I do not part the sea. I just love children."*
>
> — MARVA COLLINS

O N MY FIRST DAY as a student teacher, I was sent to observe how an effective teacher set up her classroom management system. The theory: I would reproduce the successful system six months later when I took over my first classes for student teaching. It was a great idea.

It failed miserably.

Enthusiastic in my ignorance, I entered the classroom of a veteran tenth-grade English teacher, my eyes open for every detail, my pen in hand. I was ready to learn. Throughout the course of the first week, I noticed that Mrs. Miller's classes ran incredibly smoothly. When she said to her students, "Open your books to page twenty-seven," every book opened to page twenty-seven. The students were engaged, leaning forward, attentive. I saw no evidence of hard-hitting management strategies or overbearing lists of rules. I saw nothing. My notebook was empty. I thought to myself, "This is easy. I just say it, and they do it."

Visions of my students in a Conga line behind me, their model teacher, appeared in my mind's eye. I could just see it; these kids would happily follow my lead as we journeyed into the wonders of learning. My classes would be even better than Mrs. Miller's; they would break the mold. I would have no need for discipline, because my students would tap into their natural hunger to learn. I would be their relaxed,

I thought to myself, "This is easy. I just say it, and they do it."

loving, and skillful guide, seamlessly employing invisible management strategies.

I came to Earth later that same first week while observing another tenth-grade English teacher attempting the same lesson Mrs. Miller had taught. When this less effective teacher asked the students to open their books to page twenty-seven, several students did indeed open their books. Some were on the right page. Some even had the correct book. But this simple task was torturous. Amid an outpouring of chatter, complaints, confusion, and paper airplanes, any sense of order within the room simply disappeared.

At first glance, I couldn't figure out why Mrs. Miller had been so much more effective. Since I definitely didn't want a career in dodging paper airplanes, I made it my mission to break the code. I began with a basic question, "Why can the same request — seemingly the exact same request — made to two different groups of students result in opposite behaviors?"

The answer to this — and a million questions like it — is my motivation for writing this book.

Effective classroom management is essentially invisible.

It is so seamless that unless we know what to look for, we won't be able to see it. Hundreds of thousands of student teachers, new teachers, and veteran teachers each year have this same experience: they look for effective classroom management strategies in their classroom observations, but

▲ They don't know what to look for;
▲ They don't see anything;
▲ If they do see something, they don't know how to translate it into their own classroom teaching.

As a new teacher, I became obsessed with understanding invisible management. I was desperate to survive in my classes, and I asked, begged, pleaded with, and interrogated anyone I knew who might be able to help me. Still, my first years were a struggle. Later, as a mentor teacher working closely with new teachers, my obsession remained, but in a slightly different form. Simply becoming a more effective teacher was not enough; I also wanted to find a way to make the invisible visible to others. I wanted to communicate to other teachers how to "see" classroom management and how to translate it into their teaching. To do this, I sought to make effective classroom management tangible by moving it out of the realm of instinct and into the reality of daily practice.

This book describes the key elements I have discovered along the way that help make classroom management conscious. By slowing down the camera — by looking more closely at what is happening both in the classroom and behind the scenes — we can increase our awareness of what works and why, thus providing a road map for improving our classroom experience.

Throughout the book, I refer to a fictional teacher named Mrs. Allgood. Like the effective tenth-grade English teacher I observed during my first week in the profession, she has fabulous classroom management skills. Looking closely at what she does and the thinking behind it can shed light on essential skills for managing the classroom. Imagine that she teaches your grade and subject area(s), and is just down the hall.

I also refer to a not-so-effective teacher named Mrs. Meanswell. She tries hard but is struggling. So far, Mrs. Meanswell cannot consistently make cause-and-effect connections between her management choices and her classes' behavior patterns.

Mrs. Meanswell is not necessarily a new teacher, nor is Mrs. Allgood necessarily a veteran. Teachers of all levels of experience have all levels of effectiveness in the classroom. Additionally, all of us have "Allgood moments" as well as "Meanswell moments." Even though Mrs. Allgood represents an ideal to strive for, even she has "Meanswell moments." There is no perfect model teacher. Regardless of our skill levels, we are constantly learning.

When referring to a typical student who acts out, I often use the name "Mark." This is because challenging students inevitably make a "mark" in our awareness. In cases where I refer to teachers or students other than by name, I refer to teachers in the feminine gender and students in the masculine. This is done simply to help with clarity, and is not intended to make any political or pedagogical statements. Further, I use the word "parents" broadly, referring to

A Closer Look

By slowing down the camera — by looking more closely at what is happening both in the classroom and behind the scenes — we can increase our awareness of what works and why, thus providing a road map for improving our classroom experience.

students' guardians as well as their parents. In addition, even though this book is authored by both Grace Dearborn and me, for reasons of style, it is written in the first person.

▲ ▲ ▲

How to Use This Book

This book is for any new or veteran pre-K-to-12 teacher who would like to improve his or her classroom management skills. It is also for mentor teachers and administrators who want to help their teachers to excel — for example, Chapter 16 is a new addition called "Strategies for School Administrators and Teacher Leaders." The practices outlined in this book can be effective for parents or teachers of adults as well.

A Closer Look

The combination of who we are and what we do makes for effective classroom management.

Although this book is focused on practical strategies, I have included many ideas about teacher attitude and assumptions that, at first, might seem theoretical. This is because effective classroom management is more than just a process of plugging in a series of consequences to match student misbehavior. Teachers often come to our workshops looking for an exotic new consequence — one that will work for all students in all situations. As far as I know, it doesn't exist. Classroom management is a complex of approaches that draws on an understanding of three primary areas: the students, the teacher, and the relationship between the two.[1] Success lies in awareness not only of our actions, but also of who we are as people. These two "prongs" form the basis for effective management:

Who We Are ⟵⟶ What We Do

Who we are refers to how we hold ourselves internally, and thus how we come across to our students. Are we rigid and reactive, focusing too much on our own performance to actually communicate with our students? Are we laid-back and loose, too focused on being the students' friend to consistently teach behavior? Or are we firm and soft simultaneously, assuming both the best about our students — that they want to learn classroom behavior, and the best about ourselves — that we are human beings who have the students' best interest at heart?

What we do refers to the nuts and bolts of classroom management — specific strategies for designing and maintaining a positive classroom environment, connecting with students, and taking care of business.

The combination of who we are and what we do makes for effective classroom management. It influences the manner in which we communicate with students, parents, and administrators, and it determines our effectiveness in moments of potential conflict. How do we address misbehavior? How do we hold our ground with students without appearing mean, while inviting their cooperation and sparking their natural hunger to participate and learn?

Taken as a whole, *Conscious Classroom Management* outlines a practical guide to surviving and thriving in the classroom. The "who" of classroom management can be found in the first main section, called Foundation. The "what" is divided into two more sections: Prevention and Intervention. The figure below represents these key elements:

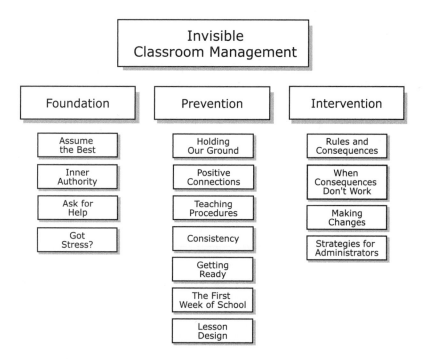

Each chapter is written so that generally it stands on its own, addressing one of these critical elements of classroom management. In addition, on the inside back cover of your copy you will find a unique

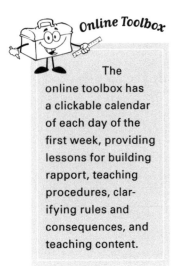

Online Toolbox

The online toolbox has a clickable calendar of each day of the first week, providing lessons for building rapport, teaching procedures, clarifying rules and consequences, and teaching content.

password that allows access to the online component of the content. By signing into the website, you can access a wealth of supporting material, including lesson plans, checklists, and videos, organized by chapter. In chapter 11, "The First Week of School," the content is formatted as a clickable calendar, in which each day of the week provides a selection of teacher-tested options in the four key areas of building rapport, teaching procedures, clarifying rules and consequences, and teaching content. Anywhere in the book you see the online toolbox icon, you know that additional resources are a click away. In addition, there's an extensive chapter-by-chapter facilitator guide to help professors and staff developers with book studies for their teachers and student teachers.

If you are truly pressed for time and are about to start your school year, go straight to Chapter 10, "Getting Ready," and Chapter 11, "The First Week of School." They will help you land on your feet in the first days of teaching.

The more I explore classroom management and the more I explore myself, the more connections I make between my growth as a person and my abilities as an educator. I've been a new teacher, a veteran teacher, a mentor teacher, and a teacher trainer. I've observed and coached hundreds of beginning and veteran teachers, and spoken to over a hundred thousand educators. I am still constantly learning. I invite you to "get lost" in this book, and discover not only some quick fixes you need for your classes, but also the deeper connection you have to yourself and your students. There is no limit to the wonder to be uncovered in this exploration.

FOUNDATION —
Who We Are

> *"You teach a little by what you say.*
> *You teach the most by what you are."*
>
> — DR. HENRIETTA MEARS

2

ASSUME
THE BEST

"You see all my light,
and you love my dark."

— ALANIS MORISSETTE

"Thank you, Johnny, for raising your hand." *HERMANSEN*

EFFECTIVE TEACHERS OFTEN internalize certain key, positive assumptions about their students and themselves, to the point where they may not be aware of what those assumptions are. We need to unearth, identify, and focus on these assumptions, because they form the foundation of our teaching experience and frame the actions we take. When we start to assume the best about our students and ourselves, teaching changes and magic happens.

1. Teachers Teach Behavior

We may have gotten into the teaching profession to teach science, music, or foreign language, but pretty soon we discover that, in reality, we are in the profession to teach people. And people have many needs beyond content areas, including learning appropriate behavior.

Mrs. Meanswell knows that she has to address her students' behavior, but she tries to address it quickly in order to get to the good stuff — that stuff called content. What she doesn't understand is that **behavior *is* the good stuff.** Students need to learn what's appropriate, what's not appropriate, how to tell the difference, and how to discipline themselves to make nurturing choices.[1] Life is about making choices, experiencing consequences, and learning from our successes and

When we start to assume the best about our students and ourselves, teaching changes and magic happens.

mistakes. Therefore, when we teach behavior, we are really teaching life skills.[2]

It's not that school behavior is supposed to be better than behavior at home or elsewhere. But it can be different, depending on one's home environment and cultural background. Knowing how to navigate the differences can be essential for student success in school and in life outside of school. The "appropriate-behavior muscle" that we can help students develop in our classrooms will help them in every area of their lives, regardless of the variety of behavioral norms they encounter in their worlds. Knowing how to focus and channel one's energy; knowing how to act non-impulsively and with consideration and kindness; holding oneself and others in high regard — all of these are navigational skills that students can use in just about any life situation.

It helps to imagine that the contract we sign to be a teacher doesn't just state that we will teach third grade or teach five classes of math. It also says in large, invisible-ink letters that we will teach our students appropriate classroom behavior. In fact, some contracts actually include a statement like this.

This behavior-is-the-good-stuff premise might cause many teachers, seasoned or not, to feel a bit of resistance. Especially if this experience sounds familiar: by the third day of a new school year, you already feel six weeks behind! There is so much material to cover; there are so many hoops to jump through — no matter how fast you go, you seem to fall further behind each day. From this orientation, teachers can tend to speed through opportunities to teach behavior with "drive-through discipline," in order to get to the content as quickly as possible. If we assume that we are here only to teach content, then the behavior situation usually doesn't resolve itself, and we find ourselves having to address the same student behaviors again and again. Paradoxically then, our "time-saving" solution costs more time, and the chaos that results from initially avoiding teaching behavior actually slows down our delivery of the content! Conversely, when we assume that we teach behavior, we put extra focus on it, students get it faster, and we have more time to teach content.

Going Under the Wave

When you swim in the ocean and want to get past the waves, you quickly discover that trying to run right through them can result in a wipe-out, as the waves drag you down. Most often the gentlest and most efficient way past the waves is to go under them. And this is true when we face the "waves" of student resistance.

When Mrs. Allgood disciplines a student from across the room, if "drive-through discipline" (a quick look or comment) won't work, she goes under the wave. Three things are evident:

▲ Her voice goes down in **volume**.
▲ Her voice goes lower in **tone**.
▲ Her body **posture** more squarely faces the student.

These three adjustments offer the student a chance to save face while shifting his behavior. There is a constant de-escalation in the way she holds her ground.

For example, if Mrs. Allgood is teaching a math lesson and Mark is playing with a magazine, she stops, takes a breath, and internally assumes the best about Mark — that he wants to behave appropriately in class. She then faces Mark squarely, and in a quiet, low tone asks him to please put the magazine away. She goes under the wave of Mark's resistance, rather than into it. He thus feels invited, rather than challenged. With her tone, volume, and posture, Mrs. Allgood communicates that she is firm in her resolve, yet soft — she is on Mark's side. Once Mark knows this, in later occurrences she often doesn't need to say anything. Just facing him can be enough. Further, whenever possible, Mrs. Allgood addresses Mark privately. This is addressed more thoroughly later in Chapter 12, "Rules and Consequences."

In a small percentage of situations, particularly with emotionally disturbed and oppositional students, square posture can cause an escalation of tension. In these cases you can still lower your volume and tone, but use "side posture," getting next to the student, or as close as is possible, and facing the same direction as he is, making sure to not look directly at his face.

As we expand our job description to include behavior, a significant change takes place. Mrs. Allgood assumes that she is here to teach behavior and that students are here to learn it. Students tend to "get it" the first time, and thus she has more time to focus on content. Both her verbal and nonverbal actions naturally reflect these assumptions. She doesn't beg, advertise, or sell. She simply addresses the behavior squarely and keeps the students focused. Later and if needed, when she's not in front of the class, she can address behavior issues as learning opportunities in more depth with particular students.

> I had one student who could even do quadratic equations in his head, while he was behind bars.

Learning behavior is at least equally as important, if not more important, than learning content. When I taught in an alternative school for at-risk high school students, some of them were quite bright. I had one who could even do quadratic equations in his head, *while he was behind bars*. He had the smarts to do the math, but not to avoid getting in trouble with the law.

As students learn appropriate school behavior, they also accumulate critical lifelong skills. In his book *Emotional Intelligence*, Daniel Goleman points to several key indicators of emotional intelligence that are directly related to behavior management[3], among which are our abilities to:

▲ address anger,
▲ soothe ourselves, and
▲ delay gratification.

When we effectively help our students develop these skills, we enhance their ability to mature. We thus teach the whole person. Teaching behavior is not a necessary evil — it is a "necessary wonderful."

2. Students Want to Learn Appropriate Behavior

Safety and structure are the two pillars of effective classroom management. Our students want both. There is an invisible covenant between Mrs. Allgood and each of her students.

The student's covenant says:

"Please teach me appropriate behavior in a safe and structured environment. I may act out, I may behave in ways that suggest I am not interested, but in truth I really want to learn appropriate classroom behavior, and I won't be satisfied unless you are holding your ground, teaching this to me."

The teacher's covenant says:

"I will do my best to teach you appropriate behavior in a safe and structured environment. I will assume that you want to learn this, no matter what evidence you may demonstrate to the contrary."

When Mark acts out in Mrs. Allgood's class, for example, it's often for one of two reasons:

1. He wants to let her know that he has not yet fully learned the appropriate behavior. She needs to teach it to him again, perhaps in a different way or by breaking things into smaller pieces. Maybe she needs to provide him a set of consequences or supports that will allow him to better see his options for appropriate behavior.

Helping Mark to learn behavior is just like helping him to learn content. Teaching is teaching, whether our students are learning to solve for x in a math problem, line up for recess, make a foul shot, or behave appropriately in class. We break things into small steps, teach the steps, and check for understanding. (This is explored in depth in Chapter 8, "Teaching Procedures.") So if Mark doesn't behave in an appropriate way, Mrs. Allgood may have to teach it to him more thoroughly or differently. She always points out what needs to be corrected and moves on. Whether she's teaching math or behavior, she'll receive little or no animosity or challenge to her authority, because Mark and Mrs. Allgood are on the same side. Please note, however: no matter how effective Mrs. Allgood is, there is no guarantee that Mark will demonstrate appropriate behavior. He will still make independent choices. All she can do is be consistent and thorough.

Wise-Apple Advice

Safety and structure are the two pillars of effective classroom management.

2. He is testing her. He wants to make sure that she will hold up her end of their covenant. He wants to know that the boundaries are clear and consistent, but not hard-edged or threatening. He says to himself, "Let's see if this teacher's class is safe and structured. I'm going to break a rule and see what she does."

If Mark acts out and she's really mean to him, then he sees that she is not creating a *safe* environment. If, on the other hand, he breaks a rule and she ignores it and he gets away with it, then she is not creating a *structured* environment. When either of these occurs, he subconsciously tells himself, "I don't think Mrs. Allgood understood. I'm going to assume the best about her. So I'll break a larger rule to give her the opportunity to come through with safety and structure."

So Mark systematically breaks larger and larger rules. Once he sees that Mrs. Allgood won't react and blame him for testing (safety), and that she won't ignore him and let him get away with it (structure), he'll know that she is honoring the contract, and he'll end his test.

If the walls — the boundaries or rules of the class — are strong yet soft, then students confirm that indeed the teacher is honoring the invisible contract. Then they can focus on honoring their end of the bargain. Simply put, when students test us, they want us to pass the test.

Another way to think of this assumption is to imagine that every moment, every one of our students has just asked us:

> ## "Could you please teach me how to behave? What do I need to do or know in order to best learn behavior?"

As we assume that students are asking this, even as they are acting out, complaining, or throwing a tantrum, we respond as if they just asked "Can you please help me with this math problem?" We are relaxed and on their side as we clearly and directly address their behavior. Even though they might be approaching us with a wave of upset or resistance or emotional energy, our relaxed reply goes under their wave.

Mrs. Allgood says

> When students test us, they want us to pass the test.

It can be quite a challenge to remember and embody this assumption, particularly when we are feeling personally attacked by a student, or we aren't noticing any improvement in a student's behavior over time. When a student is acting out, it can help to find a specific underlying message, a "subtitle" that matches what the student might really be asking for in the situation. In addition to "Could you please teach me how to behave?" a few possibilities are:

▲ I'm having personal challenges at home, and am acting them out in your class. Please be compassionate as well as firm and clear with me.
▲ What can I do right now to behave better?
▲ Please help me.
▲ I really care, but it's hard for me to admit it.
▲ Please don't give up on me.
▲ This is hard for me. Help me to succeed and let me save face, too.

Finding relevant subtitles, and thereby dropping into positive assumptions about our students, allows us to enforce a whole range of consequences without unduly ruffling students' feathers — and without taking our rough days home with us. When I first started teaching, I assumed that because my students' behavior was so negative, they must have gotten together at lunch to plot my demise! By learning to assume the best, I came to understand that students do not act out because they are trying to "get us." They are not "bad kids," intent on spreading their "badness" to their classmates.

Limiting Assumptions	*Positive Assumptions*
▲ They are bad kids.	▲ They haven't fully learned the appropriate school behavior.
▲ They don't want to learn.	▲ They want to know that the classroom environment will be safe and structured.
▲ They are trying to hurt the teacher.	▲ They are signaling the teacher to teach behavior more thoroughly or differently.

For a more thorough exploration of why students act out, see Chapter 14, "When Consequences Don't Work."

Radical Safety and Structure

Soon after I got my driver's license as a teen, I took a three-hour drive to visit my brother at his college. Like most teenage boys, I liked to drive fast. So I sped along the highway at about eighty-five miles per hour, winding in and out of traffic, alternating between the slow and fast lanes, searching out the most efficient route.

At one point in the trip I was coming uphill in the fast lane, approaching two large trucks in the slow lane. Just before I got in position to pass them, the first truck lumbered into the fast lane at about forty-five miles per hour, as if to pass the next truck. Only it didn't pass. The trucker stayed side-by-side with the trucker in the slow lane, and plodded along for several miles.

I was upset. I was mad. I was on a mission to go fast, and these two truckers were toying with me, blocking my way to driving freedom. I swerved back and forth. I honked my horn. I made it clear that I was "No One To Be Trifled With." In spite of my antics, the two trucks held their positions.

After a teenage eternity — about seven minutes — I saw a "speed trap," a large dirt parking area on the right side of the road. There were perhaps thirty cars parked there, along with six highway patrol cars! Two officers were standing on the shoulder of the highway, directing speeders into the parking area. The others were busy giving tickets to dozens of drivers.

I suddenly realized why the truckers had been blocking my way. They knew!

A half-mile later, the truck in the fast lane slowed down and took its original position behind its partner in the slow lane.

I drove by. Slowly. I turned to the first trucker, mouthed "thank you" and held my hand to my heart. He held up his CB radio mic, pointed to it, tipped his cap, and smiled.

That story has always stayed with me. That a couple of strangers would choose to be so kind as to provide me with structure and safety — both of which I had vehemently rejected — is remarkable. (Of course, some might suggest that it would have been good for me to get a ticket, as it would have provided me with a lot of safety and structure. That is a whole different story!) As teachers, we have this chance over and over again — to provide safety and structure for our students, even when they complain about it. We can assume the best about them, hold our ground, and provide environments for them to succeed and flourish.

3. Radios

Mrs. Allgood assumes that students have "radios in their heads," and are constantly tuning in to a myriad of radio stations about what it means to be a youth. These stations are different for kids of different ages, genders, and cultural backgrounds, but they mostly focus on fitting in, being cool, achieving short-term gratification, and enjoying consequence-free behavior. Often, many of our students will narrate these radio noises aloud, as if they were the truth of who they are. They will entertain ideas such as "I don't care about learning," or "My friends' opinions of me matter more than my own or my teachers'," or "Fitting in and looking good matter more than being good," or "Why bother to try?" If Mrs. Allgood isn't careful, she may find herself believing these statements. But she relies on a related assumption, which radically shifts her perspective.

Wise-Apple Advice

Our job as teachers is to focus primarily on what students need.

Radio Transmitters

In addition to having radio stations in their heads, students also have radio transmitters in their hearts. These beacons pour out the same basic message over and over again: "We want to learn and participate. Please know that we will often want to narrate the noises in our heads, but need you to honor our hearts at the same time."

The noises in their heads that they narrate are primarily in the category of what they say they want. The beacon from their heart is what they need.

Our job as teachers is to focus primarily on what students need. We witness as they tune in and narrate aloud, which is part of how they grow and mature (and often what they say they want is indeed what is needed). As we recognize and respect their explorations of the noises in their heads, we also keep our students' needs to learn and thrive as our own true north. This distinction between want and need can serve as a "road map" for us as we address the myriad issues, noises, complaints, concerns, and challenges that our students generate.

As we internalize the assumption that students want what they need — to learn and to participate — we begin to see that underneath their complaints about the lesson, the homework, or the seating chart, students are really asking for us to care for them. The gray box on page 22 further illustrates the often-silent wishes of our students.

Teaching can be like tossing a pebble in a pond. The ripples can take a while to return to where we are standing. Sometimes assuming the best about students is an act of faith, in that we don't always immediately see the results of our good work. Sometimes a student will test us for five minutes. Sometimes he will test us for the whole school year. Yet he may very well come back to visit us a year or more later and thank us for being his favorite teacher. He might not be able to articulate why, but something inside him will acknowledge that we were clearly on his side, providing what he most needed, even when he argued and complained that he wanted something else. The key is not necessarily how long a student's test lasts. It's that he knows that we are providing structure and safety and consistency. In the long run, our kind and focused attention on our students' needs can make the difference.

Our Own Internal Radios

One benefit of this orientation is that as teachers we have the same radio tuners and transmitters as our students do. Regardless of what our experience is when we come to school, whether we are feeling ready, mulling over issues at home, or anticipating our weekend, we always have the opportunity to "show up."

While teaching, we have myriad opportunities to take deep breaths and re-orient, reaching through our own noisy heads into our hearts, and making the choice to make each interaction with each student important and worthy of our full focus. As we do this, we are not only touching our own hearts, but we are also reaching into our students' hearts, connecting with them invisibly on a heart-to-heart level that truly feeds them.

This will affect all of our communications, especially the ones that address inappropriate behavior. This softening of our communication allows us to be firm when necessary, but in a way that invites cooperation, rather than inciting arguing and protests. Our students' behavior will begin to reflect these positive assumptions. What shifts is the "how" — the manner in which we communicate. Our students begin to feel that we are on their side, even as we address the "what" — their behavior. By assuming the best in the face of our own radio-station noises ("these kids don't care," "they're just lazy," "why bother?"), we can hold our ground with student misbehavior in a way that is both firm and soft, corrective and inviting. In addition, as we exercise this "muscle of positivity," we avoid the burnout that is so often associated with teaching tough kids. We create a self-fulfilling prophecy of appropriate and engaging student participation that includes their unique cultures and perspectives. Our communication becomes clear and kind, and our enthusiasm becomes contagious.

A Closer Look

Assuming that students want to learn is the difference between inviting students to engage versus dragging them into compliance.

4. Students Want to Learn Content

Mrs. Allgood assumes that students want to learn the content she is teaching, even if they don't pay attention or if they tell her that they aren't interested. This allows her to keep looking for ways to get them interested and motivated, and for teaching strategies that make the information palatable, even exciting. Rather than trying to manufacture student interest when it isn't there, her encouragement allows her students to remember and even delight in their own inner spark for learning. She is merely reminding them, rather than manipulating them. This subtle distinction isn't so subtle to our students. It's the difference between inviting students to engage and learn versus dragging them into compliance.

If Mrs. Meanswell assumes that her students don't want to learn content, then she can say to herself, "Since he's not interested, it doesn't matter what I do; I might as well not put any effort into it." She might then develop a cynical attitude toward her students and toward her role as a teacher. They'll tend to reply in kind. She will come to school ready for battle, rather than ready for teaching, learning, and wonder.

A more positive assumption helps her to keep her passion for the content she is teaching and her enthusiasm for igniting the passion of her students, making the content as real-world relevant, culturally sensitive, and engaging as possible. Chapter 12, "Lesson Design," addresses this in more detail.

Brad the Baiter

I was student-teaching a ninth-grade English "class-from-heck," at a high-achievement public school where a significant percentage of the students went on to college. However, in my class of twenty-seven students, nine of them, as it later turned out, would not graduate from high school — on time or at all. Of course, at the time I didn't know this. All I knew was that I was having an incredibly hard time managing my class, and that I must be a terrible teacher because my students acted out so much.

Of all of the tough students in that class, Brad was the toughest. Coincidentally, the word "brad" means "small nail," and Brad was a thorn in my side throughout the entire semester. He had a grating habit of challenging everything I did. He'd often play to the crowd, saying things like, "This is pointless. Why are we doing this?!?" I would then immediately feel about two feet tall, as everyone else began to consider his question. Invariably, whenever Brad spoke in class, his antics would trigger the other students to contribute complaints, chatter, and ultimately, chaos.

"Please Care for Me Today"
A Message from Our Students

Dear Teacher,

Please care for me today. I might not have the impulse control that you do, so I might not always stop myself from acting out. I ask you to be the "river banks" for my "river," even when I say or act in a way that seemingly contradicts this. Please be willing to provide the structure and safety that I need, so that I can "flow" forward.

Please have more patience with me than I seem to show for myself. Take the time to teach me behavior in simple steps, so that I have a clear road map for success. Remember that there is a lot on my plate besides the lesson that you are teaching. I may argue or get distracted or lost, but I am still teachable and worthy of kindness.

Consider that I am doing my best, even when I seem to fall short. Please don't humiliate me in front of others. Give me the chance to save face as I reorient around your positive assumptions of me.

Please honor my culture, background, life-experience, and family traditions as you help me understand what is required of me in your classroom and in this school.

Let me know as often as you can that I'm okay, that my culture is okay, that I'm acceptable and accepted, that who I am is more important than the details of what I do or believe, or what I look like.

Hold me in your heart as essential and whole, regardless of the million ways I behave, even as you take care of the million details of your day.

Allow your kind presence, in the silence between your words, to infuse me with hope and love.

Know that I am growing and learning, and part of that process includes pushing and testing and filling whatever spaces I can. Please be my silent partner in this by being firm when I complain and act out, while remembering my "soft center."

Assume that although I don't tell you directly that I appreciate your caring and consistency, I do.

In trusting partnership,

Your Student

During most nights of that semester, when lying down to sleep, the last thought I had was of Brad's pestering me. In the mornings, I would wake up and Brad's face would immediately appear in my consciousness. I tried to design all my lessons so that they would be "Brad-proof."

Brad was a smart kid. He had a sixth sense about how to push my buttons and get me right to the edge of my tolerance before he would back down and play the role of the innocent, dutiful student. My semester with that class began in late January. Sometime in early May, I finally got up the courage to send Brad to the office. It was perhaps a combination of my increased resolve and Brad's seeming over-confidence. One day he just went slightly too far, and I held my ground. After he left and the echo of his complaints receded, the class became very quiet. Things that day ran incredibly smoothly. This was, I believe, both because of Brad's absence and the students' understanding that I was suddenly willing to enforce consequences.

Brad returned the next day, and was somewhat better behaved. Although his behavior was never great, it clearly improved from that point on.

On the last day of the semester, I gave my students an evaluation form, in which they had the opportunity to assess my abilities as a teacher. On the last section of the evaluation there was a question that simply asked for comments. In that section, four students, independent of one another, wrote:

"You should have kicked Brad out sooner."

This was a revelation to me. The first thing I did was beat myself up for several days. "Oh, I'm a terrible teacher. Oh, I didn't do it right." But after licking my wounds, I examined these comments and realized something illuminating. Two students who wrote this were buddies of Brad's. When Brad had acted out in class, they had joined in, hanging tenaciously to his coattails. They were in essence saying to me:

"Although we won't admit it publicly, we want to learn. We don't have the self-esteem to stand up to Brad. We don't have the impulse control to discipline ourselves all the time. That's your job. We want you to hold the line and facilitate our learning."

Students want to learn. They want to learn content, they want to learn the procedures and routines that allow for learning content, and

Content, procedures, and behavior are the functional trinity of the classroom, and students want to learn them all.

they want to learn behavior that allows them to navigate in school and in the many situations they will encounter in their lives. If we catch them in their more "sober" and open moments, when they are not trying to impress their peers or defend themselves, they will admit this — regardless of their age, background, or apparent ability or lack of ability.

When I was a new teacher, I didn't fully embrace these positive assumptions, and it caused a painful cycle. Kids would act out. I'd use this as evidence to assume that they were bad kids. They'd get the message that I didn't respect or really see them, so they'd act out some more, reinforcing my negative assumptions. Then, by making the choice to assume the best about them — as I communicated respect and regard to my students, even when they acted out — tension decreased in the classroom, and my sanity increased.

Wise-Apple Advice

Assumptions – the Abridged Version

The bottom line on assumptions? Assume the best. Be on the same side as our students. Honor their diverse needs and cultures. Know that they want and need to learn behavior. Treat ourselves and our students with respect and dignity. Take deep breaths. Go under the wave of student resistance. Know that in the long run we will land on our feet.

3

INNER
AUTHORITY

> *"Nothing can dim the light*
> *which shines from within."*
>
> — MAYA ANGELOU

TEACHERS ARE THE PRIMARY AUTHORS of what happens in the classroom. For our visions to come to life — for our classroom environments to be smooth and harmonious — we must marshal our inner resources and write our own "scripts." Developing our "inner authority" can make all the difference in being an effective teacher.[1] Inner authority doesn't involve holding our breath or gearing up for battle or carrying ourselves in an aggressive way. It is a relaxed, natural state that permeates everything we do, in the classroom and elsewhere.

> Our inner authority affects how we give directions, pass out papers, and talk with kids one-on-one. It provides the foundation for our job satisfaction, our peace of mind, everything.

I once mentored a new middle school Physical Education teacher. He was confused because the other P.E. teachers rarely used consequences, yet their classes ran smoothly. But if this teacher didn't use consequences, his students acted out like crazy. The difference: the other teachers had already gone down that road. They had spent several years relying on consequences, until such time that they had internalized a no-nonsense, firm-yet-kind quality in their voices and postures. Their students knew that acting out was not in their best interests; these teachers had already passed their "tests." While veteran teachers are not necessarily better managers, in this case they were; they had learned from the trials that the new guy was just beginning to face.[2]

Situations like the P.E. dilemma might seem to be more obviously or visibly related to actions — "acting out leads to consequences." However, the invisible truth lies in the teacher's inner authority, something seemingly nebulous that can drive novices like Mrs. Meanswell nuts.[3] In fact, even many relatively effective Mrs. Allgoods don't know how they do it or how to explain it. A typical conversation about this might be:

Mrs. Meanswell: One of my students is constantly disrupting my class. What would you do in this situation?

Mrs. Allgood: Well, my students know that I will just not tolerate that kind of behavior.

Mrs. Meanswell, who means well, studiously takes notes from Mrs. Allgood, writing, "I will not tolerate that behavior...." Of course, that kind of advice doesn't really have a whole lot of benefit. What Mrs. Allgood is really referring to is her place on the continuum of inner authority. It's an invisible thing, but boy does it make a difference.

Inner Apology ⟵⟶ Inner Authority

We can never have too much inner authority, because it facilitates calm and harmony and imparts to the students a sense that their ship is being steered by capable hands. Moreover, we never "arrive" at full inner authority. It's a continuum on which we can always grow, and each situation that arises can help us progress along the continuum.[4] Other terms often associated with inner authority are "presence," "confidence," "naturalness," and "with-it-ness."[5] Authority doesn't translate to meanness. It simply means that we are "authors" of what happens in the classroom.

The polar opposite of inner authority is inner apology, and in the extreme it can be deadly in the classroom. Inner apology arises from acting out or repressing our insecurity, thinking that we have to be perfect. This reflects a sense that our authority is questionable, we are unsure of our decisions, and we are apologizing for being in charge. This can happen to the most effective teachers. Even Mrs. Allgood, who is seemingly in gracious command of her classroom, might stumble on her relatively advanced march along the continuum, given the right set of circumstances. Three examples clearly illustrate this continuum.

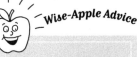

Wise-Apple Advice

We can never have too much inner authority, because it facilitates calm and harmony and imparts to the students a sense that their ship is being steered by capable hands.

Being Prepared

When a secondary teacher teaches the same new and risky lesson to three classes in a row, the first time is often filled with misgiving, question, confusion, and an undermining dynamic of apology. But by the third class, the teacher has it down and is clear and firm and right on track.

In my workshops, when I ask teachers to "please raise your hand if you've ever taught something that you just learned for the first time the night before," just about every hand goes up. This certainly happened to me. I distinctly remember driving to work, pausing at the red light across the street from school, and leafing through the textbook in a desperate attempt to put together a lesson. I'd arrive at school — and eight minutes later teach my students the "vital information" I was sharing. Of course, I did not let them know that I just learned it on the way to school! For new teachers, or teachers teaching a new subject, this experience of last-minute preparation is practically unavoidable. Even when we do our best to prepare in advance, things happen that are out of our control. (For help in preparing for the first days of school, check out Chapter 10, "Getting Ready," and Chapter 11, "The First Week of School".)

Mrs. Allgood knows that there will be days where she is less prepared than she would like. She knows it's not the end of the world, so she takes it in stride and doesn't apologize inwardly for it. Teaching is also about connecting to our students, and she allows her love for teaching and care for her students to shine through, even on days when she wished she had a more polished lesson plan.[6]

Enforcing Rules

Mrs. Meanswell's school has a rule that students are not allowed to chew gum in class. She doesn't agree with the rule, but does her best to enforce it. She tells her students, "Put your gum away, because we

Mrs. Allgood says

Mrs. Allgood
assumes that
the students will be
served by reading
chapter seven, and
that they want her to
provide that service
for them.

are not allowed to chew gum in class." But because of her lack of conviction, what her students actually hear is, "It's probably maybe better not to chew gum in class, don't you think? Should we maybe kind of agree not to chew gum? Maybe? Okay?"

The students pick up on her inner waffling about the rule, and constantly push the limit by bringing gum to class. Even though her words are clear, she is inwardly apologizing for the fact that she has to enforce the rule. She assumes that the students will disagree with her and debate her, and what she gets is a class debate on gum chewing, rather than her intended lesson plan.

To the extent that Mrs. Meanswell does not ultimately enforce the rule, she sends a message to her students that rules don't need to be obeyed if we don't agree with them. If her students internalize and apply this in other contexts, such as traffic rules, the results could be quite chaotic.[7]

Mrs. Allgood, on the other hand, discusses the gum-chewing rule with the administration. She doesn't agree with the rule, but realizes that for her, it's not an issue she wants to champion. So she decides to enforce the rule with her students *as if it's her own*. She knows that getting the kids on board and focused on learning is more important in this case than inciting protests about gum chewing. She chooses to provide the structure that her students need in order to learn in her classroom. Her clarity of conviction defuses any protests before they start.

Giving Directions

I remember observing a student teacher as she asked her class "Okay, everyone. Would you like to do some reading now?" When she received a chorus of "No's," she countered with "I think it might be a good idea, don't you?" Needless to say, the students resisted. It took twenty minutes to get the students started, and probably another twenty minutes after class for the student teacher to recover.

Mrs. Allgood, on the other hand, simply states, "Let's open our textbooks to chapter seven." Her presence doesn't offer wiggle room or equivocation. Mrs. Allgood assumes that the students will be served by reading chapter seven, and that they want her to provide that service to them. Her announcement is simple, clear, relaxed, and without apology. Her students sense her conviction and follow her lead, focusing on what they need to do.[8]

When and How to Apologize

This difference between inner apology and inner authority can be clearly seen in situations where a teacher appropriately apologizes to her class. A solid, heartfelt apology can be strong, clear, and even reassuring — the opposite of waffling. When illuminated, the process of appropriately apologizing to our students helps us to see more clearly the qualities of inner authority that are so valuable in the classroom. This is a particularly relevant issue for teachers who are immersed in inner apology.

Many teachers believe that to steer their ships effectively, they cannot appear to waver, and certainly they cannot apologize. Sometimes, however, it is appropriate, even essential, that teachers apologize to students. Mrs. Allgood has learned to do it without losing control of the rudder; her inner authority comes to her rescue.

Apologies most likely take the form of short, one-on-one conversations, during which clear communication is the key. However, when we "blow it" in front of the class and humiliate a student, it's okay to apologize to that student in front of the whole class. This action can take the form of a collective apology for our behavior to both him and the class, or an individual apology to him that is delivered in front of the class. Similarly, if we "lose it" with the whole class, it is often appropriate to apologize later, to the whole class.

There are two diametrically opposed ways to apologize, as outlined on the chart that follows. When Mrs. Allgood apologizes, she is taking the heat, and not apologizing for the fact that she's apologizing. Mrs. Meanswell, though perhaps using the same words as Mrs. Allgood, is trying to deflect the heat, and is apologizing inside — undermining herself — as she apologizes to the class.[9]

The difference in quality between the two apologies is immediately obvious. There's a weight, a presence, and a silence that permeates Mrs. Allgood's apology; this results in a more silent and thoughtful response from the students. In Mrs. Meanswell's case, the students get uncomfortable and squirmy as a reflection of her discomfort and squirminess. They don't perceive the environment to be safe and structured, and their discomfort is reflected in their actions. Further, by following Mrs. Meanswell's example, they can internalize the message that they should never apologize for their own actions, because discomfort, embarrassment, and discord will follow.

As a teacher, when I gave a "Meanswell-like" apology, the kids would often respond by acting out even more. Kids would sometimes call out,

Mrs. Allgood	Mrs. Meanswell
1. Doesn't apologize internally.	1. Does apologize internally.
2. Faces the students.	2. Looks away.
3. Makes statements. ("Yesterday, I blew it. I am so sorry.")	3. Makes statements that sound like questions. ("Yesterday, I kind of blew it? I'm sorry? Okay?")
4. Is grounded.	4. Is jumpy or visibly nervous.
5. Stands firmly and/or moves slowly toward students as she talks.	5. Bobs and weaves, and/or backs away from students as she talks.
6. Takes responsibility.	6. Blames (either herself or the kids).
7. Is self-affirming, yet humble.	7. Is self-effacing and needy.
8. Takes the heat.	8. Deflects the heat.
9. Speaks what she knows.	9. Speaks what she thinks the kids want to hear.
10. Expresses her feelings.	10. Performs her feelings.
11. Is clearly sincere, and feels empathy for what she put the students through.	11. Is questionably sincere, and is somewhat mechanical in her apology.
12. Affirms her care and concern through her demeanor.	12. Invites questions about her care and concern through her demeanor.

"You should be sorry! You did blow it!" I'd leave class that day thinking that my students were just mean kids. However, when my apology was a genuine act of self-forgiveness, the kids would be right with me. On occasion, I actually received applause from the students when I apologized, after which I thought to myself, "I've got to blow it with these kids more often…." This makes sense. If Christopher comes to school the day after I've blown up at the class, he may well be feeling incredibly resistant, powerless, and angry at having to face me again. If I apologize sincerely in a way that he knows I mean it, then he has a chance to exhale. The chip that has been lodged on his shoulder for the past twenty-four hours has a chance to dissolve.

Mrs. Allgood says

Apologizing internally for the fact that we are apologizing comes across like a "drive-by apology."

If we are going to apologize to our students, let's not do it unless we're actually sorry. Students of all ages and abilities can sniff out insincerity a mile away. Also, let's do our best not to beat ourselves up when we apologize, as this can trigger a host of responses that divert students from the essence of the exchange. As best we can, we need to simply state the obvious, take responsibility, own it, and let it go.[10]

The choice of whether to apologize internally is at the essence of Conscious Classroom Management. Apologizing internally for the fact that we are apologizing comes across like a "drive-by apology." We are never fully facing the students. We are pushing away the "charge" of the situation. That charge is twofold. First, we are literally in charge, in the sense that we are the authority figure in the classroom. Second, there's an emotional charge associated with apologizing to our students.

If we are not embracing the fact that we are literally in charge, then incoherence will build inside us — we are in fact in charge, yet we are still apologizing for it. This will tend to be reflected in incoherent student behavior in the classroom. We need to coherently hold our ground with the noise in our head that says that we should apologize for the fact that we're in charge. As we do this, we'll be able to more readily hold our ground with our students. Emotionally, if we think that good teachers never make mistakes, then we are setting ourselves up for a fall. Inevitably, we will make mistakes, and with the wrong mindset we'll tend to give self-effacing "Meanswell-like" apologies. Further, to some extent we'll be leaning in the direction of self-effacing communication — what I call teaching on thin ice — in anticipation of future mistakes that we are trying to avoid.

What if the kids' poor behavior triggered our poor behavior? Even in this case, we can unilaterally apologize for our response, offering no excuses and pointing no causal fingers. Subsequently, perhaps quite soon after, we can let the students know that their behavior was also inappropriate. One way to do this during the same lesson is to stand on one side of the room to apologize, and then move to another side of the room to point out the students' responsibility. This technique of "visual spacing" helps communicate to the students' brains that the two messages — both the teacher's apology and the kids' accountability — are separate. If we mix these two messages — by either actually blaming our students' behavior for our explosion, or seeming to — our apology isn't clear, we're not taking responsibility, and worst of all, that classroom community "exhale" that we are hoping for won't take place.

▲   ▲   ▲

Growing in Inner Authority

How do we exercise the muscle of inner authority so that we can grow along this continuum, away from inner apology? Several strategies can help, and they are sprinkled throughout this book. Each is described below in brief, and then is covered in detail in its corresponding chapter.

Assume the Best

If I assume that Mark wants to learn the behavior I expect of him, then when I teach it to him, I assume that he wants to hear what I say — and therefore, I automatically gain a certain level of self-confidence.[11] By focusing on what Mark needs, in spite of what he might say he wants, I both honor our invisible contract and grow in inner authority. In addition, when we assume the best about our role as teachers, we interpret students' acting out as opportunities for us to grow in inner authority — which, in turn, is something students actually want. See Chapter 2.

Ask for Help

The more willing we are to be human and to ask for help, the more resilient and flexible we'll be. This resiliency increases the likelihood that we'll land on our feet in times when our inner authority is challenged.[12] We won't base our inner authority on being perfect, but instead on being present. See Chapter 4.

Stress

As we reduce our stress, our level of calm increases — as do our presence, our resilience, and our confidence. See Chapter 5.

Holding Our Ground — Experience

As we gain teaching experience, we improve our ability to hold our ground in difficult moments, while still empowering our students. The more opportunities we have to hold our ground with students, the more we will tend to grow. See Chapter 6.

Holding Our Ground — Reflection

After a particularly good or rough experience, we can ask ourselves, "Where was I on the continuum? Did I hold my ground with the 'noise inside my head' that said I shouldn't be making the decisions in the class? Did I hold my ground with my arguing students — the 'noise outside my head'? In holding my ground, did I simultaneously provide my students with a sense of autonomy and dignity?" By reflecting, we naturally speed up the growth process that comes from experience. Mrs. Allgood's reflection is continuous and seamless. For her, it is mostly automatic and unconscious. Mrs. Meanswell's growth as a teacher can be accelerated by making this reflection a conscious daily practice, regardless of the quality of each lesson.

Practicing and/or role-playing in front of the mirror or with a colleague or mentor teacher also can be helpful. Just as with students, our growth accelerates as we consciously practice what we are learning. See Chapter 6.

> **A Closer Look**
>
> Each teaching situation provides us with the opportunity to "look in the mirror," examine where we are on the continuum, and mark our progress.

Positive Connections

We spiral into inner authority as our positive connections with students help deepen our positive assumptions, which in turn lead to more positive connections. In addition, our students relax as they feel a positive connection with us (as long as they perceive us as being in charge).[13] Thus, we relax as well, are less on edge, and are more willing to be in charge of the class.

In addition, when we teach students of varying cultures, we can tend to feel intimidated and out of our element. Focusing on being culturally responsive can help us to maintain our inner authority while being kind with our students at the same time.[14] See Chapter 7.

Teaching Procedures

This is probably the number-one way teachers can exercise the muscle of inner authority. Students want to succeed, and procedures are the road map to get them there. Procedures are the essential link between what we want to have happen in the classroom and what actually does happen. The more specific and thorough we are in teaching and re-teaching procedures, and the more we provide clear, concrete steps, the more our students will follow our lead — and the more we'll grow.[15] See Chapter 8.

Consistency

The muscle of consistency works together with the muscle of inner authority. Being consistent means keeping our focus on student learning despite all the distractions, sidebars, and interruptions that they can muster. As we remain focused on keeping students focused, we sharpen our skills and grow along the continuum. See Chapter 9.

Getting Ready and the First Week of School

To boost one's confidence, there's nothing like being prepared, organized, and able to anticipate student questions and concerns before they arise.[16] See Chapters 10 and 11.

Lesson Design

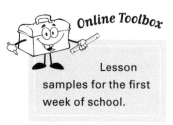

Online Toolbox

Lesson samples for the first week of school.

When our students are actively engaged, they associate our presence with a smoothly running class. This helps us relax into inner authority, which gives us the confidence to try new, more creative, engaging lessons.

Further, as federal, state, and local standards change, we are being asked to design more student-centered lessons. We can tend to feel out of control in this evolving teaching environment, and maintaining inner authority can feel challenging. Having practical strategies for helping kids drive their own learning can be a big help. See Chapter 12.

Consequences

Students often react when they receive consequences. If we can hold our ground in a firm and soft way, our presence will strengthen, and they'll tend to react less. In addition, as we internalize that consequences are less a form of punishment and more a way to help students to learn responsibility, we remain on their side, even in challenging situations. This helps our inner authority blossom.

Calling parents or guardians can help as well. I once gave a "homework suggestion" to one of my beginning teachers in which he was to call five parents a night for three straight weeks.[17] If kids were doing well, I suggested that he call their parents anyway, just to let them know. Not only did this help motivate his students, but also it helped the teacher to exercise his muscle of inner authority, because he consciously and consistently focused on student behavior. See Chapter 13.

Mrs. Allgood says

Calling parents helps exercise our muscle of inner authority because we get to practice being in charge.

Making Changes

We often feel most vulnerable and prone to inner apology when a change needs to be introduced to the class. Having clear and simple road maps for systematically making changes in the classroom helps ward off that inner apology. Implementing successful changes translates to more successful teaching, which helps us grow in inner authority. See Chapter 15.

Wise-Apple Advice

It's Worth It

Exercising the muscle of inner authority can seem both daunting and nebulous at first. Just about all teachers seem to go through a "trial by fire" where the learning curve is steep. But over time, if we continue to practice being firm with our students without reacting emotionally, while paying attention to the other elements outlined above, we will see benefits not only in our classes, but also in our lives outside of school. It's definitely worth the effort.

4

ASK
FOR HELP

*"All learning begins with the
simple phrase, 'I don't know.'"*

— AUTHOR UNKNOWN (I DON'T KNOW)

MRS. MEANSWELL IS SO SINCERE in her desire to do well that she sometimes forgets that doing well includes having bad days. She sometimes tenses up in class, trying too hard to be the perfect teacher. The result is that both she and her students need to go home and recover.

Just like everyone else, teachers make mistakes. If we walk around denying or ignoring this, not only do we set an impossible standard for ourselves, but also our students will think we expect them to pretend to be perfect. Such a set-up creates a tense and rigid environment, with students ultimately acting hard toward us as we act hard within ourselves.

If, however, we allow ourselves the "room" to be people who have feelings and imperfections, while still keeping focused on our goals as professionals, then our students will receive the message that it's okay to take risks, explore, and make mistakes in the classroom. They will consequently learn more, and the classroom will have a much better chance of becoming a vibrant, nurturing community.

If we forgive ourselves our imperfections, then ultimately our students will forgive us as well — at least when they are in the classroom. They will act soft (forgiving) toward us, reflecting our own inner softness.[1] This will have an immediate impact on our classroom management success. As our students soften, they will be more likely to be more cooperative and

Wise-Apple Advice

If we forgive ourselves our imperfections, then ultimately our students will forgive us as well — at least when they are in the classroom.

Wise-Apple Advice

Openness to others' ideas and feedback is a key to letting go of seeking unattainable perfection.

follow our directions, and less likely to act out and argue. In classroom management, who we are counts equally as much as what we do.

Openness to others' ideas and feedback is a key to letting go of seeking unattainable perfection. It is critically important for any teacher — especially any new teacher, and most mentor teachers and coaches would agree. For teachers to explore, take risks, and learn in the classroom, sometimes they need input from others. Knowing when our own resources need a boost is the first step. Being open to receiving that boost is the second.

Mrs. Allgood has a way of giving and receiving advice and suggestions that appears seamless. It's part of who she is to be open with her colleagues, even laughing at her mistakes while simultaneously feeling confident in her abilities. If we don't look closely, we might assume that she has never needed help and support from colleagues. But if we seek out and ask the Mrs. Allgoods in our schools, we'll discover that their openness and willingness to seek support are fundamental building blocks of that confident persona.[2]

Characteristics of a Good Teacher

In my workshops, I often run an activity where participants brainstorm characteristics of a good teacher. Many participants remember the Mrs. Allgoods who once taught them when they were students, or who currently teach across the hall. All sorts of adjectives are thrown about. A typical workshop might yield the following good-teacher characteristics:

Flexible	Communicative
Organized	Reflective
Knowledgeable	Firm
Sense of humor	Positive
Fair	Consistent
Patient	Enthusiastic
Caring	Honest

After this brainstorm, I then include characteristics that I suggest are equally essential. These include:

Sometimes makes mistakes   *Sometimes feels overwhelmed*
Sometimes has bad days   *Sometimes feels stressed*
Sometimes feels helpless   *Sometimes feels under-appreciated*

Many of us go into the profession thinking that we are supposed to be perfect. We think we're never supposed to feel certain feelings or have certain experiences. But the reality is that we have all sorts of experiences in the classroom. We have days where we just don't want to get out of bed. We have times when we're really angry at our students, or angry at ourselves.

If we don't allow for and welcome these feelings up front, then when they inevitably occur, we will do our best to try to hide or deny them. We will become rigid, and eventually tend to blame our students, our situations, or ourselves for why we feel the way we do. At the very least, we will tend to shy away from other teachers, because we won't want to be seen as less than stellar. Wrong move. Bad days are a signal, a special code other teachers know all too well; it lets us know it's a key time to talk with a colleague about how we are feeling and what is happening in our classes.

I've mentored many new teachers over the years, and just like me, all of them — beginners to veterans — sooner or later have had the experience of feeling inferior as teachers. They were not inferior. They just had an experience that some chose to run from. They did this by putting up walls between themselves and the students, and between themselves and me. They decided to go into "self-protection mode" and "ride out the storm." Of course, the "storm" was just life, and their decision to ride it out by retreating into their shell was what caused or magnified most of their anxiety.

Mrs. Allgood says

When we "hit the wall," it is precisely the time to reach out to our colleagues.

Openness is not a strategy. It is an orientation — a life skill that filters into every aspect of our lives, both professional and personal. Our openness to sharing our thoughts and experiences with colleagues and friends softens us, so that when we hold our ground with students, our firmness is matched by our kindness.

Countering Isolation

Let's look at the italicized list above, and focus more closely on the teacher quality "sometimes feels helpless." As a teacher, this simply means, "doesn't always know what to do." Let's say Mrs. Meanswell is in the staff room between lessons or classes. She's got fifteen minutes before she goes back to class, and she realizes that her lesson plan is not going to work. For whatever reason, what looked good last night is now clearly a bomb waiting to go off. There's another teacher in the staff room who may just be able to help. Mrs. Meanswell basically has three choices.

- ▲ She can apologize internally for the fact that she's not quite sure what to do, and do the "duck and cover" routine by avoiding that teacher and keeping to herself.
- ▲ She can apologize internally for the fact that she's not quite sure what to do, and put on a false bravado by pretending that everything is "great!"
- ▲ She can choose not to apologize internally for the fact that she's not quite sure what to do, and simply ask for help.

This last option can be a lifesaver.[3] We need to find people whose opinions we trust, and then ask away without holding back, talking with mentor teachers, master teachers, supervisors, peer coaches, colleagues, foremen, or whatever name our fellow teachers go by.

There's no way we can be expected to know what to do in every situation. There's no way we can do it all, know it all, and make all the right decisions. There is no way that the experiences of our one lifetime-as-a-teacher can match the combined experiences of all of the other teachers in our building, our district, or our workshops. We need help! This is true for all teachers, regardless of their level of experience.

My Bumpy Start

When I was a student teacher, I was working in a county that had a glut of teachers and very few available teaching jobs. I spent my four months of student-teaching focused not on improving my craft as a teacher, not on learning the mechanics and subtleties of the art of teaching, not on cementing relationships with mentors, but on *getting a job*. I walked around for four months trying to prove to everyone that I was the right man for the job. I focused on my mantra: "I know what to do, thank you very much, and any staff would be proud to have me as their colleague." When April / May rolled around and it became apparent to me that my classroom management system had huge holes in it, I had a very bumpy time getting help because I had isolated myself from my much more experienced colleagues.

Conversely, one of my student-teacher friends at the time had a similar assignment at a similar school. Sometime in the first week of her student teaching, she fell apart crying in the presence of her colleagues, asking some of the staff members of her department for help. The next day when she came back to school, her mailbox contained lesson plans, invitations to dinner, and encouraging and heartfelt cards. She was willing to show how she felt that first week, while I tried to cover it up. Two years later she was a tenure-tracked teacher at that school, and I was interviewing for teaching jobs. It was a hard lesson, but one that I'll, thankfully, never forget.

Synonyms for Help

If the word "help" is intimidating, then there are synonyms listed below that may be easier to stomach. The main thing is not the word choice — it's that we ask!

Help

Advice

Collegiality

Collaboration

Educational Consulting

Professional Development

All these words describe the same thing: "show and tell." Working together is an essential element for teachers to survive and flourish. However skilled and inspired we feel inside, we will tend to become stilted and burned out if we don't get in the habit of reaching out. In addition, sharing with colleagues, looking at student work, and figuring out together what we can do differently will have a great impact on our students' ultimate academic achievement.

We Receive the Help We Ask For

No matter what we name it, when we ask for help, magic happens. The first indication is that we receive the help we ask for. I have been asking for help from colleagues, administrators, and students for many years — sometimes many times a day — and I have never once been turned down.

One time, when I was a first-year teacher, I was about to be evaluated by the principal. I was anxiously reviewing my lesson plan during my prep period when I realized trouble was ahead: I had planned my lesson around a book that I had forgotten to ask the students to bring to school! There was another teacher in the staff room at the time, but she was on the phone with her back to me. I meekly interrupted to ask if she could help me with my lesson plan, to which she replied, without turning around, "Sure. Why don't you check with me after school?"

"After school," I thought, "I'll have plenty of time, because I'll be out of a job." Aloud I said only, "Thank you." Something in my voice, some squeak or fluctuation of desperation, got through to her. She turned around, took one look at my face, and barked into the phone, "Gotta go. Teacher down! Hold my calls! Medic!!"

Needless to say, I received the help I needed just in the nick of time, and was able to keep my job. Otherwise this might be a manual on burger-flipping strategies.

Openness is Win-Win

We've established the benefits to the teacher on the receiving end of assistance in a teaching environment, but there is also a flip-side in this exchange. Our openness can improve the experiences of the teachers on the giving end, who will appreciate not being cornered with a defensive colleague. If receiving help at first is challenging, think of the untenable position of a mentor offering help to a struggling, resistant, know-it-all, "Teflon teacher" — who allows suggestions to slide off unreceived and untried.

And then remember the magic. Those who give us help blossom even more than we do. When they share their expertise, colleagues begin to reflect on their craft and appreciate what they know. Many principals and administrators seek to hire brand new teachers for this reason — to enliven a grade level or department with the collegial interaction that occurs when new teachers come on board.

Mrs. Allgood says

Those who give us help blossom even more than we do.

Years ago I was asked by board members at a school district to help them design a mentor program. They told me that they had enough money budgeted for one full-time director. I suggested that instead of hiring one full-time person, they hire two half-time people (they could spend the other half continuing as classroom teachers). That way, the co-directors could talk to each other, and model the collegial spirit that they would be trying to instill in their mentors and new teachers. This is indeed what happened, and the two co-directors worked together successfully for years. Their collegiality both served them and acted as a model for the teachers and mentors in their program.

I believe that we learn most by teaching, whether it is teaching students or other teachers. Further, as professionals, we are all hungry to be acknowledged and appreciated. When asked for help, we receive that recognition and deepen our understanding and appreciation of our own skills as professionals.

▲ ▲ ▲

Helpful Strategies for Beginning Teachers

There are several areas where new teachers don't yet know the ropes. Having a heads-up beforehand can make things a lot easier.

Share Evaluations with Trusted Teachers

After receiving your evaluations from the administration, please share them with a mentor teacher / support provider, regardless of what the evaluations say. One or more "needs improvements" can provide opportunities for your mentor to help you hone in on the solutions. If the evaluation is excellent, then you and your mentor can share a well-deserved sense of pride. Either way, discussions centering on evaluations are often rich and insightful.

Read Between the Lines of Evaluations

Like mentor teachers, administrators know that teachers like Mrs. Meanswell need encouragement. If a first evaluation were totally negative, Mrs. Meanswell might shut down and go into a shell, thereby limiting her opportunity for growth. Some administrators often use the first evaluation more as a carrot than as a stick. They emphasize the positive, with only a small percentage focusing on the negative, *even if the negative is enough to warrant end-of-the-year dismissal.* The potential problem is that Mrs. Meanswell needs to know clearly what is not satisfactory. Many times I've had to walk new teachers through their first evaluations, pointing out areas for improvement that the teachers thought to skip over, because the overall tone of the evaluation was so positive.

Document Everything

Being open doesn't mean being naïve. In addition to asking for help and sharing successes and challenges, being open also means being aware of potentially sticky situations, and dealing with them proactively. One strategy is to document all potentially controversial decisions, conversations, and actions. A simple way is to have a notebook or online document in which to record conversations and interactions with parents, administrators, students, and others. Simply note the date and time, a basic summary of the content of the interaction, and any direct quotes that might help down the line if someone might remember a conversation differently. Another way is to use an index card for each student. This makes it easier to gather notes for parent conferences.

A Closer Look

Some administrators often use the first evaluation more as a carrot than as a stick.

Giving Students Chances to Ask for Help

Teachers are not the only ones who need help in the classroom, but it is their job to pave the way for students to feel safe in accepting that essential direction. In Chapter 7, "Positive Connections," there are several suggestions for encouraging openness in students. Among them: suggestion boxes; community circles; and designated signals, such as objects placed on desks or hand signals for students to utilize if they need us.

However we go about it, our mentorship in this area is crucial to addressing the needs of the student as a whole person. Our modeling openness certainly starts the process, but there is more we can do.

Remembering that We are Role Models

We know that being open takes the edge off the challenges of being human. But being a teacher means being open to more than asking for help; it also means being a role model. Our students learn about themselves by measuring their experiences against those of people in their community. One of our jobs is simply to be seen as an imperfect, kind, and ideally self-forgiving adult out in the world.

Our openness to taking on this task is a quality that rubs off in our teaching and in our personal relationships with our students. This is true regardless of how old our students are. I remember one of my high school students once spotted me in the grocery store:

Student:	"MR. SMITH!! WHAT ARE YOU DOING HERE?!??!!"
Me:	"Shopping."
Student:	"SHOPPING!! OH MY GOODNESS, MY TEACHER IS SHOPPING!!"
Me:	"Well, the school lets me out on Saturdays for good behavior…."

In that silly moment, I realized that the student had never thought of me outside the classroom. I had to let it be okay that he could look in my basket and see that I had a secret passion for organic, GMO-free, gluten-free pasta. This open approach helped immensely when the stakes were higher, when problems arose and feelings got hurt and solutions were necessary. My students began to trust the person I was, and to know they were safe with me.

5

GOT
STRESS?

"Life is what happens to you while you're busy making other plans."

— JOHN LENNON

HERMANSEN

HOWEVER PROFICIENT WE ARE, however prepared, positive, effective, and resilient, we are going to spend some up-close and personal time experiencing stress. How we address this can make a big difference in our overall outlooks, attitudes, and successes as teachers — and as people. There certainly seems to be a correlation between how effective we are at reducing stress and how effective we are at managing our classes, regardless of our level of experience.[1] Taking the time to address the causes of our stress and some possible antidotes isn't a luxury; it's a necessity. Veteran teachers please note: although this chapter is primarily oriented toward minimizing the stress of the new teacher, it's applicable across the board. The stress of the new teacher, if gone unchecked, can manifest in patterns that result in the burnout of the veteran. Regardless of our level of teaching experience, we always have opportunities to slow down, exhale, shift those patterns, and renew our enthusiasm for teaching.

Expectations

In my workshops I often ask participants what they think is the biggest source of stress for teachers. I get the full gamut of responses, ranging from writing lesson plans and grading papers, to talking with irate parents or handling challenging situations in the classroom.

I suggest that none of these is the prime culprit. Nor is writing Individual Education Plans (IEPs), dealing with unyielding adminstrators, implementing the new standards, or trying to teach an engaging lesson. I suggest that the single biggest source of stress for teachers is:

Unrealistic expectations of themselves.

Each of the individual stressors mentioned above is certainly part of teaching. But each of them can be stressful or not, depending on what we see as the measure of true success as a teacher.

Granted, we need to work a lot of hours a day in order to teach well. But those hours can be more relaxed if we aren't constantly looking over our shoulders — wondering if we're good enough, doing it right, pleasing the administration, or getting the students to like us. And of course it's tough for new teachers because they don't really know what to expect. Here's a potent analogy:

Being a new teacher is like trying to fly an airplane…while building it.

New teachers have to take care of the daily "doingness" of teaching, such as planning lessons and grading papers. But at the same time they have to figure out the big picture. Have you ever tried to put together one of those do-it-yourself bookshelves? Frustrating nightmare! Ever built a second one right after the first? Piece of cake! This is because we had to go through the process of learning the directions as we put the first one together. By the second time, the secret was out.

A Closer Look

Our job description is infinite — and this is the good news.

For the entire first year I taught, I was wrangling a dismantled Boeing 787. I was generally one day ahead of my students. I didn't mention to them that I had learned their day's lesson the night before; I naturally tried to impress upon them only how vital the information was and how they couldn't live without it (see "Being prepared" in Chapter 3, "Inner Authority"). I kept this desperate approach as an embarrassing secret until I later learned that I was right on track for a new teacher. My 787 was wobbly, with only two engines firing, but it was in the air.

With experience, teaching becomes easier. But how much experience does it take until we know the air-traffic controllers by name? When I was getting my credential, I was told:

▲ The average teacher teaches the same thing three years in a row before "feeling comfortable" with it.

▲ The average teacher doesn't plateau in ability for seven years.

I would suggest that excellent teachers don't plateau at seven years. They never plateau. Such is the blessing and the curse of teaching — we can always do it better.

Our Infinite Job Description

The job description of a teacher is infinite. We can always give more feedback on our students' work. We can always devote more time to our bulletin boards. We can always make more phone calls to parents. Our job is never-ending.

This is the *good news*. Why? For several reasons. First, if we find ourselves going to bed at night with a sense of incompleteness about our work, then we know we're right on track. Teachers who thrive in the profession know this feeling well, and have learned to accept and embrace it. Second, because we can't do everything, we shouldn't try. We will never dot every "i" and cross every "t." The nature of our job demands that we make choices, that in some areas we work as impeccably as we can, and in other areas we only do what is essential. Mrs. Allgood rarely complains about the fact that her job is never done. She recognizes the feeling of incompleteness as part of what it means to be a successful teacher. She picks her priorities, focuses on them, and lets the rest go. Third, crucial to our emotional health, we need to realize that however good we are at classroom management, sometimes nothing we try seems to work. To recognize this, to ask for help, and to try again is simply part of what it means to be a teacher.

This news is especially pertinent for new teachers, because they often come into the profession thinking that they have to do it all flawlessly. Since by definition "all" is unachievable, a rethinking is necessary. Otherwise, the new teacher will feel as if she is falling further and further behind some mythical signpost of competence. Unlike actual planes, that classroom 787 may never have all its parts, but it flies well anyway.

My Criteria for Success

When I first started teaching, **I measured my success by how successful my students were.** While laudable, this turned out to be quite stressful. Why? Because I ultimately had no control over their success! I could certainly make a difference, but my students made their own choices and their own pathways through life. In truth, sometimes students do poorly even when teachers are rock stars, and sometimes students do well even with less than stellar teaching.

After riding a roller coaster during my first couple of years — with my sense of personal value soaring and plummeting with my students' successes and failures — eventually I developed a second, seemingly more stable criterion. Instead of relying on my students' choices and results, I based **my sense of success on how available I made success to them.** Soon, however, I realized that this was problematic as well, because I could always make more effort! No matter how hard I tried, I could always do more. Even if I was working fourteen-hour days, grading papers with copious comments, working on bulletin boards on the weekends, conducting parent visits at night, I could always do more to make success available to my students. There was no limit, so I found myself constantly falling short of some unachievable goal of perfection.

Finally, after several years, I developed a third way to measure my success, which I use to this day: **"How relaxed am I?"** That's it! The key is that I can't be relaxed unless I am doing a really good job. Not a perfect job, but a really good one. After a few years in the classroom, I internalized what makes sense in terms of my efforts, given the limitations of time and resources. In that "sweet spot" lies my integrity. I don't serve anyone if I burn out after six months, and I can't look myself in the mirror if I am not working hard to make a difference. Relying on this inner compass has reduced my stress level immensely, while allowing me to both thrive and rejuvenate in my role as teacher.

The Bottom Line: Expectations for New Teachers

With all of this focus on reducing stress, what's the bottom line? What realistic expectations might a new teacher have for her first year?

If, after your first year of teaching, you want to continue in the profession, and if, after your first year of teaching, the administration wants you to return, then you have had a successful first year.

Granted, there is a lot of room for new teacher performance above and beyond this bottom line, but these are the "bones." Sometimes in working with new teachers, I see them get so concerned about the minutiae that they forget to take a look every once in a while at the big picture. Yes, it's important to give each student the proper grade, and yes, it's important to fill out all of the various forms correctly. But in the end, the bottom line is: Do you want to come back? Do they want you to come back? You'll improve dramatically in your second year. You'll improve dramatically in your third year. As long as you leave open the possibility of returning so that you can improve and continue to support students, you're on the right track.

Ask Mrs. Allgood how her first teaching years were. She will most likely laugh to herself or sigh, and admit how difficult they were. In the next breath, she'll affirm how glad she is that she stayed with it.

> **Wise-Apple Advice**
>
> Our caring gets us into stress — our caring can get us out.

Emotional Nurturing

Focusing on our emotional health can dramatically reduce stress. Below are several approaches and strategies.

Caring for Ourselves

On a Boeing 787, or even on a puddle-jumping prop, just before takeoff the flight attendant tells us that in the event of sudden cabin air-pressure loss, an oxygen mask will drop from the ceiling. The kicker: if we are traveling with a small child, we should put on our masks first, and then take care of the child. Why do we put on our own masks first? If not, both parent and child might lose consciousness.

The main reason we get so stressed as teachers is because we care so much about the success of our students. Therefore, it can be said that our caring gets us into stress. And, I would suggest, our caring can get us out. We have, inside us, a "laser beam" of caring that we often focus on our students. By adjusting our laser beam to also monitor our own well-being, we can greatly reduce our stress, without losing sight of our students' success and without losing our integrity. We need to slap that oxygen mask on our faces. Period. Even though we're in this for the kids. Even though education and schools are all about the kids. We can't give what we don't have. If we fail to monitor our own levels of stress and we

Mrs. Allgood says

We are human beings, not human doings.

burn out, then we are doing ourselves and our students a disservice. Ultimately, teachers who are good to themselves deliver the best teaching.

How do we take care of ourselves in the classroom? We can start by making the "unconscious" conscious, the "automatic" intentional. When you experience a rough or problematic school situation, ask yourself "How do I feel?" as well as "What should I do?" Both questions are valid and essential, and they unravel our autopilot responses in stressful situations that are over before we've had a chance to think or reflect. Yes, we need to take care of business, often right away. Equally as important, we need to take care of ourselves in the process, so that we are calm and resourced moving forward.

My approach is to "check in" regularly with my feelings — the good, the bad, and the ugly — with a trusted colleague, mentor teacher, or friend. Others prefer a more solitary approach. For example, some choose to keep a journal — whatever works best. The point is to balance our emotional responses with our actions so that we are responsive and resilient, and our students receive consistency. Also, our willingness to feel our feelings, even if they are uncomfortable, can be quite a release — especially as we let go of our efforts at holding back how we feel.

Five Minutes a Day

During my last teaching job, the bell would ring to end third period, and the kids would go flying out the door to be the first ones in line at the cafeteria. I would follow them, get my bagel and cream cheese, walk to the staff room, eat my bagel and cream cheese, and return to class just before the bell rang for fourth period. At some point in this cycle, it dawned on me that during break, *I was never resting*. I had stopped assuming the best about myself and was being a robot, doing the "robot-break thing." So I decided to try something different, which worked so well I did it in one form or another every day from then on.

When the bell would ring to signal break, after the kids had flown out of the room, I would do nothing. I would simply stand still, and begin to notice my feet — I tended to forget that I had feet when I taught. So I stood still; I walked slowly around the room; I took off my shoes. Gradually I'd begin to notice my breath. What part of my body was receiving breath? I would walk over to the window and look out at the trees to the right, not at the traffic to the left, and maybe gaze at the birds' nests that had been built in the corner of my windows. I would not return phone calls, make lists, grade papers, or check on lesson plans — nothing to do directly with teaching. Invariably, after a few minutes, something shifted. I stopped being a machine on auto-pilot, and returned to being a person who had chosen to teach. I could once again access positive assumptions about myself — that I was whole and innocent and inspired to work with students. This five-minute shift was an invaluable vacation. I could then get my bagel and cream cheese and join the staff or join the students, but I would be so much more relaxed and resilient.

So my suggestion is:

Sometime during the day, take five minutes of unstructured time for yourself.

Disengage from the job description and remember yourself. Metaphorically step away from your role as teacher, and reconnect with yourself as a human *being*, rather than a human *doing*.

This is not as easy as it may seem. Finding five minutes during the school day is often quite difficult. It needs to be a priority. Once at a school district function I shared this five-minute idea with a principal of a neighboring school. He decided to try it, and reported great results. The only problem was that whenever I needed to contact him for school-related business, his reply was always, "Not now, Rick; I'm doing my five minutes!"

Mindfulness

Mindfulness is a research-based practice that is rapidly gaining ground as a way for students to lower anxiety, increase memory, and improve connections with themselves and others.[2] You'll find more on mindfulness for students in Chapter 11, "Lesson Design."

Mindfulness also works for teachers as a tool for self-care. Many find noticeable shifts in their awareness, attitude, and stress level in about a minute. So, here's a practice, similar to "Five Minutes a Day," described above, that you can do right now — even before you finish reading this chapter.

Sit comfortably and close your eyes. For a minute or so, pay attention to your breath, without trying to change it. Notice the passage of air through your nostrils or mouth, and the rise and fall of your rib cage and belly. If your attention wanders, simply notice, and then gently bring your attention back to your breathing. Again, there's no need to try to adjust your breathing pattern. Just observe what happens naturally as you witness your breath.

After a minute, what do you notice? Do you feel calmer? More energized? Many teachers find that even though they haven't checked anything off of their "to-do" lists, an item called "my own well-being" hovers closer to the top. This gentle exercise allows their perspectives to realign.

Another breathing technique is to sit quietly and take ten slow, deep, relaxing breaths. This can work at school as well as at home. Gently focus your awareness on your breathing as you do this. This simple technique can work wonders.

Inspiring Messages from You to You

Several quick and effective reminders can enhance your classroom experience. For example, try keeping a book of inspirational quotes with you at home and at school, and refer to it often, especially when overwhelming feelings are knocking on your door. As a classroom teacher, Grace compiled a personalized notebook with positive quotes from students, parents, administrators, and other teachers. Anytime someone said or wrote something positive about her teaching, she put it in the notebook, and would read it whenever her self-esteem needed a boost.

A Closer Look

Our minds know the difference between real laughter and made-up laughter, but our bodies don't!

In addition, you can find a picture that makes you feel good inside. It could depict loved ones, someone you admire, an image of a student graduating, or perhaps a scene in nature. Keep the picture somewhere in your classroom, and glance at it whenever you need to relax.

When I first started teaching, I didn't have my own classroom, and thus didn't have my own desk on which to place a calming, inspirational photo. Instead, I wore a necklace that I got while traveling in Thailand. Whenever I started to feel stressed in the classroom, my hand would reach to my necklace, and I would think to myself, "warm tropical breezes, warm tropical breezes…."

Setting Boundaries Around School Focus

Many teachers need to talk about their school experiences in order to relax. Find colleagues you can confer with, vent with, and plan with. Also consider making dates with colleagues to spend time talking about things that are not school-related! The shift can be a great stress reliever. In addition, consider making dates with friends and family members during which you consciously focus your attention away from school and teaching. This can be challenging, particularly when you are a new teacher, and are feeling overwhelmed. By the way: no worries if it makes more sense to you to focus on school stuff in order to relax. Please — no need to stress about finding ways not to stress!

Laughter

Laughing can bring huge benefits to our immune systems, as well as increasing our mental clarity and retention. But you don't necessarily need to watch funny videos or movies. You can just start laughing. Our minds know the difference between real laughter and made-up laughter, but our bodies don't! We still get the benefits, even if our laughter isn't spontaneous.[3]

There are thousands of "laughter clubs" in more than sixty countries in the world, where people get together and simply laugh. Invariably, once the laughter starts, it becomes more and more genuine and spontaneous. The real laughter gets "kick-started" with fake "stand-in" laughter, and takes on a raucous life of its own.

Positive Attitude

A single situation can be viewed from many different perspectives; a positive perspective can reduce our stress. Below are strategies and approaches that illustrate this simple principle.

Acts of Kindness

According to research reported by Allen Mendler, author of *When Teaching Gets Tough: Smart Ways to Reclaim Your Game,* happiness can increase simply by counting one's own acts of kindness for one week. By consciously focusing on kindness, we tend to be kinder to ourselves.[4]

Focus on What's Working

Also from Mendler, track the positive by keeping a "three-good-things journal." Every day, document three things that went well in school and in your personal life, and what caused them.[5] Research on this approach suggests that this type of documentation — done for just seven days in a row — can reduce depression and increase happiness for months.[6]

Intention

In the morning, try setting an intention or goal for the day, as well as an intention for your connection with kids at school. These goals are more likely to occur if you can *feel* the satisfaction of your day as you set the intention — not just *see* it in your mind.

In addition, try setting a positive intention for each class or lesson that you are about to teach. That is, instead of "gearing up for a tough class," you can prepare for the possibility of wonder. Finally, try focusing before bedtime on what you are grateful for that happened during the day.

Note: If we try to "wallpaper over" our negative feelings by forcing positive feelings to take their place, our stress will likely increase. There is, I suggest, a "sweet spot" in consciousness, where we can notice and welcome all of our feelings — including sadness, anger, frustration, fear, and the feeling of being overwhelmed — while leaning in the direction of the positive. This perspective expands our overall authentic positivity.

Appreciation

Choose three colleagues at school and share one or two things that you appreciate about each of them. Start with people you know and with whom you feel comfortable. Then, for a challenge, consider choosing colleagues that you don't often speak with, or even colleagues with whom you may have conflicts. Make sure that the appreciations you share are genuine and from the heart. Even with your most challenging colleagues, you can always find genuine appreciations. Reminder: this isn't a "gratitude exchange." It's quite possible that you won't receive appreciations in return. No worries — it's our expression of gratitude that is itself the biggest reward.

Another option is to spend time with colleagues, consciously sharing things we appreciate about students. This is often an easier first step than sharing what we appreciate about each other directly.

Rejuvenation

Zoning out in front of the television can be just what the doctor ordered when we are feeling stressed and overwhelmed. But we also can try channeling our energies differently. Create something. Your project could be a song, a tree house, new dance moves, a collage, or working in the garden. Paint, write, sing, play music, sculpt — whatever allows you to access your creative juices. These activities can work wonders in giving you a broader perspective and alleviating work pressure.

In addition, try playing. Playing? When I was a child, I would go over to my friend's house and ask, "Wanna play?" We didn't know what we were going to do, but we knew it would be creative and fun. What form of "play" works for you?

Wise-Apple Advice

> In the morning, try setting an intention or goal for the day, as well as an intention for your connection with kids at school.

Perhaps you have a religious or spiritual practice that helps you center and remember your own well-being and goodness. Maybe it's prayer or meditation or reading a spiritual text.

Make an effort to connect with nature. The rejuvenating effects are often immediate. Here's a confession: When I travel to other cities to work (which I do constantly), I often find a grassy spot outside the hotel, take my shoes off, and plant my feet on the ground. I know, you're thinking, "He's from California — of course he does something goofy like that!" Well, I'm a convert. My embarrassment at being caught with my shoes off has become outweighed by the immediate relief I feel, as the stress of the plane flight and the time-zone shift drains out of my body and into the earth.

While at school, consider changing your patterns. Try varying where and with whom you take breaks and eat meals. Take a chance on expanding your circle, and see where you can share and receive new insights and inspirations.

Physical Nurturing

Our bodies are equipped to deal with tremendous stress and strain. But they could use our help. There are a number of things we can do for our bodies to prevent and alleviate stress.

Movement

In Chapter 11, "Lesson Design," I write about the importance of movement for our students. This is just as true for us. Movement increases the flow of oxygen and glucose to the brain. Create a daily movement practice. It could be jogging, swimming, aerobics, dancing, yoga, cycling, walking, or my favorite — Ultimate Frisbee™. After work, we often have a choice between napping and exercising. If you consistently choose the nap option, and aren't getting any movement in your days, try switching to exercise. The first few minutes can be challenging, until the endorphins kick in and you feel a sense of aliveness and energy.

Shoes and Clothes

Dedicate a healthy percentage of your clothing budget to comfortable shoes. Wear clothing that is professional and feels empowering, at the same time allowing you to relax and feel at ease when you teach.

Touch

Our bodies benefit when we safely give and receive touch. Schedule a massage for yourself. Offer to massage someone else's shoulders. As counterintuitive as it seems, massaging someone else can be a great benefit to you. If you're in a relationship, make dates with your partner to snuggle and hold each other, even when you don't think you have the time. Hug your friends. Hug yourself. Hug a pet. Find ways and excuses to regularly make safe physical contact with living, breathing bipeds and quadrupeds.

Food and Water

Whatever your water intake is, you will probably benefit by doubling it. I'm not a doctor — so please take this with "a grain of salt" (pun intended!).

Take the time to consciously plan your meals for the week, perhaps shopping on Sunday to get things ready. Do your best to avoid caffeine and processed sugars, particularly during stressful times.

This practice can be particularly valuable during the December holiday season. Even though the kids seem excited about the holidays, they are often more stressed than usual. Their vacation expectations are too high, or they may have tough family situations and fear losing the stability of the school schedule during the break. But they are not alone; many teachers ruefully admit that they don't get sick except during vacations. This seems especially true for the December holidays. In each of my first three years, I got swept up in the stress and drama of pushing myself to make it to the "finish line" of the Friday before vacation, fighting a cold or sore throat, only to lose the fight on the first day of the break.

After years of struggle, I came up with a solution. I made a conscious decision not to eat any sweets between Thanksgiving and the December break, because the influx of holiday sugar seemed to lower my immune system. I kept my hands off parents' cakes, the PTA's pies, and the kids' candy canes and chocolate. I seemed to cope better with all of the stresses of the vacation and the new winter germs — and I stopped getting sick.

Stress in the Staff Room

Teachers often gather in the staff room to vent about their students. This "off-the-record" emotional download can help give teachers a chance to exhale and release stress from the day. However, without assuming the best, venting also can take on a life of its own, leading to teacher cynicism and burnout. When we are tired or stressed, we can lose track of our positive assumptions about students. This can lead to a kind of self-destructive form of complaining, rather than a self-creative form of emotional navigation. If this venting isn't balanced with more positive expressions, staff rooms can become stressful environments that take on a negative atmosphere as their default culture. Just like any habit, it might feel good in the moment to join in the venting, but over time, we can find ourselves boxed in by the excessive expression of negativity, making it challenging to "stem the tide."

Wise-Apple Advice

In the staff room, consider placing a sign next to you that says "Positive-Talk Zone" or "Good News Only."

On the other hand, it can be a courageous and vulnerable act to "swim upstream" in a staff room by expressing positive regard for students. Try pointing out successes of your students or others' students. Express the silver lining about students. Consider placing a sign next to you that says "Positive-Talk Zone" or "Good News Only."[7] Let staff members know that that section of the staff room is reserved for discussing appreciations and positive perspectives. The conversations can be about anything, as long as they are positive.

If you are shy about doing this, try planning to do it with a colleague, or try doing it only on Fridays at first, and see what happens. The "positive-talk zone" works best when we assume the best about our colleagues and ourselves, and recognize that even though we are tired or overwhelmed, we hold our students close to our hearts.

The familiar dynamic of over-venting in staff rooms often applies to conversations about parents, administrators, or other teachers. The same solutions are possible, as we take courageous steps to infuse the staff room with a more inclusive and positive tone, assuming the best about all the stakeholders at the school or district. I remember early in my teaching career when a twenty-year science teacher was made my school's assistant principal. The teachers were thrilled that "we finally have someone on our side." This sense of triumph was soon followed by dismay, as the new assistant principal made decisions that were no different from those that the previous administrators had made! We are all well intentioned — wanting to care for students — but our job descriptions can make it seem as if we are on opposite sides. Remembering this can soften animosity in a school or in a staff room, thus reducing stress in our teaching environment, and ultimately benefiting ourselves, one another, and our students.

Time Management

Imagine it's a Tuesday evening at about eight o'clock, and you're at home with a stack of papers to grade. The phone rings and it's your friend asking you to drop everything and "go out." The "good teacher" on your right shoulder says, "Stay home and be responsible. Grade the papers." The "rebel" on your left shoulder shouts, "GO OUT!"

"Grade papers," says the good teacher.

"Go out," implores the rebel.

What should you do? My answer? At least every once in a while, go out! Not only will you be benefiting yourself, but you may be benefiting your students, as well. Research suggests that the more positive students' perceptions are of their teacher's feelings, the better the academic achievement — and the more desirable their classroom behavior, as rated by the teacher.[7]

In plain English, this means that if students sense that their teacher feels good, then they will exhibit positive classroom behaviors and perform better academically. So if going out every once in a while allows us to exhale in our lives, puts smiles on our faces, and brings us back into the classroom more relaxed and resilient, then please, by all means, let's go for it. Even though we won't have the students' papers corrected, our presence will be a much more positive factor in the classroom. We can always cite the above research and tell them that we were helping them succeed by not grading their papers!

Another strategy is to bring home, each day, only the amount of work that you can realistically grade/give feedback on that evening. Once that "short stack" is graded, then you are done! Psychologically, you've eliminated that imposing stack sitting on your desk at home that calls out to you to feel bad until you make a superhuman effort to take care of it. There also will be a tangible reward of free time in the evening, once you're finished with your allotted stack.

Along these same lines, schedule breaks for yourself, and make those breaks as much of a priority as your work time. Even if one effective technique is spontaneity, then schedule it in: "Tuesday, 8 p.m., be spontaneous for 1.3 hours…." Otherwise, teachers may end up like I was during large parts of my first few years as a teacher. At times, I made schoolwork so much more important than my "life" that periodically I'd wake up in the morning over the edge, in what I call "machine mode." No longer was I a person who taught. I had become a machine-teacher who was never quite good enough, and who was in constant need of repair.

> **A Closer Look**
>
> If students sense that their teacher feels good, then they will exhibit positive classroom behaviors and perform better academically.

One strategy to help alleviate this scenario is to set a timer when you are working at home, and schedule breaks during your work time. Also, consider setting a solid boundary whereby you don't focus on schoolwork for a minimum of half an hour (or an hour) before bedtime.

Speaking of bedtime, try getting to sleep earlier in the evening, and working in the morning before school, if you need to. The benefits of Ben Franklin's practice of "early to bed and early to rise…," are becoming verified by research into Circadian rhythms and sleep patterns.[9]

For tips on saving time in grading student work, check out the "Time-Saving Strategies" archived newsletters on our web site. A half-hour of reading can save you a dozen or more hours of labor during the school year.

Wise-Apple Advice

A Final Word on Stress

Make the effort to take care of yourself emotionally and physically. It's the only way you can truly serve your students. Remember to be as soft with yourself as you are with your students in your very best moments. Welcome all feelings of incompletion and inadequacy that inevitably come from this profession, but don't listen to them too closely. We are role models. Modeling this awareness, resiliency, and openness — while truly enjoying ourselves — is one of the greatest gifts we can give our students.

DOG TRAINING SCHOOL
(Homework Excuse #1)

PREVENTION —
What We Do
Proactively

*"An ounce of prevention is
worth a pound of detention."*

6

HOLDING OUR GROUND

*"What gives light
must endure burning."*

— VIKTOR FRANKL

Finish reading
Chapter 5
· Questions 1-9
· Test Friday

HERMANSEN

WHEN MRS. ALLGOOD TELLS a student to do something, he does it. When she gives a student a consequence for inappropriate behavior, the student does not erupt with unnecessary protests or complaining. Although we might not be able to see obvious reasons why students respond so well to Mrs. Allgood's directions, there is something going on under the surface that is making all the difference. I call this Mrs. Allgood's ability to hold her ground.

Holding our ground is challenging, regardless of the system of rules and consequences we have, regardless of the grades we teach, and regardless of the abilities or attitudes of our students. This invisible quality, this willingness to be firm without being mean, spills into everything we do as teachers. It influences the way we enforce consequences, impart information, describe procedures, talk with students about their lives, walk down the hall, and even how we feel about ourselves and our jobs.

I was once told that teachers make, on average, about fifteen hundred decisions each day. I'm guessing that a majority of them involve some form of holding our ground, as students provide us with a myriad of questions and situations that we need to address. Imagine a typical classroom situation where the students want one thing and we want another. If we can hold our ground with our students without discouraging them, without beating ourselves up, without having to go home that night and recover, and in a way that invites student cooperation, then we have succeeded at the hardest element of classroom management.

Saying "No"

How does one learn to hold one's ground effectively? While various components are sprinkled throughout this book, perhaps the most primary is our ability to say "no" when necessary, while remaining on our students' side.

In my classroom management workshops, I create an artificial situation where participants pair off and role-play. One person becomes a teacher, and another becomes a student in that teacher's class. The student's job is to get the teacher to allow him to leave the classroom, using whatever compelling reasons he can think of. The teacher's job is to communicate that the student can't leave, no matter what. Even though the role-play itself is unrealistic (we often say "yes" to students), I implement this role-play to make conscious the very real emotional charge that teachers can feel in moments of conflict with students. These moments are where we can best examine our strengths and challenges in learning to hold our ground with kindness and discernment.

A Closer Look

Our willingness to be firm without being mean spills into everything we do as teachers.

At one point in the role-play, I limit the teacher's vocabulary to two possible word-for-word responses:

No
I understand, and the answer is no.

Afterward, we talk about the teachers' experiences and identify several successful approaches.

Don't Over-Explain

First, most of the time, teachers don't need to explain why they are holding their ground with their students. In situations where they do need to explain, most likely they don't need to explain right away.

When we explain our reasons right away, invariably the student will provide a reason that he feels is better, even if his reasoning is biased on his own behalf. This can happen so often, it might seem as if students have "argue!" built into their genetic code! And they're not alone; all human beings prefer to hear a "yes" when they ask for something. Our students often respond to our "no" emotionally, before reason has a chance to kick in, exclaiming "WHY?!?" We are providing riverbanks, and their river initially protests at having to flow in an adverse direction. If we try to answer the question in the heat of the moment, the student may slip out of "right-brain-emotive" mode and jump into "left-brain-logical- debate-and-argue" mode. Before long, this debate can become the class lesson. Twenty or thirty pairs of eyes are watching it unfold. Pretty soon, kids will be calling out from the back of the room, "Let him go! He's right! Let him go!" Or just as bad, "Let's vote!" If this sounds familiar, then welcome to the teacher's nightmare: the "Land of Reasons."

The solution? Delay explanations until later. **Get the conflict off center stage.** Ask the student to approach you "in ten minutes when the bell rings" or "in four minutes after we start the artwork" or "in six minutes when we line up for recess." Getting the discussion out of the "moment" will keep more students on task, eliminate the involvement of "student lawyers," de-escalate issues to a time when cooler heads will prevail, and allow you to remain in charge. Let's remember to put the responsibility on the student to approach us, rather than committing to finding that student later. This will help in case we forget or get sidetracked (leaving the student feeling slighted), will teach the student the responsibility of following up on his concern, and will indicate to us more clearly if the student has a legitimate need that we need to address.

Giving the student options, such as, "Talk to me after school *or* at lunch tomorrow," puts an additional ownership on the student, and can soften the impact of your decision to delay the explanation. If and when you do explain, speak one-on-one to your student, out of earshot of others. When explanations are tabled, however, most of the time students won't end up coming up to us later and asking why. The reason is not that they are intimidated or cynical, but because once they have a couple of minutes to allow the dust to settle, they realize why you made the call — or they realize they don't particularly care why — and they settle down to work. On the other hand, if we offer a reason in the moment, while they are in emotive-blurt mode, we are essentially fighting a losing battle.

Mrs. Allgood says

Delay explanations until later — get conflicts off center stage.

Alternatives to delaying explanations include repeating the initial answer, or simply waiting silently. The silent option can be accompanied

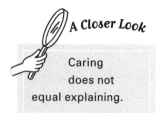

A Closer Look

Caring does not equal explaining.

by gestures, such as pointing to or looking at whatever the student should be doing.

The word "no" isn't what's critical; it's what it symbolizes. As long as we're not in the land of reasons, we don't need to use "no." We can answer in the affirmative: "Yes, Mark, you can discuss the homework assignment with me as soon as the bell rings." "Yes, Sally, you can sharpen your pencil in about three minutes when Omar finishes his oral report."

Avoiding an explanation does not correlate to a lack of caring for students. To underscore this fact, add simple sentences that go a long way: "I hear that you are very concerned, Maria. I see that this matters to you. I'll tell you what: please do have a seat now, and then come talk to me as soon as everyone starts working on their projects. Let's see then what we can work out." Caring does not equal explaining; Our commitment to fairness and compassion does not mean that we have to invite open, class-wide debates with our students about decisions we've made.

Characteristics of an Effective "No"

At first glance, we can't see why Mrs. Allgood's "no" is so effective. However, when we carefully compare her technique to Mrs. Meanswell's, we can start to discern vital differences.

An effective "no" has **no blame**. Mrs. Allgood doesn't blame Mark for the fact that he wants to page through a magazine, or leave the classroom, or talk with his neighbor. She simply communicates to him what needs to happen instead.

An effective "no" has **no complaining**. She doesn't complain, either under her breath or aloud, when Mark talks out of turn. She simply communicates in a matter-of-fact way that it is not appropriate.

An effective "no" has **no automaticity**. If we generally look for ways to accommodate our students by saying "yes" to them when we can, then when we say "no," their reactivity will remain minimal. Students will tend to trust us, knowing that if there was a way we could say "yes," we would.

An effective "no" has **no animosity**, **baiting**, **antagonism**, **waffling**, **sarcasm**, **attack**, **equivocation**, or **humiliation**. It is simple, clear, to the point, and kind.

Often, Mrs. Allgood will attach a consequence to her "no:" "Mark, if you continue to surf the Web instead of staying on task on the computer, you will be choosing to give up your computer privileges this period." There is nothing wrong with connecting consequences to holding our ground. This is explored in-depth in Chapter 12, "Rules and Consequences."

Ambiguous Characteristics of an Effective "No"

There are some surprising, even counterintuitive characteristics of an effective "no."

An effective "no" might include initial **hesitation**. Sometimes a student asks us something, and we honestly don't know what to decide. No problem. We can simply ask the student to ask again at a later time: "I'm not sure, Latisha. Please ask me again at the end of group work and I'll let you know then." If we assume that we should never be unsure of an answer, then we might pick an answer right away that we'll end up having to defend later. There's nothing wrong with changing our minds, either. Holding our ground is not about being rigid. It's more about our presence and inner authority as we respond flexibly to various situations.

An effective "no" may or may not have **wiggle room**. In general, when Mrs. Allgood holds her ground, she doesn't leave open any loopholes for Mark to try to squeeze through. She simply and clearly communicates that the answer is no. However, there are always exceptions. Sometimes there are circumstances that arise that are too hard for our students to reckon with. Be sensitive to discovering the unique situations of each of your students as you hold your ground with them, being open to conditions that might not fit the mold. It may be that Mark, for example, would best be served with a "yes," rather than a "no."

And yes, sometimes the kindest, most efficient choice a teacher has is indeed to offer a "no" packaged with an **immediate explanation to one student**, even as the whole class listens. There is no "one-size-fits-all" rule about this. It's just Mrs. Meanswell tends to over-explain, thus getting her into unnecessary trouble.

▲ ▲ ▲

When We are Angry in the Classroom

As we hold our ground, we might have feelings such as **anger**, **frustration**, or **guilt**. Just about all teachers have felt these emotions in the classroom, and they don't have to be a problem. The key is how we are with ourselves as we have these feelings. If we push them away, the feelings can come back to us magnified, ultimately undermining our effectiveness. Let's examine this more closely by focusing on teacher anger.

Let's say Mark is tapping his pencil, giggling, and calling out, thereby triggering a feeling of anger inside us. If we think, "Good teachers are never supposed to feel angry," then we'll try to overcome our anger by squelching or avoiding it. As we spend our energy this way and Mark continues to bother us, we will inevitably start to see him as the enemy. He is the one who is forcing us to feel inappropriate feelings. Soon blame will follow, along with either our snapping at him or being sarcastic. It goes something like this:

Externally:	"Mark, please stop talking and have a seat."
Internally:	(I won't be angry I won't be angry I won't be angry Anger isn't okay. Anger is for bad teachers.)
Externally:	"Mark, I said please stop talking and have a seat."
Internally:	(Stop making me angry! Anger is wrong! Stop doing this to me!)
Externally:	"Mark!!!"

This type of response is what I call **reactivity.** It is different from anger in that anger is a feeling that we all have from time to time. Like the weather, it comes and goes. Reactivity, on the other hand, is a *choice* that we make to take our anger out on someone — often ourselves.

What's the alternative? We simply take a deep breath and count to ten before responding. In that time of counting to ten, we re-assume the best about Mark and ourselves: that he wants to learn behavior, and that part of our job is to teach him appropriate behavior (this is explained more fully in Chapter 2, "Assume the Best"). We should remember that he is not out to get us, but instead he is simply communicating that he hasn't fully learned how to behave appropriately. We need to remind ourselves that there may be difficult situations in Mark's life that we don't know about or understand.

After counting to ten, we look inside, welcome the anger, and simply state in a calm voice what Mark needs to do. We acknowledge our anger internally, but don't act out of the anger. We simply note it to ourselves, avoid blaming anyone for it, and then act calmly and professionally.

Importantly, counting to ten, in and of itself, is often not enough. Many teachers tell me that the longer they count, the angrier they get! This was certainly the case for me when I first started teaching. Sometimes at night I'd get a phone call from a friend asking to go out, but I'd respond, "I can't. I'm too busy counting!" The key is to remember while we count that our students want to learn behavior. Further, our deep breaths oxygenate our brain, and help us to move our focus from reptilian "fight-or-flight" mode to the neocortex's higher-level thinking. Now, if I have feelings of anger in a teaching situation, it's no longer as big a deal as it was. I find I usually don't have to count to ten. I just need to take one deep breath, during which I make the choice to assume the best about my student, affirming that he wants and needs safety and structure, and then I express what I need to — without blowing up, without blaming the student for making me angry, and without blaming myself for being angry.

> **A Closer Look**
>
> Anger is a feeling — reactivity is a choice.

We can allow ourselves these natural feelings of anger, guilt, or anxiety, and yet not indulge or act them out. When these feelings knock on our door,

Let's let them in for tea —
but not serve them a seven-course meal!

The RRR Technique

Grace has come up with an approach she calls the "RRR" Technique. She advises teachers that when they feel angry, it's easy to remember the technique because they feel like growling ("R-R-R"). The first "R" stands for "Recognize" that we are angry, because often we lash out before we even realize what we are feeling. The second "R" prods us to "Re-orient" before acting out or making a decision we'll regret later. This involves calming down through taking a deep breath and assuming the best about our student — that he wants to learn appropriate behavior. The third "R" is "respond" to the situation, rather than react to it, going under the wave of resistance rather than into it.

Soft Eyes

All teachers feel frustrated from time to time. When our frustration spills into our voices and body language in the classroom, students feel it. Our frustration generates tension and increases the likelihood of an escalation of exactly what we're trying to stop in the first place. How do we take the frustration out of our voices? We soften our eyes. Specifically, we soften the muscle between the eyebrows (the "corrugator supercilli" muscle). Dr. Alex Korb writes:

> The facial expression of a furrowed brow is a large part of what it means to feel, and create, negative emotions. When you start to feel anxious or stressed or angry, notice if your brow is furrowed. Try relaxing your forehead, and it will help diminish the feeling.[1]

In our workshops, Grace and I give teachers a chance to conduct a simple role-play with a partner, in which they take turns trying to express frustration and anger — at the same time softening the muscles around the eyes. Kolb calls it using a "soft peripheral gaze," which requires noticing what is happening on the periphery of your sight while looking straight ahead. So far, with thousands of teachers making the attempt, no one has been able to keep frustration in her voice while her eyes are soft. It works like a charm! So, when you are doing your best to be calm in the classroom, but you can hear the tension escalating in your voice, take a moment to consciously relax the muscles around your eyes. Rather than squinting or staring or furrowing your brow, just let it relax, and watch the magic happen. Students will not only respond to your softer voice, but they'll also respond to the softer look on your face.

What about situations where we can't calm down quickly, and yet we have to discipline a student? If it's not a question of physical safety, I'd suggest leaning in the direction of not talking until it's possible to speak non-reactively with the student. If we react, regardless of our good intentions, we will communicate to the student that:

▲ we are frustrated at our own feelings of helplessness;
▲ the classroom is not safe; and
▲ the student is not welcome.

We will win the battle. That is, the offending student will most likely do our bidding. But we will then find ourselves in a land of battles. We will come to school on the defensive and preparing for confrontation instead of magic.

What happens if we get into a pattern of reactivity with our students? Hopefully, we'll be able to break the pattern by being responsive rather than reactive. But if we continually react with students, several things might happen:

▲ We will start to assume the worst about our students, rather than the best.

▲ They will become "bad kids" to us, rather than good kids making inappropriate choices.

▲ We will start looking for and seeing evidence to support this.

▲ Our students will start to reflect this negative assumption, by acting out more and challenging more, or by ceasing to participate in class discussions and activities.

▲ Ultimately, if they feel powerless and intimidated enough, it's possible that our students will start spreading rumors, possibly accusing us of things we haven't actually done. Ironically, when students do this, they are acting as "mirrors," reflecting that by not assuming the best about them, we are in essence "accusing" them of things they haven't done.

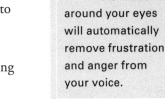

A Closer Look

Relaxing the muscles around your eyes will automatically remove frustration and anger from your voice.

These symptoms aren't the end of the world. But they are "yellow lights" in our universe. They are warning signals to take full responsibility for our feelings, to re-choose positive assumptions about ourselves and our students, and to regain their trust step-by-step through calm, clear, firm, and non-reactive communication and use of consequences.

In this circumstance, we also may need to explore our use of apology. Recognizing when and how to incorporate the dynamic of apology is a fine art. Please refer to Chapter 3, "Inner Authority," for an expanded discussion of this.

Finding an appropriate method and place outside of class to process our feelings of anger or anxiety is a critical component of self-care. This is addressed in Chapter 5, "Got Stress?" and Chapter 7, "Positive Connections."

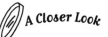

A Closer Look

If we react, we will win the battle. But we'll also find ourselves in a land of battles.

A Rite of Passage with Holding my Ground

When I was a beginning teacher, I took over as varsity boys' soccer coach at the high school where I had student-taught. In the summer before the season officially started, I played pickup soccer with the guys. There was a particular player named Justin, whom everyone agreed was the best player at the school, and who was needed in order for the team to have any chance of success.

This moment between his request and my reply was, I realized, a key rite of passage for me as a teacher.

At the end of one of the games, he came up to me and said, "Hey coach, I got a job working at a restaurant on Mondays and Thursdays starting at 4:30 p.m. Would it be okay if I missed the last half-hour of practice those two days during the season? Since all our games are on Tuesdays and Fridays, I won't miss any games."

When I asked him if there was any way he could adjust the hours of his job by thirty minutes, he said, "No. I already asked. They need me then, and I really need this job to save money for a trip to Mexico over spring break." I asked if it might help if I spoke to his employer, but Justin said that it wouldn't make a difference. Finally, he added, "If I can't miss those thirty minutes of practice twice a week, I'm going to have to skip soccer altogether."

In that moment between his statement and my next reply, time slowed down, and a wave of thoughts passed through my mind: That seems reasonable. He's the best player on the team, works hard and gives his all. It's only a half an hour. No big deal. I wouldn't want to see him miss his senior year of soccer. He will be the captain of the team, and his presence will help everyone play better and work better together.

But then the tone of my thoughts shifted: If Justin gets permission to leave early, then everyone is going to want to get similar permission. I'll start the season with my hands tied, because none of the players will believe that my rules and my authority matter. My heart goes out to him, but I need to be careful of what I say now, as it will set the tone for the entire season, even though it doesn't start for another three weeks.

This moment between his request and my reply was, I realized, a key rite of passage for me as a teacher. My insecurity about being offensive, inflexible, inhumane, mean, hurting the team, losing camaraderie with the players — all of that was right there on the surface in that five-second window. Without Justin, what would have been a mediocre team would have been downright awful, and a terrible win-loss record wouldn't bode well for my future as a soccer coach.

I decided to hold my ground.

So, inwardly shaking but outwardly calm, I told him that if he couldn't find a way to make it to the full practices, he would have to choose between his job (and perhaps his spring break trip) and soccer. He argued, and I calmly repeated my decision. He reacted, told me it was a stupid rule and that I was making a big mistake, and then he stormed off.

It took me a day or two to relax into the decision that I made. I was, after all, passionate about coaching soccer. I wanted to win every game and be "The Best Soccer Coach Ever."

I didn't see Justin again at any of the pickup games that summer, and I resigned myself to putting my all into having a fun, albeit losing season that fall.

Three weeks later, on the first official day of soccer practice, Justin showed up on time, dressed and ready to play. He said, "Hey coach, I was able to change the hours of my job. I'm in, and ready for a great season!"

The season rolled out in fine fashion. The boys respected my authority and we got along great. Although we didn't win every game, we played together all season as a coherent team.

I realized that if I had yielded to Justin's request, the season would have been a struggle from the start, with constant testing and complaining from the other players (and probably from Justin as well) about the rules.

Wise-Apple Advice

The Gray Area of Holding Our Ground

This is not to say that we need to be robotic and rigid in our responses or decisions. Often there is no clear-cut, right decision. Perhaps, for example, Justin needed to work in order to help his family pay for rent and groceries, rather than for a spring break trip (or perhaps the fact that Justin had a job at all would be enough for me to make an exception). What if Justin needed to attend 12-step meetings after school, or rehearse for the school play, or help with his little sister two afternoons each week when her day care was closed? In each unique situation, we can be both open-minded and in charge, as we look to support individual students as well as the whole. In making a choice in our role as teacher (or coach), it helps to anticipate what the ramifications of our decisions will be. The message we send with one decision will affect how our students respond, and can influence their challenges and successes, and the challenges and successes we have with them down the line.

7

POSITIVE CONNECTIONS

*"We can do no great things —
only small things with great love."*

— MOTHER TERESA

EXTENSIVE RESEARCH underscores how the teacher/student relationship impacts student learning and satisfaction.[1] How students feel about their learning environment has a huge effect on how much attention and effort they expend in the classroom[2] and profoundly affects their readiness to learn[3]. In other words, students "may not care about what you are teaching until you demonstrate that you care about them."[4]

In order for Mrs. Allgood to work her magic in the classroom, to create an environment where students trust and learn from her, she cultivates positive, healthy connections with her students. These connections are a frame of mind and a series of decisions that together — with practice — meld into intuition and then into action. Let's break positive connections into visible, workable pieces.

A Closer Look

If we genuinely care for our students, they'll know it, regardless of how they behave.

The Ingredients — Caring

If we personally and genuinely care for our students, then they'll know and appreciate us — no matter what classroom management menus we use, no matter what our teaching style.

As a new teacher I wanted to communicate to my students that I genuinely cared for them. I discussed this at length in university credential courses. But

Mrs. Allgood says

When we act to get the kids to like us, we give them our power. When we choose to be kind, we exercise our power to help our kids.

it wasn't until I had my own class that it slowly dawned on me: caring isn't a strategy; it's a choice. I began to realize that my students knew I cared for them, even when my lessons bombed and when they walked all over me. The hard part was realizing that even though they knew I cared for them, they still acted out and took advantage of my management loopholes.

Some of the Mrs. Allgoods out there are tough. How can they be so firm and yet convey to their students that they care? It's because their genuine caring underlies all that they do, and because they channel their caring into the safety and structure that their students need.

Doing What's Best, Not What's Easiest

It's our job to assume that regardless of what they claim, our students want what serves them best — what they most *need*. This doesn't mean that we shouldn't consider student opinion. It just means that we shouldn't be giving kids ice cream and cake for every meal.

Teachers often confuse being *nice* with being *kind*. This can get them into trouble. In my vernacular, being nice means doing things to get the kids to like us, and being kind means doing things that are truly in the students' best interest. Sometimes a specific action translates into both "niceness" and "kindness," but the key to how an action is interpreted lies in the reason *why* we make the decision. Students can read the energy behind our decisions, even if they do so unconsciously.

For example, Mrs. Meanswell's students are obviously struggling with a new lesson, which triggers her feelings of insecurity. ("I don't want my students to be mad at me.") So she gives the kids a break — choosing to be nice to them. On the other hand, when Mrs. Allgood teaches the same challenging lesson to her students, she might also give her kids a break — in order to give them an opportunity to approach the lesson from a new and fresh perspective later. She might make the same decision, but the reason she makes it is more in line with being kind.

Even though these two decisions appear to be the same, the difference in motivation is critical. The kids in Mrs. Meanswell's class are in charge of aspects of their classroom that they should not control, using a silent (or even blatant!) threat of dissatisfaction as a way to manipulate her. Ultimately they will exercise their power — through some of their reactions to her choices — in ways that are off-task, and thus confrontational. And, because the students actually do want to learn, they will eventually start acting out because they won't be satisfied. They will complain about all sorts of things, as a veiled communication that the things they really want are structure, direction, and learning. They want Mrs. Meanswell to steer in a way that's in their best interest.

Steering includes discipline, and Mrs. Allgood's direct, matter-of-fact style reflects her understanding of this truth. Her words leave very little wiggle room, and while students might make a show of wiggling, they respond to her. This is because she focuses on what's best for them, and knows that the students need it.

The underlying message here is that teachers need to be firmly committed to what the students need, even if that means occasionally experiencing feelings of being disliked or under-appreciated. The students will be better served, and they will actually appreciate the teacher more, even if they don't express it. Loving teachers care more about their students' well-being than about whether or not they are liked. Later, these caring teachers are likely to be the ones at the top of their students' "favorite-teachers-of-all-time" list.

Head, Heart, and Gut

This is another "road map" option for navigating the sometimes-bumpy landscape of teacher and student experiences. While this technique differs from the analogies described in Chapter 2, "Assume the Best" — where our heads were likened to radio stations and our hearts to transmitters — its essential message is the same.

In this scenario, the head refers to what we *think*. The heart is what we *feel*. The gut is what we *know*. Often, students speak from their head or their heart, wanting something that isn't always what they know they need. As teachers, we do the same, jumping from one modality to another. What I sometimes do in situations of confusion is to "check in" with my gut to see what I know needs to happen. It can help me cut through all the noise about wanting to be liked or wanted. It also works as a guide for my students, particularly when they need support in areas of conflict. I can ask them what they think, what they feel, and what they know about a given situation. It's surprising how often I will get disarming answers from students when I frame things this way.

As I improved as a classroom manager, I found myself speaking more directly to what my students knew, rather than getting into a debate about what students thought they wanted or who did what. For example:

Mark:	Mr. Smith, I don't think you're being fair. Lots of other kids were talking. Why did you pick on me?
Mr. Smith:	Mark, you and I both know that you want to learn and do well in my class. Right?
Mark:	Well, I guess so….
Mr. Smith:	That's why I'm here talking to you, so that we can work together to achieve that.

Because I'm speaking directly to what Mark knows (his gut), he has to struggle in order to disagree with me. Often his complaints are short-circuited before he even knows what happened. If I come at him, then I run straight into his wave of defenses. But if I assume the best about him and speak to what he knows, I can come in *under* his wave, providing clarity and support simultaneously.

> Because I'm speaking directly to what Mark knows (his gut), he has to struggle in order to disagree with me.

Using these tools — from the analytical to the emotional to the instinctual — we can make good, solid choices when interacting with our students. From this foundation, we can implement strategies to create strong, positive connections with them. Distinguishing between what our students think, feel, and know has an additional benefit: it increases our inner authority, which makes everything easier in the classroom.

The Recipe — Strategies

When students feel a positive connection with the teacher and the class, they are more likely to participate and less likely to act out. Ongoing personal connections between teachers and students serve as continual invitations for students to step out of resistance and into cooperation and learning.

The Two-by-Ten Strategy

Choose the student in your class whose behavior is the most challenging for you. If you have six or eight kids in mind, choose the kid whose absence seems to allow everyone else in class to do better! With this one student, for two minutes per day for ten days in a row, have a personal conversation about anything he is interested in, as long as the conversation is PG- or G-rated.

This strategy, also referred to as "the two-minute intervention," was researched extensively by Dr. Raymond Wlodkowski and several educators thereafter.[5] Wlodkowski found up to an eighty-five-percent improvement in the behavior of whatever student he focused on. In addition, all the other students in the class behaved better.[6]

This research can seem counterintuitive. Although Mark seems to have a negative attitude, he actually needs a positive personal connection with his teacher. It's as if our most challenging kids walk into our classrooms with a constantly cramping muscle. The muscle says, "I want a positive personal connection with an adult authority figure — namely, my teacher." This need for connection is generally more primary than

Bright Ideas

Specific Things We Can Do

To put all our good intentions into action, we need to implement specific strategies. Try some of the following to nurture positive connections and to make your lessons relevant for each student:

▲ Relate the lesson to students' lives and interests.

▲ Give students questionnaires about themselves.

▲ Ask students about their lives.

▲ Tell students about your life.

▲ Share personal artifacts, photos, and anecdotes with students.

▲ Take an interest in what your students are interested in.

▲ Attend extra-curricular events in which your students are involved, such as soccer games or theater productions.

the need to learn content. Our challenging students want to feel safe,[7] and a good portion of their energy is focused on this need — through acting out, disrupting, and distracting, rather than on focusing in the classroom. If we assume the best and read between the lines, then we can see that these students are saying: "Teacher, I'd really like to be able to focus in class today — so could you please make a positive connection with me?" As we connect with them over time, the muscle uncramps and relaxes, and then they can focus on learning.

For Mark, the positive connection with his teacher may be his only positive interaction with an adult authority figure, in or out of school. One single, positive connection can have a huge effect on his behavior, his attitude, and his ultimate success.[8] Think about your experience in college. Most college graduates I've surveyed chose at least one college class based on who was teaching it rather than what the topic was. Your personal connection with

Bright Ideas

- ▲ Visit student homes.
- ▲ Write letters, emails, and/or journal entries back and forth with students.
- ▲ Make phone calls home to students to let them know how well they are doing in your classes.
- ▲ Have class meetings or community circles to discuss various issues, including conflicts in the class, without discussing specific students.
- ▲ Have appreciation circles in class meetings.
- ▲ Provide time for students to engage in mindfulness practice (See Chapter 11, "Lesson Design").
- ▲ Involve students in making rules and consequences (See Chapter 12, "Rules and Consequences").
- ▲ Have a "Student of the Day" or "Student of the Week," allowing the class to learn more extensively about one student.

a professor or your student's personal connection with you can have a powerful impact on motivation and learning.

Many veteran teachers recall a student who began the school year as a negative influence, and then changed so much that toward the end of the year he was a positive ally in the classroom. The Two-by-Ten Strategy is a rigorously researched way to bring about this kind of change consistently with some of our most troubled students.[9]

How do you decide what to talk about with Mark? Find out what he likes. You can give an interest inventory survey to your students and use the data to find a topic that will get Mark to talk with you. You can start with what he says to his friends, what he's wearing, or what is written on his notebook. Once you find a topic that he's drawn to, if you don't know anything about it, then try an Internet search. You

A Closer Look

One single, positive connection can have a huge effect on student behavior, attitude, and success.

Bright Ideas

- ▲ Honor students on their birthdays, or half-birthdays if they were born in the summer.
- ▲ Create a student bulletin board where each student can fill one square foot with pictures, stories, photos, and writing samples.
- ▲ Invite students to create a section of bulletin board to document highlights of the school year-to-date.
- ▲ Create a pen-pal assignment with students from another country or state.
- ▲ Find out what video games your students like to play, what websites they like to visit, or what apps they have on their phones. Use these to support classroom activities whenever possible.
- ▲ Ask students to create personal timelines of key events in their lives.

can prompt him to tell you stories or offer you snippets about his world. Become Mark's "student" on the topic.

If Mark is so resistant that he won't speak to you, then approach a classmate who is seated next to him. Strike up a conversation with that student about something you know might grab Mark's attention. Eventually you can pull him into the conversation. I've gone so far as to find out my student's schedule, and "randomly bump into him" in the hallway between classes, just to keep a connection going. Although this takes time on my part, if it helps Mark to feel more connected to school, feel better about himself, calm down, and focus in my classroom, it's worth it!

It's relatively easy to be sincerely interested in what Mark is interested in, because you are primarily interested in getting to know him and his world. So, you don't, for example, need to buy a skateboard in order to be sincerely attentive to Mark when he talks about skateboarding. Your genuineness is the key. Humans of any age can easily sense authenticity, and they respond positively when it comes their way.

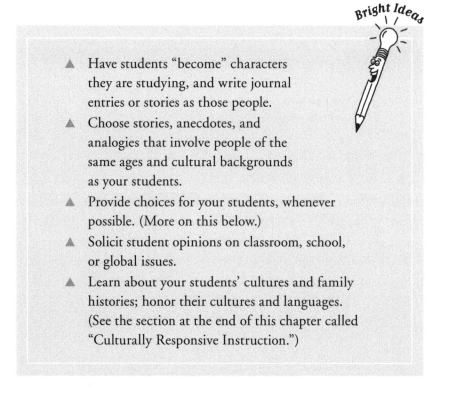

Bright Ideas

- ▲ Have students "become" characters they are studying, and write journal entries or stories as those people.
- ▲ Choose stories, anecdotes, and analogies that involve people of the same ages and cultural backgrounds as your students.
- ▲ Provide choices for your students, whenever possible. (More on this below.)
- ▲ Solicit student opinions on classroom, school, or global issues.
- ▲ Learn about your students' cultures and family histories; honor their cultures and languages. (See the section at the end of this chapter called "Culturally Responsive Instruction.")

Secondary teachers can find it challenging to block out even two minutes per day, because they might teach 150 or more students each day. In this case, it's better, I suggest, to have half-minute conversations each day for ten days in a row, rather than to have one longer conversation. The ongoing nature of the connection is what seems to make the most difference.

Similarly, if you don't see your students every day, do the best you can. The research was done based on connecting daily with students. But every other day, or even every week, if that's all you have time for, can still make a big difference.

Choices

The more we can build in choices for our students, the more likely they are to feel energized as participants in their learning processes. According to William Glasser and others, students have a fundamental need to explore and exercise their power.[10] Providing tailored options motivates them to use their power in positive and creative ways.

Bright Ideas

- ▲ Create community-service opportunities for students.
- ▲ Give students jobs and responsibilities in the classroom.
- ▲ Set up cross-age tutoring for students.
- ▲ Provide regular opportunities for listening to students.
- ▲ When talking privately with individual students about their misbehavior, use compassion and kindness, along with firmness. You can listen to them and encourage them, following up when they behave well.

Mrs. Meanswell can start by asking herself the following question every time she finishes designing a lesson:

Where can I build in choices for my students in this lesson?

Often, the answer to this question is "nowhere." But by asking consistently, we can usually find ways. For example, Mrs. Meanswell can say to her class, "We're going to do three things in this lesson. Which would you like to do first?" Students can vote, or a "Student of the Day" can decide. Mrs. Meanswell can give a quiz with twelve questions, and ask the students to pick their favorite ten questions to answer. When assigning homework, instead of assigning problems 1 – 10, she can let the students vote on doing either the evens or the odds for problems 1 – 20. Or, she can let each student pick any eight problems of the twenty to do for homework. (Most students will look at all twenty, trying to find the eight easiest!) Even these simple options give students an added sense of participation and connection.

Wise-Apple Advice

> With community service, students access an awareness of their own generosity and kindness, which can spill into all areas of their lives.

Small steps at first will lead to bigger steps later, such as choices in assignments and activities, project-based learning, students teaching one another, and community service projects. This last one — community service — can be a game-changer when students reach out to help others. Rather than challenging and disrupting, they get a chance to use their energy to help others and learn to appreciate themselves. They access an awareness of their own generosity and kindness, and that kindness can spill into all areas of their lives.

The "4-H strategy" combines choices with personal connections. When the teacher greets the students at the door, the kids choose one of four greetings: hello, handshake, high-five, or hug (secondary teachers often forego this last option). Students make their choices depending on their moods. Regardless of what they choose, they get a personal greeting from the teacher each day. Though a simple daily routine, teachers often find that even their high school students look forward to the "4-H" or "3-H" ritual each day.

Grace had an experience that highlights this. When she taught eighth grade, she was struggling with her fifth-period class, so opted to try the

3-H strategy with them. One day her biggest and toughest kid, Carlos, came up, head down, and tried to walk past her. She was blocking his entry, though, so he stopped. She said, "Hello Carlos, what can I give you today? A high five, hello, or handshake?" He replied, "I don't want none of those." "Okay, why don't you go back down the ramp and think on that some more." He stomped down and she greeted the rest of the kids behind him. Finally he came up once more, and again she asked him which H he would like. Again he said "none."

"Come on Carlos, anyone can say hello. How about we do hello." "Fine" he blurted, with disdain in his voice, and then with all kinds of attitude he said "hello." She replied in her most genuinely kind voice, "Hello. I'm so glad to see you today. Come on in and have a seat." But he didn't go in. Instead he started to get choked up, on the verge of crying. She asked him several times what was wrong but he kept saying "nothing." Finally he murmured, "it's just that... nobody said nothing nice to me today but you." Sometimes we forget that kids like Carlos can spend their whole day hearing nothing from adults but "stop that," "enough," and "I'm talking to you." One teacher's small effort to connect can have a profound effect.

When giving choices to students, remember to make sure that you can live with whatever options they choose. This is addressed in more detail in Chapter 12, "Rules and Consequences."

Applause

One teacher describes an experiment he did with his ninth-grade class of twenty-five students. For twenty-five consecutive school days, a different student received a hearty, robust, standing ovation from the rest of the class. Four years later, all graduating students filled out a questionnaire about their high school experience. Seven of the students from that ninth-grade class cited receiving a standing ovation as a major highlight of their schooling. How could this be? They hadn't earned the applause; it was given for no reason. When I've done this with my students, the effect has been remarkable. Just receiving that amount of energy boosted their esteem and deeply affected many of them. It also gave students a chance to safely and loudly express appreciation for each other.

In addition, when students are supposed to applaud for each other, such as after oral reports, make sure that every student applauds.

Otherwise, the applause can become a smattering and then a trickle by the time the last student presents. This is addressed in more detail in Chapter 8, "Teaching Procedures."

Listening

Many of us describe a key attribute of our good friends as "knowing how to listen." Just the willingness to pause and listen and receive someone can have powerful positive and lasting effects. This is also true with our students. In a private conversation with a student, even if it only lasts half a minute, take the time to pause, put your things down, face the student who is speaking, and provide your undivided attention. We don't necessarily need to give advice or try to fix things — just our simple attention and presence is often all that is needed. And this doesn't need to last an hour for each student. It's more the quality of attention than the quantity.

Writing vs. Speaking

When I taught at-risk high school students, I would often give them evaluation forms to fill out regarding units or projects that we had just completed. One day I included an optional question: "Is there anything that you would like me to know about you, this class, or anything else?" More than half my students left this question blank. But I did receive answers like, "Mr. Smith, I had a huge fight last night with my mom," or "Mr. Smith, I haven't slept at home in three days," and even "Mr. Smith, I really like this class."

Mrs. Allgood says

> The more willing we are to be firm and hold our ground with our students, the more personal we can be with them, without crossing that line.

I had previously met with these same students one-on-one and asked them how they were doing and what had been happening in their lives. In our personal conversations, all I heard was, "Fine. I'm doing fine." Somehow, students felt more comfortable confiding in me through the written word. Needless to say, I spent time with each student who had confided to me in writing, and a lot of good came from those conversations.

From then on, I always included that optional question at the end of all my unit evaluations, making sure to follow up personally with students who had confided in me. And each time, I received answers that surprised, enlightened, or tickled me.

▲ ▲ ▲

Avoiding Pitfalls

Connecting with our students can have its challenges. Below are a few that seem to be woven into the fabric of teaching.

Getting Too Personal

With rare exceptions, personal equals positive. The exception is when we cross a privacy line, by asking too much of our students or revealing too much about ourselves.

We all have a desire to connect personally with our students. Where, then, is that line between being friendly and being intrusive? There is no clear-cut answer. But paradoxically, the more willing we are to be firm and hold our ground with our students, the more personal we can be with them, without crossing that line. Our firmness allows the students to relax when we are soft, because they know that we are not abdicating our responsibilities to teach content and behavior, and will continue to provide safety and structure. It is a balancing act, much like the seesaw below. The more weight put on one side, the more weight needs to be put on the other.

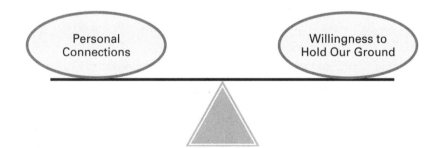

Let's look at how this works with Mrs. Meanswell. She is still new at developing her inner authority, so she is close to the center of the seesaw on the right side. She tries to compensate for this by being quite personal with her students, and going far to the left side of the seesaw. Sometimes this backfires. Perhaps she talks about things that are uncomfortable for the students, and they express their discomfort through acting out at odd times. Or perhaps the kids feel overly friendly with her and make it hard for her to quiet them down. She discovers, for example, that if she tells a joke, several minutes of chaos often follow as kids go off-task to tell their own jokes. She has them in good spirits, but she can't establish sufficient focus. (For a solution to this issue, see "Joke Recovery" in Chapter 8, "Teaching Procedures.") On the other hand, Mrs. Allgood's students seem quite comfortable with her "personalness." Even though she rarely draws a line in the sand with her students, they know that she is willing to do so, and that she is committed to holding the line. Therefore they tend to act out less.

Prepare for the Worst, Even as We Assume the Best

The art of teaching involves a kind of "realistic optimism" or "idealistic pragmatism" or "gullible integrity." I remember when I was Trick-or-Treating as a kid with my friends, coming upon a house that had a bowl of Nestlé Crunch™ bars outside the front door with a note that read, "Parents: Happy Halloween. Sorry we couldn't be here personally to hand out candy. Please take one for each of your children." Did we take one each or empty the bowl? Suffice it to say that my bag had an overabundance of Nestlé products that night — and for many nights afterward.

Mrs. Allgood says

The sooner we embrace being the boss, the sooner we can succeed.

Did I know better? Yes. Did I feel guilty? Yes. Did I take the candy anyway? You betcha! As teachers, we need to structure success for our students. Part of this means building in tailored options for our students, being realistic about how much independence our students can handle, and anticipating worst-case scenarios.

What could go wrong? Am I ready for it? If I word my questions/ directions a certain way, what are possible misinterpretations that my students might make? Are my deadlines clear? What if some students finish early? What if they arrive late? What if the technology doesn't work? What if my substitute teacher isn't strong? What if kids fight in my room? What if there's a fire? Am I prepared for all these possibilities? Do I know what to do? Do I know what to say? How can I be ready in advance? Who can help me prepare?

Part of structuring success is addressed in the Before-School Checklist in Chapter 10, "Getting Ready"; part of it is addressed in Chapter 8, "Teaching Procedures"; and part of it is an attitude or orientation that we can bring to each situation.

We Are the Boss. Period.

One key to a successful, proactive attitude is gaining comfort with our position as teachers. We are in charge. In other words, there is a certain emotional or psychological charge that comes with being responsible, the keeper of the guidelines and the grades. Being in charge doesn't mean that we should be mean — just clear and firm in our resolve.

Authority is a double-edged sword. It's *great* because ultimately, as "authors" in our classrooms, we have more ability to craft our classroom environment than we might think. It's *difficult* because we are responsible for our classroom climate, no matter which students we teach. Even teachers who promote democratic and/or consensus-based classrooms are still ultimately responsible for what happens there. They are the ones with veto power. They are the ones who have held their ground so that their students respect them enough to feel safe in a democratically run classroom. This is also true in classroom environments that are student centered and filled with independent learners. We don't need to be authoritarian. On the contrary — we can be open and kind and encouraging, as long as we are willing to hold our ground when it serves our students.

> **A Closer Look**
>
> Kids dump their emotional charge on us if we take the bait by reacting when they push our buttons. We go home exhausted, and they go home ready for more.

The sooner we embrace this part of our job description, the sooner we can become successful teachers. But it isn't always easy. The fact that we are the ultimate decision-maker can give rise to many feelings, both positive and negative — and feelings drive actions. How we address our feelings can make the difference between a bumpy teaching experience and a smooth one. Let's look at some common scenarios.

There Will be Times When We Are Not Liked — Hated, Even

This is inevitable, at least in our experience. Students may respond to us by blurting out, "You're mean," or "I hate you." It helps to know that this may happen from time to time, and that it doesn't necessarily mean that anything has gone wrong. Expressing feelings such as hatred or anger can be an essential part of a student's growth. If he feels received and not attacked for it, he often is so appreciative that his "negative" feelings transform rapidly into gratitude. Below is an all-too-common example.

Teacher: Mark, please put your pictures away and have a seat.

Mark: You're mean! My other teachers are a lot nicer!

At this moment, if a teacher were to resist Mark's opinion of her, it could lead to her being reactive, arguing with him in class, and generally creating the worst-case scenario that she is trying to avoid:

Mrs. Meanswell: MARK! I'M TIRED OF YOUR ATTITUDE! SIT DOWN!!!

In this example, Mrs. Meanswell ends up acting mean, just as Mark predicts. Her reactivity can be classified under many headings, such as "taking the bait," "having one's buttons pushed," "attacking," or "losing it." In defending herself from being seen a certain way, she is resisting certain possible judgments or opinions: "I can't be seen as mean. Therefore I need to cut out the source of those opinions quickly." Then Mark, who is perceived to be the source of those opinions, feels cut out.

Mrs. Allgood *responds* to Mark, instead of *reacting*.

Mrs. Allgood: Mark, please put your pictures away and have a seat. Otherwise you and I will need to meet after class.

Here, Mrs. Allgood allows the consequences to speak for her — and Mark knows that meeting with her after class may entail further consequences. She doesn't react to Mark's reactivity, nor does she attack him back. After the dust settles, she can talk to him, letting him know that his antagonistic language is not acceptable, and perhaps exploring the causes behind his unrest.

A Closer Look

Secondary teachers become masters of the meaningful twenty-second conversation.

Circumventing potentially reactive situations is discussed in more detail in Chapter 6, "Holding Our Ground." A few reminders: take a deep breath, count to ten, re-orient to the positive assumption that the student wants to learn behavior, soften your eyes, use the RRR Technique, and go under the wave. Know that if we can wait to talk with our student until we are calm, we've got a much better chance of genuinely communicating with him, thus decreasing tense classroom scenes in the future.

The Emotional-Charge-Transfer Game

Question: Why is it that sometimes we leave school at the end of the day feeling beaten up, like we want to go home, close the blinds, and sit in the dark? Answer: Kids dump their emotional charge on us if we take the bait by reacting when they push our buttons. We go home exhausted, and they go home ready for more.

Let's look at the above example with Mark. Say he has had a huge fight with his parents that morning. He comes to school feeling angry, hurt, and bottled up with a strong emotional charge. When he lashes out at Mrs. Meanswell in class, he is signaling that he doesn't quite know how to address this charge in a healthy way. When she reacts, his experience "sticks" to her. It's as if she starts to feel his feelings. Mrs. Meanswell ends up feeling beaten up, as if she just went the wrong way over a driveway that reads, "Do not enter — severe tire damage." If she forgets to assume the best about Mark, then his negativity is reflected back to her, and she takes home with her the brunt of her own negative assumptions. Mark feels justified in blaming her and has a temporary reprieve from his own negative feelings, whereby he feels permission to "dump" on others to get rid of his feelings. In this exchange, Mark loses out on the opportunity to address his emotional needs directly, and Mrs. Meanswell loses out on the opportunity to support him by modeling responsive behavior. And although his antagonism may be a cry for help, she misses the chance to talk to him about what is happening in his life.

In my first three years of teaching, it seemed like I did PhD work in reacting to students. I'd argue with and threaten them, yell out of frustration, or blame them for not participating. Only after years of teaching was I able to reorient, assume the best about them, and discover that many of my conflicts with students were actually opportunities to serve them.

Secondary Teachers' Built-In Challenge

Secondary teachers generally have a tougher job at making connections with individual kids because they have so many students each day. If a teacher of 150 students spent all day speaking privately with one student after the next — without spending any time teaching lessons — she would have less than two minutes to spend with each student. Because we have to teach, that time is reduced to just a few seconds per day per student. Sad as it is, this is often all the time we have to make and reinforce a personal connection with each student (I sometimes joke that as a high school teacher, I became a master at the meaningful twenty-second conversation, which helped to support my cocktail party skills).

In spite of this built-in limitation, meaningful and valuable personal contact can and does happen between teacher and student in ten- and twenty-second connections. It's not always apparent based on the content of the conversations, since nonverbal communication is equally if not more significant. As we assume the best about ourselves and our students, these brief connections, and our warm and positive tone throughout class, can communicate our caring in significant ways.

Classes Have No Memory (Although Kids Do)

Although some individual students will remember strong positive or negative classroom experiences — even if they don't let us know — the class as a whole is another animal. It has a short memory, which can be both a blessing and a curse.

We can have a rough experience with our students on Tuesday, and on Wednesday they return as if the slate were totally clean. This in itself can be a bit unsettling, as we arrive at school on Wednesday ready for resistance, and find none. Similarly, no matter how wonderful our lesson is and how engaged and excited the students are, when the bell rings, they are ready to go. We can count on a built-in resiliency in our classes, and therefore we are generally best served not "riding" on the good experiences or making too much of the bad ones. Our best recourse for success with our classes is to consistently cultivate strong, positive connections over time. This will help "smooth out" any rough moments in the classroom.

▲ ▲ ▲

Culturally Responsive Instruction

For students to feel safe and connected to their teacher, classmates, classroom, and what they are learning, they need to feel welcome. And this includes their cultures. Students don't drop their cultures at the door like a coat they're wearing, and neither can their teachers.[11] Understanding this can allow for a deeper, more authentic connection between our students and us.

Culture is made up of the underlying structures, information, and messages that inform our students' upbringing, makeup, sensitivities, and how they see and fit into the world. It includes their age, gender, ethnicity, skin color, primary language, sexual orientation, religion, socio-economic background, and ancestry, and how these have translated into and shaped their lives. It is the lens through which they see the world, and often through which the world sees them. If we don't connect to students' cultures, then we increase the likelihood that they will feel misunderstood, lonely, and uncomfortable; misunderstand our expectations; and disengage from learning, thus increasing the chance that they will act out in our classrooms. Conversely, when students feel that their cultures are welcome, relevant, and represented in our classrooms and in our hearts, then they can become staunch allies for a positive learning environment.

Mrs. Allgood says

We can examine what we don't know we don't know, looking for ways to unearth our own biases.

How do we connect to students' cultures?

The process starts with examining ourselves.[12] Just as classroom management is essentially invisible — and is a combination of what we do and who we are — so cultural responsiveness in the classroom can be invisible. Although plugging in strategies is a place to start, it isn't enough. We need to take stock within ourselves. My appreciation goes to Bonnie Davis, author of *How to Teach Students Who Don't Look Like You*, for her wealth of contributions to this section. She suggests examining "what we don't know we don't know," looking for ways to unearth our own biases. By recognizing our built-in assumptions, we can transform our teaching to truly embrace students who are different from us. We can't fully know another's culture, but we can continually reach toward that knowing. Our own views are inevitably shaped by our own culture and upbringing, and our growth trajectories as teachers include admitting where our limited lens falls short. This self-exploration (which is itself a strategy) requires welcoming our own feelings that arise in the process, which in turn allows us to be kind and open to our students, even when they don't look or talk like us. This process is not only challenging, but also it is ongoing. Some alarming statistics in the United States point to a huge disparity in the percentage of students of color who are referred to special education, suspended, or expelled from school.[13] In large measure, I suggest, this disparity is caused by well meaning teachers who unknowingly treat their students differently because they don't share their cultures. Taking the time and the emotional energy to look honestly at ourselves can pay huge dividends for our students. And, there are numerous practical things we can do to help bridge the cultural gap, thus assisting all of our students in thriving in our classrooms and schools.

Strategies

If it's true for you, be willing to sincerely acknowledge that you can't fully know your students' cultures, but that you are willing to stretch and learn and appreciate them. The key to success: you care about your students and want to learn from them. This is often "the elephant in the room" that inhibits student learning. If, for example, you are white and teaching African American students, then acknowledge your differences, and recognize that there is no "normal" or "ideal" culture. Let your students know that you are committed to doing your best to honor them and their cultures. Treat them fairly and with high expectations, even though you have a different cultural lens.

Let your students teach you what their lens looks like, so that your ability to reach them is enhanced. Learn about the cultures of your students, including finding out about the histories of the countries of your immigrant children. Remember that singling out a student as a "representative" of a particular culture can be very uncomfortable for that student, and that we cannot know a student by what he looks like or where he comes from.

- ▲ Share news, especially positive news, about relevant countries or territories with your students.
- ▲ Learn simple words and phrases in your students' primary languages.
- ▲ Integrate poetry from your students' cultures and give students the option to share the poetry in their own languages.
- ▲ Have students write personal narratives about their lives, families, and family customs. They can bring in photos to share.
- ▲ Post images and quotations of role models of diverse cultures on the walls of your classroom.
- ▲ Post student self-portraits on the walls of your classroom.
- ▲ Learn how to pronounce your students' names, teach your students to pronounce each others' names, and have students share what their names mean.
- ▲ Consider slowing down during class discussions. Some students' cultures may teach them to pause before replying, in order to

weigh all options. By allowing for this, you increase the likelihood that they will contribute meaningfully to class discussions.

▲ Use cooperative learning, Tribes™ strategies and ice-breakers to get kids to connect with one another.

▲ Reach out to students' families through school organizations, through visiting students in their homes, or through welcoming families in the morning in front of school.

▲ Let students know that you are available to be invited to dinner in their homes. Enjoy the rich cultural exchanges and free meals that follow!

Teaching Children of Poverty

According to Eric Jensen, author of *Teaching with Poverty in Mind*, students who live in poverty tend to undergo chronic stress. They are in fight-or-flight mode on a consistent basis, which affects their brain chemistry and emotions. Students in poverty are more likely than other students to demonstrate the following[14]:

▲ acting-out behaviors;
▲ impatience and impulsivity;
▲ gaps in politeness and social graces;
▲ a more limited range of behavioral responses;
▲ inappropriate emotional responses; and
▲ less empathy for others' misfortunes.

Schools in low socio-economic areas are often challenged by a lack of resources, as well as by a high percentage of students burdened by poverty. The combination can seem overwhelming. Changing the economic landscape in our country is the ultimate solution. Barring that, there are a few things that can help.

▲ Be especially aware and sensitive to your students' underlying needs for physical and emotional safety. For many children of poverty, school may be a place of refuge.

▲ Respond rather than react when your students act out or display some of the behaviors listed above.

▲ According to Jensen, there are six emotions hardwired into our brains: joy, anger, surprise, disgust, sadness, and fear. The rest, including cooperation, patience, embarrassment, empathy, gratitude, and forgiveness, can be taught to our students.

▲ Investing energy in teaching these skills to your students can make all the difference. It can take longer than you think to "teach your students to be students."

▲ Be kind to yourself by modeling the patience, empathy, gratitude, and forgiveness for yourself that you want your students to learn.

Wise-Apple Advice

Positive Connections — the Abridged Version

Students tend to thrive more if they feel a positive connection to their teachers. Teachers tend to enjoy teaching more if they feel positively connected to their students. The class environment tends to blossom if all students of all cultures feel respected and welcomed.

8

TEACHING PROCEDURES

> *"A teacher is one who makes herself progressively unnecessary."*
>
> — THOMAS CARRUTHERS

We're going to keep on doing this until we get it **right!**

BAXTER BULLDOGS

HERMANSEN

MRS. MEANSWELL PUTS HER FULL FOCUS on teaching content to her students. She doesn't know about the invaluable secret Mrs. Allgood has worked seamlessly into her system. Procedures, far from being "busy work" or a distraction from content, are her best friends. Spending time on procedures in the classroom not only makes the environment run more smoothly, but also actually facilitates teaching content.[1] Mrs. Allgood puts a tremendous emphasis on procedures, regardless of what grade level she teaches. Her procedures — ranging from how students enter the classroom, to how paper is distributed, to how pencils are sharpened — are taught, reinforced, practiced, and reviewed throughout the school year.

When you're on an airplane, don't you sometimes wish the flight attendant would stand up at the front of the plane before it takes off, and say, "Please raise your hand if you already know the safety-belt procedure"? And then after seeing 100 percent raised hands, he or she would say, "Good news! Looks like we can skip it today!" This never happens! On airplanes, they are amazingly thorough and consistent in teaching the safety-belt procedure. They use auditory (tell you), visual (show you), and kinesthetic (you do it) modalities to make sure everyone reviews the procedure every time. This is the spirit with which we should be teaching procedures to our students — thoroughly and with multiple teaching

A Closer Look

The "tracks"
of procedure
will determine the
direction—and the
speed!—of the
"train" of content.

modalities. It is almost impossible to teach procedures too much. Well, I imagine it's possible, but with the hundreds of teachers Grace and I have observed and coached, we've never seen it. By trying to teach procedures too much, teachers begin to appreciate the amount of emphasis procedures actually need.

If students complain, "We already know this — why are we doing this?", then remember that it's often one or two students who complain, while the rest are engaged with practicing the procedure. You can simply reply, "Do you think Olympic champions ever practice? We are honing our procedural edge to stay in tip-top procedural condition." What you'll probably notice first is that things actually run more smoothly in your class when you try to over-teach procedures. You may also discover that you end up teaching more content, because the students are focused when the classroom procedures are clear.

Procedures are the Railroad Tracks; Content is the Train

I used to have to drag my "trainful" of brilliant lessons along bumpy terrain, uphill both ways. However, once I clearly laid down the "railroad tracks" of procedure, the "train" of content ran much more smoothly in the direction I wanted. Consequently, I learned to start the process of teaching procedures on the first day of school; consistent maintenance and "polishing" were essential throughout the year.

A Closer Look

Mrs. Allgood
addresses
procedures before
disruptions; Mrs.
Meanswell addresses
them afterward.

When Mrs. Meanswell assumes that her kids are supposed to already know most of the class procedures and routines, or if she is so overwhelmed by the amount of content the students are supposed to learn, then she may fall into the trap of giving only a quick, cursory overview of procedures. Bad move. The tracks of procedure will determine the direction — and the speed! — of the train of content. Because of this, procedures come before content. And in that sense, they need to be given more priority than content. Additionally, timing is paramount. Mrs. Allgood addresses procedures before disruptions occur, trying to "head problems off at the pass." Mrs. Meanswell addresses procedures after the chaos has ensued.

What Procedures Do We Need?

Below is a partial list of procedures typically used in K-12 classrooms.

Beginning Class

▲ Entering the classroom

▲ Using cubbies

▲ Putting away cell phones

▲ Starting the lesson

▲ Turning in homework

▲ Tardies

▲ Excused absences

▲ Unexcused absences

▲ Make-up work

During Class

▲ Getting student attention

▲ Listening to P.A. announcements

▲ Passing out papers

▲ Writing headings on papers

▲ Using the bathroom

▲ Using the water fountain

▲ Going to lockers

▲ Checking out books

▲ Passing out classroom supplies

▲ Using classroom supplies

▲ Collecting classroom supplies

▲ Turning in class work

▲ Asking for help during direct instruction

▲ Asking for help during independent work

▲ Asking for help during group work

▲ Checking for understanding

Bright Ideas

- ▲ Sending students to the office
- ▲ Sending students to another teacher
- ▲ Using hall passes
- ▲ Sharpening pencils
- ▲ Sharing pencils
- ▲ Raising hands during class discussions
- ▲ Working in pairs
- ▲ Working in small groups
- ▲ Watching videos
- ▲ Sustained silent reading
- ▲ Taking tests
- ▲ Taking quizzes
- ▲ Organizing notebooks
- ▲ Using technology
- ▲ Sharing technological devices
- ▲ Moving around the room
- ▲ Giving oral reports
- ▲ Giving incentives for positive behavior
- ▲ Giving consequences for inappropriate behavior
- ▲ Addressing put-downs
- ▲ Addressing student conflicts with each other
- ▲ Addressing student conflicts with the teacher
- ▲ Listening attentively
- ▲ Participating in classroom community circles

Special Situations

- ▲ Fire drills
- ▲ Field trips
- ▲ Events in the auditorium
- ▲ Library or computer lab
- ▲ Guest speakers
- ▲ Parent/guardian volunteers in the classroom

Bright Ideas

Ending Class

- ▲ Assigning homework
- ▲ Dismissing class during the day
- ▲ Dismissing class at the end of the day
- ▲ Putting materials away
- ▲ Cleaning up the room
- ▲ Lining up for recess, lunch, or an assembly
- ▲ Using cubbies
- ▲ Putting notebooks in backpacks and backpacks on backs

The difference between the two approaches is a key to successful teaching. Mrs. Allgood knows that it is much easier to polish and maintain railroad tracks than to fix a derailed train, so she takes the time to minimize the derailments in her classroom by keeping the tracks of procedure well polished and grooved throughout the year.

Each procedure needs to be learned, so each needs to be taught. Although it may seem overwhelming to have to teach all of the procedures listed above, most of them are simple and don't take long to establish. Others don't need to be emphasized in the first few days. We should put our attention first on the key procedures that will establish order and focus, and follow up later with the rest. Generally speaking, students' entering and leaving the classroom, starting class, and getting student attention are the primary procedures to start with. We can add the others systematically in the first few weeks. Check Chapter 10, "Getting Ready" for a "Before-School Checklist" that can help with organization before the school year starts. Also take a look at Chapter 11, "The First Week of School," which addresses in more detail the initial procedures that need to be taught.

Mrs. Allgood says

> Each procedure needs to be learned, so each needs to be taught.

▲ ▲ ▲

How Do I Teach Procedures?

Procedures, like behavior, are taught in the same ways that content is taught. Teaching is teaching and learning is learning, no matter whether we are teaching calculus, singing, foul shooting, lining up for recess, or appropriate behavior during an assembly. The components are still the same. Here's a formula that works for teaching procedures, behavior, and content:

1. Give a vision of the intended goal of the lesson.
2. Break the lesson into simple steps.
3. Teach the steps one by one.
4. Have the students connect the steps, as needed, to the goal of the lesson.
5. Check for understanding and make adjustments throughout the process.

Simply put, teachers need to break things into steps, teach the steps, and connect them. Students need to do the same: learn the building blocks and put them together through inquiry, experiential learning, collaboration, and/or direct instruction. For example, most students are exposed to the quadratic equation in math class in the eighth or ninth grade. In actuality, they start learning it in kindergarten. Their learning begins with the number line and moves through addition, subtraction, multiplication, and division — until, eventually, they can wrestle with the quadratic equation. It is a complex lesson, taking about nine or ten years to implement. Similarly, in teaching procedures we need to find a first step that is small enough to allow our students to "get on the escalator." Once that step is established, we can continue to add steps that are appropriately challenging for our students' abilities.[2]

Mrs. Allgood says

> Procedures, like behavior, are taught in the same ways that content is taught.

To summarize, there are several steps to teaching procedures effectively:

▲   Determine what procedures are needed.
▲   Break them into simple steps.
▲   Teach them visually, orally, and/or kinesthetically.
▲   Check for understanding.
▲   Practice them.

▲ Reinforce them.

▲ Periodically review them.

A simplified version of this is the "I do, we do, you do" approach:

1. **I do**. Model what students will be expected to do.
2. **We do**. Students practice in pairs, small groups, or as a class. Teacher provides feedback throughout the process.
3. **You do**. Students try to accomplish the task independently in real time.

Regardless of which step-by-step approach we use to teach procedures, the process is helped when we assume that students want to succeed, and that procedures are the road map for that success.

Below are four examples for teaching or re-establishing procedures.

1. Practicing Procedures: Group Work

If Mrs. Meanswell were to ask her students on the first day of school to "get into groups of four and discuss the story that I just read," she'd more likely than not have total bedlam. Group work is a complex task and needs to be taught. In fact, group work is so multi-faceted that most adults in the workplace are still learning it, even though they've been doing it for years. Human Resources Departments of major corporations have reported that many of their employees have a hard time working in teams.[3] They should watch Mrs. Allgood. By the time her students are ready to practice group work — "working in groups of four" — she already has completed the following steps.

First, she determines what procedures the students need to be taught to work effectively in groups. Her partial list includes how to:

▲ move their belongings;

▲ move their desks;

▲ move their bodies;

▲ know where to sit, and with whom;

▲ interact with the other moving bodies in the room;

▲ listen to the teacher once in groups;

▲ take turns discussing and staying on task;

▲ record responses;

▲ encourage one another to participate;

▲ construct valid arguments and critique the reasoning of others;

▲ respect one another's opinions;

▲ verbally report results;

▲ listen to others when they report;

▲ take notes on others' reports;

▲ thank and appreciate their group members;

▲ move their belongings back;

▲ move their desks back;

▲ move their bodies back;

▲ refocus their attention once they are moved back.

Before tackling groups of four, Mrs. Allgood teaches her students how to effectively work in pairs, focusing on how she wants them to talk with each other and making sure each student participates in the discussion. Once students can work effectively in pairs, then they are ready to tackle group-work procedures.

Mrs. Allgood says

The first part of group work is getting the students into groups.

Mrs. Allgood breaks the new procedure into parts. The first part is getting students into groups. On the board or screen is depicted an aerial view of the classroom, showing all of the desks labeled with students' names and gathered into groups of four with the corners touching. This can be done with Powerpoint, an overhead, a SMART board, document camera, or hand-drawn. She tells the students to get into their groups according to the map. She times them. Once they are in groups, she debriefs students on the lesson by noting how long it took and giving any commendations and recommendations. "Excellent work, class. It took you forty-five seconds, which is good for a first try. There were two students bumping elbows too much, and one group didn't have their desks touching…."

A Closer Look

Once she feels that the students are getting the procedure, she will "lightly season" the lesson with content.

Then the room is rearranged into its original configuration, and Mrs. Allgood asks the students to try the grouping procedure again. This time she offers them an incentive as a class. "I know you all want extra time today to work on your projects. We'll be practicing getting into groups several times. You can earn time by saving time. Each time you get into groups in fifteen seconds or less, with the corners of your desks touching, I'll give you an extra minute at the end of class to work on your projects."

They practice getting in and out of groups several times. Once she feels that the students are getting the procedure, she will "lightly season" the lesson with content. But the procedure is still paramount. Whenever she debriefs the students on their group lessons, she always talks about the procedure of group work first, before discussing whatever topic the students talked about.

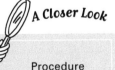

Online Toolbox

Video of high school students moving their desks into groups.

This policy that "procedure precedes content" is one element of invisible management, something Mrs. Allgood does consistently. During a discussion, she'll say, "Yes, Bao-yu. Thank you for raising your hand (procedure). What is your comment (content)?" Or, "Thank you, class, for being so quiet while Jose was speaking (procedure). Let's look at his idea (content)." As Mrs. Allgood focuses on procedures first, she is polishing the railroad tracks to allow the content to flow smoothly.

2. Reviewing Procedures Periodically: Timing Is Everything

Mrs. Allgood and Mrs. Meanswell each have the same ten-day lesson that involves daily group work toward completion of a project. Each class goes smoothly for the first six days. Then on the seventh day, for no obvious reason, Mrs. Allgood takes three minutes at the start of the lesson to ask a student or two to review the procedure for group work. She asks them to clarify their roles and comment on positive things that are working. The lesson resumes, and once again things go smoothly.

A Closer Look

Procedure precedes content.

In the other classroom, however, Mrs. Meanswell follows the same schedule as in the previous six days and has the students go straight into their groups. Pandemonium ensues. Disorder, jostling, off-task chatter, loud noises, complaints! Kids get out of their seats en masse.

After the lesson, Mrs. Meanswell thinks, "I don't understand it. They've been so good for the last six days. It must have been something with the weather, or with their astrological signs, or a weird biochemical aberration…." The next day, or later that day, depending on the grade that's being taught, she has to do her twenty-minute "Sermon on the Mount" — thou shalt not disrupt class, thou shalt respect each other, and thou shalt listen to the teacher. She has to make phone calls to parents and guardians, keep kids after school, basically try to stuff the mushroom cloud back into the canister, all because she didn't spend

Online Toolbox

Samples
of teacher-made
procedure quizzes.

three minutes at the start of class polishing and maintaining her railroad tracks.

Did she miss something? Nothing obvious. Effective managers have a sixth sense of knowing when things are about to fall apart. Mrs. Allgood simply knew that it was time to polish the tracks, even though there was no obvious evidence that the kids were about to act out.

Because none of us has a perfectly developed sixth sense, it makes sense to err on the side of caution. When in doubt, we can take two or three minutes to go over procedural expectations. In the above example Mrs. Allgood reviewed the procedure for group work. She could use several methods, such as those listed below:

▲   Remind students of the written directions for the procedure and key points to remember.

▲   Informally or formally quiz students on the procedure [i.e.: Question 1, multiple choice: "When I ask you to open your books to page 27, you should A)…].

▲   Ask students to recite key steps in the procedure to each other.

▲   Ask students to repeat the procedures back to the teacher.

▲   Ask students to reflect (aloud or in writing) on the process — what is working, what needs improvement.

▲   Implement a fishbowl model whereby a group of students simulates the desired procedure while the rest of the class watches, takes notes, and reviews afterward.

The more complex the procedure, the more the students need to focus kinesthetically and visually (not just verbally) in the review. An example might be to have the kids practice lining up for recess, or practice setting up and cleaning up labs.

However we choose to remind students of the appropriate procedures, it makes sense to do it regularly, before the students act out.

3. Two Procedures per Class or Lesson: "The Budweiser Approach"

Research once done on middle-school students suggested that more could spell the word "Budweiser" than the word "Eisenhower." My belief is that even if the students had the same number of minutes of exposure to both words over the course of a school year, they would still be able to spell "Budweiser" better. That's because they get Eisenhower once, in a two- or three-week block called "WWII and the Fifties." It's like asking kids to learn content by going through a cave with a flashlight: they don't know Eisenhower is coming, and they don't think about him when he's gone. On the other hand, kids are exposed to Budweiser in fifteen- and thirty-second spots throughout the year. Even though these days many kids use technology to skip TV ads altogether, the concept still applies — kids report their impressions of the year's coolest ads, many of which they've seen on the Internet. So let's take advantage of "the Budweiser Approach" in teaching and maintaining procedures and routines.

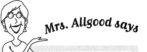

Mrs. Allgood says

Because none of us has a perfectly developed "sixth sense" of knowing when things are about to fall apart, we should err on the side of caution, by periodically reviewing procedural expectations.

When I taught one class per day of P.E. in an alternative school for at-risk high school students, we had a simple routine. We would meet in my classroom to start the class, and then we would migrate to either the field or the gym. (My students didn't change into gym clothes for P.E.) Every day I would take attendance, and then I would make some simple announcements. Here is a typical one:

"Class, yesterday we went up to the gym to play volleyball. I want to commend you on how well you walked through the halls. There was no banging of the lockers and nobody stuck their head in the doors of classes that were in session. As a group you all walked quietly and efficiently to the gym. That was wonderful. Today, we will be playing volleyball again, and I want to remind you that volleyballs are for hands only. Any questions? No? Let's go."

I had about six key guidelines for volleyball, one of which was that they were for hands only. If I didn't mention "hands only" at least once every three days, by the fourth day balls would be kicked all over the gym, with offending students pleading temporary insanity.

Mrs. Allgood says

The more complex the procedure, the more the students need to focus kinesthetically and visually (not just verbally) in the review.

Using little spot-check "Budweisers" throughout the school year was so successful in cutting down chaos that I suggest it to all teachers. Every class period or lesson, try to consciously teach at least two procedures — regardless of what the lesson is. They don't need to be new procedures — they can be ones that the students already know. This sometimes entails more than

simply thanking a student for speaking in a nice, loud voice. Teachers can mix up modalities, rotating between auditory, visual, and kinesthetic reminders. Although I had to teach the procedures in the beginning of P.E. class to avoid yelling procedures across the field, classroom teachers don't necessarily need to. Choose appropriate points in each class or lesson. Sometimes it will take a five-second reminder, and sometimes it will take a two-minute run-through. The ongoing nature of the reinforcement over time will help keep the train on the tracks.

If you write lesson plans, then I suggest that you write the two procedures into each plan. And rather than writing a phrase for procedures and a page for content, write out the procedures fully, since they are taught in the same step-by-step ways that content is taught.

By teaching a minimum of two procedures per class in secondary, or per lesson in elementary, not only will your classes run more smoothly and your kids learn content faster, you'll also consciously exercise your muscle of inner authority, and the dividends will pay off down the line in all aspects of your teaching.

4. Rubrics and Visuals for Procedures

A rubric strategy will work for any elementary or secondary classroom requirement that can be modeled, drawn, photographed or otherwise illustrated. For example, elementary students can be shown a rubric for lining up. A very poor line would be a "one" and an excellent line would be a "three." Students need to exhibit a "three" before they are ready to leave the classroom. With sufficient modeling, they will tend to self-monitor their lines by referencing the quality of the line to a number: "C'mon everybody, we look like a two!" They'll need little or no direction from the teacher.

To make it even clearer, a teacher can take pictures of the students in the three different "lineups," number the pictures, and then put them over the door to the classroom. Students can then reference the pictures as they form their lines. All the teacher has to do is stand under the door facing the kids and hold up her fingers to correspond to the quality of the line. When she holds up three fingers, the class is ready to go. This can be done with students modeling a lining up rubric (shown) or with teachers doing it! Both can work quite well.

3   2   1

Another procedure for students of any age involves getting them to straighten desks and clean the room before they are dismissed. The teacher can provide a one-through-five rubric for a clean and straightened room. The kids know that unless the room is a "five" they won't be dismissed. Pictures of the room can be taken in various stages of cleanliness — and the teacher can enjoy a moment of camaraderie with students who "help out" by messing up the room for the photos, or are assigned to help to capture it in its various states of disarray. Student readiness also can be communicated in pictures; for example, even if all the desks are lined up and the paper is thrown out, backpacks must be on the floor and students seated before the room is a "five." Again, the students will self-monitor, talking among themselves rather than arguing with the teacher. In the example below of high school students, if the bell has rung and the teacher holds up four fingers, the students will look at the photos, look at each other, and blurt out to Sally, "Your pack — take your pack off!" Once Sally removes her pack, the teacher holds up five fingers, and the class can be dismissed. This eliminates a lot of the "shuffling" that students do in the last few minutes of class. It also eliminates kids' gathering in front of the door before the bell rings.

Wise-Apple Advice

A teacher can take pictures of the students in the three different "lineups," number the pictures, and then put them over the door to the classroom. Students can then reference the pictures as they form their lines.

Rubrics can be applied to procedures including lab or art set up and clean up, P.E. activities, and forming groups. In addition to posting photographs, the teacher can project them onto screens and display them in front of the room when appropriate. Sometimes, rubrics aren't necessary. Just show a picture of the ideal behavior or bookshelf or room arrangement, for example, and students will know what they need to do. Three samples are below. Multiple rubrics and visuals can be placed on a "Wall of Readiness" on the side of the room, motivating students to know and follow the class rules and procedures. We've put hundreds of usable

photo examples into our book called *Picture This! Visuals and Rubrics to Teach Procedures, Save Your Voice, and Love Your Students*. Each book comes with a unique password for online access to digital versions of the photos and videos. Information is on our web site.

▲ ▲ ▲

Teaching Key Procedures

Often particular classroom challenges or problems can be solved with a focus on procedures, rather than on consequences. Below are a few chronic classroom issues — or "itches" — that can be "scratched" by teaching and reinforcing classroom procedures. Also included are innovative approaches and strategies for maintaining student focus, even during transitions.

Students Entering the Classroom

If our kids enter our classroom in a rowdy, disruptive manner, then during class we can have them practice the procedure for entering the classroom. We can:

▲ Review the correct procedure by describing it or modeling it.
▲ Check for understanding by calling on students to describe the procedure.
▲ Direct students to pick up their belongings and leave the classroom, wait for the signal, and then walk back into the room as if the class were about to start.
▲ Time them and debrief what they did well and what they can improve.
▲ Have them practice it again, trying to improve their behavior and beat their time.

These approaches will work with kids of any age. Once they learn the procedure, classes consistently will start more smoothly. This is addressed in more detail later in Chapter 15, "Making Changes."

A Closer Look

When students' dissatisfaction is acknowledged, they tend to relax and focus on the lesson at hand.

Class Complaints

When I taught social studies to at-risk high school kids, we'd often play games on Fridays. Therefore, I established a procedure for those

Fridays when, for whatever reason, we didn't play a game. At the start of class, I would announce that we wouldn't be having a game, and then I implemented our procedure — called "Complaining aloud for up to three seconds in a G-rated manner." First I counted aloud to three, then put my hand to my ear and listened to three seconds of complaining, moaning, and whining. When I'd give the stop signal, by moving my hand across my neck, the complaining would cease. All they needed was for me to acknowledge their dissatisfaction; after that, I'd proceed to teach a much more relaxed and focused group of students. Conversely, if I didn't give students three seconds of "official" complaint time, some of them would complain off and on for the entire period!

Joke Recovery

Many teachers find that when they tell a joke or a funny story, the kids seem to think that they are allowed to take several minutes to indulge in jokes of their own. Mrs. Meanswell concludes that she can't make any attempts at humor in her class, because she'll lose control. Mrs. Allgood creates a nonverbal procedure for students to "recover" from jokes in the classroom, placing her thumb and forefinger on her earlobe to let the kids know when the time for a natural laugh is over, and it's time to quiet down and refocus. She clarifies that it's totally acceptable to laugh and feel good, but that they need to get back on task when she gives the special signal. After they practice responding to the signal, they are much more likely to get back on task faster in the future, and she has a new license to be funny in her classroom.

Mrs. Allgood says

If kids are acting out while sitting in groups or circles, and you need for them to be quiet, rows will tend to quiet them down and focus them up front.

If students can't easily see the "earlobe signal," then try something bigger, such as moving your arms in a circle and bringing your hands over your mouth.

Tattling

Some of our students, especially in elementary school, are chronic tattlers. It's often not enough to simply tell them not to complain about each other. We need to teach them appropriate alternatives. For example, we can establish a procedure during classroom community circles to address student conflicts and concerns. We can ask students to role-play appropriate ways to address conflicts. We can teach them to differentiate between that which is their business and that which is gossip. Or between that which is a safety issue, either physical or emotional, and that which is not. One way is to ask a student "Are you saying this to me to help get someone out of trouble or to get someone into trouble?" Helping someone is "reporting." Getting someone into trouble is "tattling." This distinction will encourage the student to reflect and reconsider whether to approach you the next time. We can also create a suggestion box where students can place their tattles. This will allow the tattlers to get their concerns off their chests without disrupting class. In our book *Picture This!* we show several approaches, including examples of teachers having younger students "tell it to the ear (drawn on the board)" or "tell it to the president" (whose photo is taped to the wall) when the student clearly is in "tattle" and not "report" mode.

Mrs. Allgood says

Try to get within three feet of each student one or more times per class or lesson.

Seating Arrangements

Teach your class a step-by-step procedure for switching between the various seating arrangements that you use, such as rows, groups of four, pairs, and horseshoe. Seating arrangements are discussed in more detail in Chapter 10, "Getting Ready."

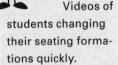

Online Toolbox

Videos of students changing their seating formations quickly.

Please note: many new teachers, especially at the elementary level, believe that they should never put students in rows. From my perspective, if kids are acting out while sitting in groups or circles, and you need for them to be quiet, rows will tend to quiet them down and focus them up front. Seating students in rows establishes a safe environment for direct instruction. So at least as an occasional measure, let's not hesitate to go for it.

Proximity

Proximity during direct instruction tends to improve behavior and learning.[4] Let's take advantage of this by circulating throughout the classroom often. One way to ground this concept: Try to get within three feet of each student one or more times per class or lesson. Some teachers already do this naturally. Some don't. Some classroom designs make it difficult. Either the student desks are so close together that the teacher can't circulate, or the desks are screwed into the floor, and the teacher is a virtual prisoner in the front of the room. Do what you can to make access to your students easier. For example, if you have desks arranged in rows, then put some space between the desks. Below is a seating chart for rows for thirty students. Notice the two vertical gaps and the one horizontal gap. During direct instruction, the teacher can easily teach from several areas in the room. The students in the back are no longer a vague rumor in an outpost on the horizon — they are in the teacher's zone of connection.

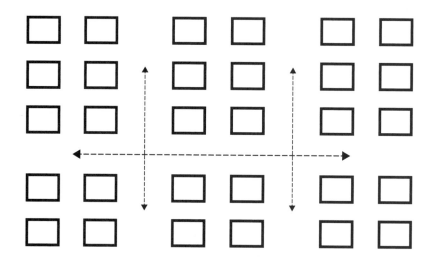

See page 231 in Chapter 13, "Rules and Consequences," for more on the use of proximity to redirect student misbehavior.

Music for Transitions

A first-grade art teacher plays the song "Whistle While You Work," signaling students to begin cleaning up. When the song is over, the room is clean, the supplies are put away, and the students are seated in circle for the closure activity. The students are so used to the procedure that one day when the teacher forgot the music and asked the students to clean up, they asked, "Where's the song?"

This procedure works for any grade level. One year I worked as a consultant, teaching and coaching teachers in an inner-city middle school in Northern California. I shared the music-for-transitions strategy with the teachers, and one took the idea to heart. Her approach for her eighth-grade class was the most remarkable example I have ever seen. She greeted her students as they walked in the room — at the same time handing each student a copy of the current reading book. Students went to their desks, sat down, and read in silence. About seven minutes into the silent reading, the teacher played the upbeat song "Hot Hot Hot" by Buster Poindexter. Every student then did the exact same thing at the exact same time! First, all heads popped up in unison. Then, every student closed his book, stood up, book in hand, and starting bopping back and forth to the music! The teacher opened a cardboard box in the front of the room, and students filed forward, while dancing, to put the book in the box. It was a conga line to the front of the classroom! Each student put the book in the box, gave the teacher a high-five, and bopped back to his seat, high-fiving other students on the way. They all stood in front of their desks, swaying to the song. When the song ended, they all sat down, and were totally quiet! Now, this may not be your style, but if it is, it can work wonders for transitions, positive connections, and an overall, positive class environment.

Mrs. Allgood says

Pick a song that your students like — and that you can live with! — and designate it as the signal for a given transition.

How do you set it up? Pick a song that your students like — and that you can live with! — and designate it as the signal for a given transition. If the transition is to last thirty seconds, then play only the last thirty seconds of the song. You can use different songs for different standard transitions, but use each for a month or more, so kids get used to the connection between each song and its corresponding transition, along with the timing for each song. You can also give incentives if all students have completed a given transition by the time the song is over.

Playing fast-paced music can speed up transition time. Many restaurants play fast-paced music in the background to make their customers subconsciously eat faster, thereby increasing the number of patrons per day.

Sound Signals

When Mrs. Meanswell uses her voice to try to get student attention, often she has to raise it to the point of irritation, aggravation, and escalation:

Mark:	"Mrs. Meanswell, why did you yell?"
Mrs. Meanswell:	"Well Mark, the first four times I said your name, I started at a very low volume and systematically moved up the ladder, until on the fifth try I reached a volume that got your attention."

In this scenario, Mrs. Meanwell is doing everything in her power to be patient and kind, and yet Mark feels yelled at and defensive. The other students in the class also feel tension because of her raised voice. This happens in part because Mrs. Meanswell's voice competes directly with their voices, and they can't hear her at low volume.

Sound signals, on the other hand, don't compete directly with student voices, and can be heard clearly at relatively low volumes, even while students are talking. Squeaky toys, electronic sounds — anything that can be bought at a toy store — can work well to get student attention.

Consultant Rick Morris (www.newmanagement.com) suggests using several different sounds, with each one geared toward a specific class procedure. For example, for third graders he uses a train whistle to get students to line up, a hotel bell to signal group leaders to come up for handouts to distribute to their group members, and a puppy squeeze-toy for "stop, look and listen."

> **A Closer Look**
>
> By using these hand signals, the teacher receives more information about what kind of comments are hiding behind the raised hands of her students.

Hand Signals

Also from Rick Morris, this strategy has proven quite useful, especially in elementary and middle schools. If a student has a **question**, he holds a fist in the air with pinky extended — American Sign Language for "I," as in "I have a question." If a student wants to **answer** a question, he holds his fist in the air with thumb pointing up — sign language for "A," as in "I have an answer." If a student has a **comment**, he holds his hand up in the form of the letter "C." If a student needs to use the bathroom, he holds up his hand with the middle finger crossed over the forefinger — "R," for restroom, or a fist with thumb inside the forefinger — "T," for toilet. If he wants a drink of water, he holds up his hand with the three middle fingers extended — "W," for water. The teacher can then respond with a gently knocking fist for "yes," or the index finger and middle finger tapping the thumb for "no."

By using these hand signals, the teacher receives more information about what kind of comments are hiding behind the raised hands of her students. Students feel safer asking questions because they know the teacher won't call on them unless it's an appropriate time to address questions. Plus, students will no longer interrupt class to ask permission to use the bathroom or get a drink of water.

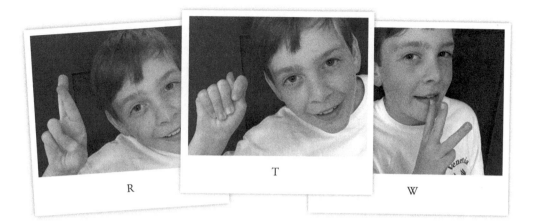

R   T   W

If a student is disruptive, either by interrupting a private conversation with another student or by doing the, "Oh-oh-oh, call on me call on me" raised hand strategy, another signal we can use is the extended index finger. When we hold it up at about a 45-degree angle, we signal the student that we acknowledge his desire for our attention, and we'll address his issue shortly. He can then put his hand down or back away from our private conversation, without worrying that no one will acknowledge his life-or-death need to tell us a story about a cool insect he saw this morning.

Directions, Questions

There is an art to giving directions, as well as asking questions. As we grow in teacher presence, many of the strategies below naturally occur. Nonetheless, it helps to lay down our own tracks.

Clarity

When Mrs. Meanswell asks, "Does everyone have a copy?" she'll get a chorus of yeses, but not from the students who need one. As an alternative, she can ask, "Who needs one?" Instead of, "Would you like to read now?" she can say, "We're going to read now," or better yet, "Please take out your books and open to page twenty-seven."

A Note on the Word "Please"

Many teachers have asked me if I think it's okay to use the word "please" in giving directions. My answer? Absolutely, as long as it is spoken as a statement rather than a question. Correctly imparted, "please" simply communicates respect, rather than loopholes, inner-apology, or weakness.

Check for Understanding of Procedures

Mrs. Meanswell assumes that when students don't ask questions about the upcoming activity, they already know what to do. Not the best assumption. A lack of questions doesn't necessarily indicate student understanding and readiness; it could occur for many reasons. These include students': 1) mistakenly thinking they know what to do; 2) hoping another student can tell them what to do once the activity begins; 3) not wanting to reveal that they don't know the procedure; or 4) not paying attention to either the directions or the check for understanding of the directions.

Mrs. Allgood says

Correctly imparted, "please" simply communicates respect, rather than loopholes, inner-apology, or weakness.

There are a variety of techniques to counter any of these circumstances, including writing directions on the board, a flip chart, or a handout, or projecting them onto the screen. With these tools, we can periodically and systematically refer to the written directions, and our visual learners will love us for it. Our book *Picture This!* has several examples of how to use photographs for these tasks. For involved procedures, our students can do several "walk-throughs" before they complete the actual activity.

It's a good practice to ask specific students to repeat back to us what we've said — regardless of whether our focus is about procedure, behavior, or content — to make sure that everyone is on the same page. Below is an example where Sally hasn't been paying attention and Laniyah has.

"In a moment, Laniyah, I'm going to ask you to please repeat back to the class exactly what I just described is going to happen next. Before you do, I'm going to ask two people to serve as monitors, to make sure that what you say is complete and accurate. Let's see…Sally, will you serve as a monitor? Great. And the other monitor? I'll decide after Laniyah has finished talking. So everyone listen closely to what she says."

First, this process avoids singling Sally out with, "Sally, what did I just say?" — and then the inevitable, "Why weren't you paying attention?" She isn't embarrassed for not knowing the procedure, because she gets to learn it from Laniyah. Not only does she avoid embarrassment, but she's also empowered, because she now is seen as the authority or judge of Laniyah's response.

Second, the class gets to listen to the directions' being repeated by someone other than the teacher, the novelty of which will tend to increase their attention.

Third, Laniyah is empowered because she was paying attention and will be able to repeat back the correct procedure.

Fourth, everyone will tend to listen closely because they don't know who will be called on at the end to be the second monitor. The teacher can raise the stakes a bit by letting the class know she'll ask a follow-up question of the second monitor, a twist that goes beyond Sally's responsibility.

Break Complex Procedures into Digestible Chunks

Often teachers try to give all the directions to a complex procedure beforehand, and students end up lost in the doing. It makes more sense to give the students only what they need to know first, and then add to the procedure as they are ready for more. Imagine following a complicated cooking procedure and being allowed to look at the recipe only once before starting.

For Simple Group Procedures, Give Directions Beforehand

This will eliminate the need to silence the class right after they form their groups. Plus, when students are in groups facing one another, their attention naturally goes in the direction of their group members, making it harder for them to focus on our directions. As above, if group-work directions are detailed, give chunks at appropriate intervals. Also, when possible, dissolve groups before having them report their findings to the class. They'll have an easier time paying attention to each student speaker.

Give the Most Distracting Directions Last

Mrs. Meanswell tells her students "You're going to be forming groups of four. You'll get to choose your groups. What you'll be doing is…." Before she ever gets to the details of the lesson, the students are completely distracted, focusing on who gets to be with whom in which group. What Mrs. Allgood says is: "In a moment I'll be putting you in groups of four. What you'll do in your groups is the following…. Are there any questions before I assign your groups? None? Great. For this one activity, you'll get to choose your groups…." By putting the most distracting step last, Mrs. Allgood avoids the inevitable "You! Me! You! Me!" that her group-seeking students would have whispered to one another while she was still giving the directions.

During student presentations, have students listen for key words or phrases that they can report on afterward.

Similarly, Mrs. Meanswell tells her students: "You'll be reading in the textbook from page thirty to page thirty-six. Before you open your books, let's review the questions you want to be asking yourselves as you read…." As soon as Mrs. Meanswell says the page number, students are opening their books and distracting themselves from the next direction. Mrs. Allgood, on the other hand, says: "In a moment you'll be reading seven pages in the textbook. Before I give you the page numbers, let's look at the questions you want to be asking yourselves as you read. Are there any details you need other than the page numbers? No? Okay. The reading begins on page thirty and ends on page thirty-six." Again, there is less distraction with Mrs. Allgood's directions, because she knows that had she mentioned the page numbers first, several of her students would have been so focused on the textbook that they would have missed her directions.

If you don't know which direction will cause the most distraction with your students, then you'll discover it right away — once you give it! You can use this experience as good information for the next time you need to give similar directions.

Limit the Number of Group Presentations per Lesson

Too many presentations will lead to restlessness and acting out. It's also helpful to consistently reinforce appropriate audience behavior throughout any lesson where students need to listen to one another. We can remind students what's appropriate, thank them when they listen attentively, and stop them in their tracks if they don't. One procedure I like to use goes like this: I remind students to listen with their eyes (on the speaker), mouths (closed), and hands (quiet), as well as with their ears. In addition, I ensure that whenever a student speaker is finished, all class members applaud. Applause serves several purposes. First, it makes the speaker feel good. It instills a self-induced mood change of wellbeing that stimulates serotonin to the brain.[5] Second, it focuses the class as a group. Third, clapping involves movement, which introduces numerous related benefits, including raising the flow of oxygen and glucose to the brain[6] and increasing student focus and alertness.

In many classes, students tend to applaud for the first student speaker and then "space out" for the remaining speakers. It's one of my pet peeves. I always make it a point to teach all my students to applaud each time; otherwise what is intended to be a positive, community-building experience can come across as a put-down for a given speaker.

As an alternative to applause, you can teach your students to send one another positivity, support, and love by silently stretching their hands toward the student or toward the ceiling and wiggling their fingers. Or, you can ask your students to come up with a class-wide alternative way to show support.

When I Say "Go"

When Mrs. Meanswell gives directions, particularly ones that involve active student movement, her students often get started before she is finished talking. They move and disrupt, and chaos can ensue, because not all the students know yet what to do. A simple formula she can use is the "Go" Procedure. There are four steps:

1. "When I say the word 'go'…";
2. "You will…" (or "Please…");
3. Check for understanding;
4. "Ready, and, go."

For example, if Mrs. Meanswell wants her students to clean up their desks and put the art supplies in the cabinet, she can say to her students "When I say 'go,' please clean up your desks, putting things away in the following manner…. Jose, can you please model what to do by putting your supplies away first? Thank you, Jose. That was excellent. Everyone else, now that you've seen Jose's model, are there any questions? No? Okay, ready, and, go."

By using the formula consistently, students get used to it, and it becomes part of the class culture to wait until the teacher says "go" before starting activities. This allows for more clarity, and keeps the chaos in check.

Many Mrs. Allgoods don't use the "Go" Procedure. Somehow, whether it's through subtle inflection, eye contact, gesture, or tone, they communicate to the students when to listen, when to clarify, and when to move. But many Mrs. Allgoods do use the "Go" Procedure, because they don't want to have to rely on subtle messages when a clear formula can work every time.

Some teachers prefer to use a different word than "go." This is primarily for one of two reasons. First, they use the word "go" in describing the directions ("You will go to the supply cabinet…"), and they don't want "student lawyers" to have a loophole built into the system. Second, the word "go" can get kids too energized. Instead, they might use, "When I say the phrase 'peace and quiet,' everyone quietly move to the carpet on the floor and sit in a circle." Or, as a fun alternative to "go," they might use a word from the content of the day: "When I say the word 'photosynthesis'...." Whatever word or phrase you use, the "Go" Procedure can help build your consistency and keep kids focused and on the same page.

Nonverbal Messages

Online Toolbox

Video showing how we can align our nonverbal and verbal messages.

Sometimes, it seems we say everything exactly the right way, and our students still get too active too fast. This is often because our nonverbal messages to students are the opposite of our verbal messages. If we say "When I say GO," putting emphasis on the word "go," then we can unintentionally spark students to get up and move before they even know the full directions. Or if we ask students to raise their hands to be called on to speak, but our manner and/or mannerisms seem excited, then we cause students to blurt out.

Bathroom Procedure

Check with your school administration about bathroom policies, as they vary widely from school to school and district to district. Some see limiting bathroom use for students as potentially punitive, if kids need to go (especially for young children). Others restrict bathroom use, whereby students are not allowed to use the bathroom during the first or last ten minutes of the class, thus encouraging them to use the bathroom between classes.

One strategy that works well for secondary classes: teachers give students a certain number of non-transferable bathroom passes per quarter — usually two. If a student has used all his passes, then each subsequent time he needs to use the bathroom, he owes the teacher three minutes at lunch or after school for each minute he is in the bathroom. At the end of the quarter, students can pool their unused passes and "cash them in" for something special. Some teachers report that when the class has the opportunity to "buy" something with their unused bathroom passes, the peer pressure to keep kids from using the bathroom generally ensures that kids go only when they really need to.

Wise-Apple Advice

A Final Word on Teaching Procedures

Students can meet our high expectations for following classroom procedures if we:

- ▲ assume the best — that our students are capable and determined to learn them;
- ▲ provide a crystal-clear road map for students, such as rubrics and visuals or the many other strategies offered in this chapter; and
- ▲ offer students a chance to practice, so that they can internalize the steps necessary for their success.

As the railroad tracks of procedure are laid down and consistently polished and maintained, the train of content can go full speed ahead.

9

CONSISTENCY

Mrs. Meanswell:	"Mark, didn't you promise to behave?"
Mark:	"Yes."
Mrs. Meanswell:	"And didn't I promise you there'd be a consequence if you didn't?"
Mark:	"Yes, but since I broke my promise, I don't expect you to keep yours."

The following text is inside the image: "I MEET WITH STUDENT LAWYERS ON FRIDAYS AT 4:30", "Test Wednesday!", "solve for X", "$\sqrt{2 + Y(27 - X^2)} = \frac{Y}{X^3}$", "Do problems 1-23", "pgs. 115 - 120", "HERMANSEN"

T HERE'S AN OLD SAYING: "Once the camel gets its nose in the tent, the rest of the animal is sure to follow." Another, more modern version is, "Give a mouse a cookie and he wants a glass of milk." Or you may be familiar with, "Give them an inch, and they will take a mile." Our inconsistency can send our class mixed messages that invite camels into the tent for afternoon tea — and students into inappropriate behavior. Since we are the primary authors of what happens in the classroom, students follow our lead, and they will behave in ways we unconsciously allow. The trick is to get conscious and consistent.

Here's a conversation that I once had with a teacher who was struggling in her classroom management:

Me:	What do you think you need to do to improve your classroom management?
Teacher:	I need to be more consistent.
Me:	Great. How do you need to be more consistent?
Teacher:	I just need to be more consistent.
Me:	Do you know the specific areas where you want to focus?
Teacher:	I just need to be more consistent.

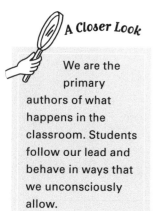

A Closer Look

We are the primary authors of what happens in the classroom. Students follow our lead and behave in ways that we unconsciously allow.

Mrs. Allgood says

When students call out, we need to honor the procedure rather than the content.

I left the conversation thinking: "Well, she certainly is consistent about thinking that she needs to be consistent!"

In truth, knowing the details and where to put our attention in order to grow in consistency is not that easy. The story below and the strategies that follow will help fill in the gaps and ground the focus on consistency into simple, practicable strategies.

In March several years ago, I began mentoring a first-year fifth-grade teacher. She had been teaching since the beginning of the school year, and was struggling. I sat in the back of the room while she taught, and in ten minutes I wrote down twenty-five suggestions. Honestly, in her repertoire, I didn't see a whole lot she should continue to do. Transitions seemed to elongate and blend into one another so that there really wasn't a whole lot of teaching going on between them. The kids interrupted constantly, redirecting the flow of the class easily and often. The "camel" of student interruption hadn't just gotten its nose in the tent; it was reclining on a chaise lounge.

As I sat looking at my notes, I knew that if I shared my twenty-five suggestions with this teacher in our first post-observation meeting, I was toast. Not only would she resist any of my suggestions, she would probably sever what few ties we had to each other. Just as students balk when they receive their essays back with twenty-five suggestions in red ink, so do teachers balk when they are already overwhelmed and get a bunch of ideas thrown at them.

I realized that I needed to pare down my ideas to a few. This teacher needed a manageable handful of threads to follow, threads that would tie her to some basic strategies for classroom survival. I came up with three. I introduced them one at a time over a period of weeks, which allowed her to start experiencing success in her classroom. All three ideas, as it turns out, have three things in common. Each is:

- ▲ immediately applicable to all Pre-K–12 teachers;
- ▲ focused on teacher consistency;
- ▲ practical and doable.

All the other aspects of good teaching — holding our ground, effective lesson design, teaching procedures — are supported by these three suggestions, which are described below. Don't be fooled by their simplicity; consistency takes a lot of focus and practice before it becomes second nature. If she works hard at it, Mrs. Meanswell can discover a new teaching "muscle," one that will keep the wildlife outdoors.

> I suggested that when she woke up in the morning, rather than focusing on content or student misbehavior, she should focus on hand raising consistency instead.

Hand and Mouth Dis-ease

Just about every teacher has a procedure in place where students are asked to raise their hands and be called on before they speak.[1] However, in all my years as a mentor, I have never seen any teacher be absolutely consistent with this simple procedure. Students flow through the gaps, loopholes, and inconsistencies like water. Maria will raise her hand and call out the right answer. Manny will yell out the right answer without bothering to raise his hand. Even Mrs. Allgood isn't absolutely consistent in this. After years of practice, she can proudly state that about ninety-eight percent of the time, she is aware when she is being inconsistent.

The solution involves bringing awareness to the procedure and practicing consistency. When students call out, we need to honor the procedure rather than the content. In Manny's case, we can respond with something like, "That's a great answer, Manny. Could you please raise your hand, let me call on you, and then you can repeat it so the whole class can hear you."

Especially if Manny is normally a reluctant participant, it can be a temptation to acknowledge his good answers even when they are called out of turn. But giving in will send a mixed message to students about procedures, penalize those who don't call out, and ultimately lead to adding the camel's name to the mailbox.

A clear hand-raising procedure is one of the hardest things for teachers to enforce consistently. It takes practice and self-discipline, but it makes a huge difference in the noise level in the classroom. For the struggling fifth-grade teacher, this may well have been the most valuable tip she focused on. I suggested that when she woke up in the morning, instead of thinking "I'm going to cover such-and-such content today," or "Today, I'm going to be a better classroom manager," she should focus on, "Today, I will be more consistent about hand raising than I was yesterday." I gave

After two students asked if they could help, she had the "hand police" on her side!

Online Toolbox

Video showing how to align verbal and non-verbal messages in hand-raising directions and other areas of consistency.

her a clip-art picture of a hand and she posted it on the back wall where she could easily see it. The students asked her what the hand was for, and she replied, "To help me be consistent in asking you to raise your hands to be called on." Two students naturally asked, "Can we help?" — so then she had the "hand police" working on her side! She gave them a special hand signal — left hand flat on the desk, with all five fingers spread wide — to remind her when she had "missed a consistency opportunity." Ultimately, her awareness and her "muscle" of consistency began to grow. By focusing on one area, she became much more conscious of the whole realm of procedures and consistency, and this ultimately began to spill into other key areas of her teaching. Indeed, hand raising is at or near the top of the list for many who are looking for one thing that will help them improve their classroom management. It serves as an "anchor" to spread our awareness to many key management elements.

Arguing with the Ref

Have you ever come back to your car during a shopping spree to put more money in the meter, only to discover that you're too late, and there's already a ticket on your windshield? At that point you think to yourself that you might as well not move your car or put money in the meter. Simply keep the ticket on the windshield, and go back to shopping. No parking officer is going to give you two tickets.

In a similar way, students often feel that once they've received a consequence from us, all bets are off. They figure there's no way we're going to give them a second consequence for arguing about the first consequence we gave; they've already hit bottom, so they have every right to argue about it. This "arguing with the ref" applies to all those times when students argue with teacher decisions, and it can drive teachers crazy.

For example, Mark is interrupting class by talking to Susie. Mrs. Meanswell has warned him several times to no avail. She then tells him that he has to change his seat. Does he pop right up and walk to the new seat, thanking Mrs. Meanswell profusely for teaching him appropriate behavior? Forget about it! Instead, he argues with her. She then "takes the bait" by explaining to Mark what he already knows — why he needs to change seats, attempting to justify her decision. Or, she doesn't explain, but does end up verbally warning, cajoling, and/or threatening Mark until he saunters — taking his sweet time, noisily complaining — across the room.

In this example, Mrs. Meanswell is the ref and Mark is arguing with her. What she needs to understand and enforce is that his arguing is in itself a disruption, deserving a second consequence. Mark's first consequence is a temporary change of his seat. His second consequence could be that he stays in his new seat longer. (For other consequence ideas, see Chapter 13, "Rules and Consequences.")

Mrs. Allgood addresses student arguing proactively. She establishes the procedure for when a student disagrees with her decisions and makes it clear that "arguing with the ref" is in itself a misbehavior that will warrant a separate consequence.

Let's look at how she handles Mark's disruption. If Mark disagrees with her decision to change his seat, he holds his hands up to form a "T" (for "talk") — like a time-out signal. She nods to acknowledge the signal, and silently directs him to his new seat. Mark quietly changes seats. Later, they have a private conversation where Mark can voice his protest. If it turns out that Mark has a legitimate point, she thanks him for waiting to talk to her and asks him to return to his seat. She can then publicly acknowledge how well Mark followed the procedure for disagreeing with her decision, and remind students: "Even though I was wrong, had Mark argued with me, he still would have received a consequence because in this classroom, there is no arguing with the ref." The whole process with Mark will thus become a model for all of her students' future behavior.

> **A Closer Look**
>
> Student arguing is in itself a disruption, deserving a second consequence.

An alternative to the "T" signal is a special "teacher-student conversation pass" that students pick up at the back of the room and "cash in" when they want to talk privately with their teacher. One middle school teacher uses a great variation of this. She has a sign on her wall that says "Arguing Appointments." When a student begins to argue with her, she says, "I argue by appointment only. Please put your name on the appointment sign and I will call you up later to discuss it." Students rarely if ever make an appointment!

Whether or not we decide to use the "T" signal or another variation through which students can voice their protests, we can still benefit from an increased consciousness about arguing with the ref. The main element is simply to be aware that students do not have the right to protest our decisions whenever they choose. Conversations about the details should be on the teacher's timetable — not the student's. We have the right to table their protests until such a time that twenty or thirty pairs of eyes are not watching the debate.

One benefit of tabling student arguments is that students will often not follow through with their protest, because their original concern was more of an emotional outburst than a logical disagreement.

What about when a student argues on behalf of his friend? His arguing is equally disruptive, and needs to be addressed as such. Mrs. Allgood spends time early in the school year to define "student lawyers." Her mini-lesson is engaging and funny, yet also informative, as she and her students brainstorm examples of "student lawyering." She then posts a permanent sign on the wall of her classroom, which reads "I meet with student lawyers on Fridays at 4:30" or "This is a student-lawyer-free zone." Whenever a student argues for his friend, she simply points to the sign and moves on.

A Closer Look

We have the right to table their protests until such a time that twenty or thirty pairs of eyes are not watching the debate.

To reinforce the "student-lawyer" policy, I describe to my students an analogous policy from the National Basketball Association (NBA). If there is a fight on the court and a player on the court gets involved in that fight, he may get fined or worse, depending on his level of involvement. If, however, there's a fight on the court, and a player who is sitting on the bench jumps in, the moment he steps foot on the court (he could be fifty feet away from the fight), he is immediately suspended for the entire next game. In other words, it is much more severe in the NBA to jump into a fight than to be initially involved. And this is what I tell my students:

> ## "Student lawyers" start on a higher level of the consequence hierarchy than those initially involved.

When Mark disrupts class by arguing about someone else's issue, I may forego the "reminder" and "warning" consequences and go straight to an actual consequence within the classroom. (See Chapter 13, "Rules and Consequences.") As I consistently address students who argue on behalf of others, pretty soon those students tell their friends "I can no longer afford to be your student lawyer. The price has gotten too high!"

Remember, our aim is to include all students in the learning process as much as possible and to avoid student distractions. With more awareness and practice, we will naturally take the bait less when students argue, and our classroom disruptions will settle down.

> Two seconds after the teacher turned her back, the students were wrestling on the asphalt. Three seconds after that, they were picking up loose pieces of asphalt and throwing them at each other.

The Popcorn Effect

Imagine that you're making popcorn on the stove. You've got a pan full of unpopped kernels on low heat with the top off. One kernel pops and flies behind you onto the kitchen floor. You turn around and bend down retrieve it, and by the time you come back to the stove, dozens of kernels have popped, and they are all over the kitchen because you forgot to put the lid on the skillet. How does this translate to the classroom?

Get all students actively on task before having individual conversations with any of them.

A couple of years ago, I observed a middle school P.E. teacher who broke this guideline three times in about twelve seconds. The kids had run a lap and were standing on their numbers on the asphalt. As the teacher was about to announce the basketball activity, Mark raised his hand. The teacher committed her first mistake when she called on him before starting the activity. "I wasn't here yesterday when you gave us our grades," he said. "Could you tell me my grade?"

Her second mistake: "Sure. Come on up." A better answer would have been, "I talk to students about grades on Tuesdays and Thursdays at three o'clock. Please see me then." When Mark walked up, the teacher turned her back to the class in order to privately show him his grade. Mistake number three!

I was in the back observing and taking notes. About two seconds after the teacher turned her back, these eighth-graders were no longer standing on their numbers. They were wrestling on the asphalt. Three seconds after that, they were no longer just wrestling — they were picking up loose pieces of asphalt and throwing them at each other. Three seconds

Mrs. Allgood says

Minimize the number and length of private conversations held during class, while maximizing the opportunities for them.

later, the teacher turned around to see total "popcorn" bedlam. After class, she remarked to me, "These are just bad kids." It was unfortunate that she drew that conclusion from the lesson she taught. (For more on the unique challenges of teaching P.E., go to Chapter 13, "Rules and Consequences.")

Getting and keeping kids on task without having to constantly put out fires is a tall order for many of us. Keeping the "camel" of student disruption out of the tent begins with two guidelines. First, minimize the number and length of private conversations you need to have during class. This will help your students stay on task. Second, when you must have private conversations, make opportunities for them by building in activities where the rest of the class will be focused for at least a few minutes; perhaps show a short video, assign a reading or writing task, or have a competition among pairs, something sure to keep them on task without your constant attention. Numerous strategies (we call them "Fifty Ways to Leave Your Lecture") are offered in Chapter 12, "Lesson Design."

It can be quite a challenge to hold off in responding to individual students' needs. We want to help our students. We want to be fair and kind and caring. Yet when we attend to one student's apparent needs at the expense of all of our other students, trouble is sure to follow. It can help if we ask ourselves if what the student is asking for is a "need" or a "want." "Does it need to be addressed now, or can I do it later, at a time when I am not on stage with the rest of my students?" Often, the student is expressing a want, and that want can be addressed at a later time.

Other Consistency Keys

As we follow the three threads of consistency outlined above, our effectiveness in all areas of consistency will increase. Other keys to consistency, addressed in various chapters in this book, include:

▲ Holding our ground without over-explaining.
▲ Staying focused on the topic even as students try to change it.
▲ Teaching and re-teaching procedures.
▲ Starting and ending class on time.
▲ Enforcing and following through with consequences.
▲ Talking with parents/guardians.

▲ Welcoming and encouraging students.

▲ Aligning verbal and non-verbal messages to students.

Schoolwide Consistency

While it can help for the entire school to be consistent with procedures, rules, and consequences, it isn't a necessary ingredient for an individual teacher's success with her students. Getting every student in your classroom on the same page can be less of a challenge than getting every staff member in your school on the same page. For example, Mrs. Allgood believes that gum chewing adversely affects her students' pronunciation in her seventh-grade foreign-language class. She has no problem being consistent with her "no-gum-chewing-in-class" rule, even though many other teachers allow gum chewing. Her students learn very quickly what works and doesn't work in her class, regardless of the differences between their teachers.

Nonetheless, Grace and I have seen many schools adopt one or more of our classroom procedures school wide, with great benefit. For example, many schools that we have worked with now have teacher "walls of readiness" in every classroom. In some schools, every teacher uses a three-tone chime to get student attention in the classroom. Others have all students use hand signals for using the bathroom or getting a drink of water. Many secondary schools play music in the hallways between classes, timing the end of the song with the start of class, or use images of student attire that meets the school dress code. (See Chapter 8, "Teaching Procedures," for more details about these strategies.)

Wise-Apple Advice

Relaxing into Consistency

Being consistent doesn't mean being a robot or a machine. It arises out of our caring for our students, and caring for their learning. As we combine an open, resilient quality with a commitment to teach students content, behavior, and procedures, we naturally become more consistent — without losing our humanity or spontaneity.

10

GETTING READY

> *"Everything should be made as simple as possible, but not simpler."*
>
> — ALBERT EINSTEIN

You must be the new teacher. Here are your room keys,
roll sheet, lesson plans and spit-wad deflector suit.

O NE THING MRS. MEANSWELL won't see when observing Mrs. Allgood is what she does to get ready before she ever gets to the classroom. Her organization and preparation are keys to smooth teaching and smooth management. These are particularly important skills to learn for a new teacher, or one who is transferring to a new school or district, because there are so many things to do and consider. This chapter lays out much of the nitty-gritty of getting ready before the students arrive, as well as what to do in the first weeks of school. And Chapter 11, "The First Week of School," along with the online toolbox, provides detailed lesson plans for what to do in the first five days.

What to do Before School Starts

Online Toolbox

The list on the next page is available in the online toolbox.

Suppose it's June and you just got hired at a new school for a new teaching job that begins in August. Whether it's your first job or your tenth, there are certain preparations that can help take the edge off those first days and weeks of school.[1] They help us get organized, get to know our students better, deal with district and school issues, and answer classroom and procedure questions.

Bright Ideas

Before-School Checklist: Questions to Consider

Notes

Assistance from Other Teachers

1. Do I have a buddy teacher and/or a mentor I can ask for help?
2. Do I have the phone numbers of teachers I can call for help?

Schoolwide Management Policies

3. What are the school policies about rules and consequences?
4. How should I present these to students?
5. What are the school policies about suspensions, detentions, referrals, and keeping students after school? Are teachers encouraged or discouraged to make use of these options?
6. What are the school policies about student use of cell phones in classes and on campus?
7. What are the school rules about notifying parents about inappropriate student behavior?
8. How do I get assistance from the office for emergencies, illness, or discipline problems?
9. Is there a schoolwide management plan?
10. Is there a policy concerning the number and types of warnings given before sending a student to the office or counselor?
11. What are the expectations about behavior during transitions such as going to lunch or recess?

Notes

12. What are yard and lunch duty rules? How do I enforce them?
13. What should I do if there's a fight in my classroom? On the playground? In the parking lot?
14. What should I do if a student reports another student's misbehavior?
15. What is the emergency plan for violence on campus and natural disasters, such as fires, earthquakes, tornados, or floods?

Schoolwide Issues and Concerns

16. When is the principal available? About what should s/he be contacted?
17. When is the school nurse available and what are appropriate reasons for making a referral?
18. Is a counselor available? What types of referrals are appropriate?
19. How can the school or district help with diagnosing or working with students who have severe learning or behavior challenges?
20. What janitorial services are available for my room? How do I make requests?
21. Do I know the bell schedule? Is it posted?
22. Do I have a district and school calendar?
23. What is the procedure for taking roll?
24. What is the procedure for using hall passes?
25. What are all the different pieces of paper that go back and forth among the office, the counselors, the attendance staff, the students, and the teachers?

Notes

In the Classroom

26. Have I determined the class rules, or will I include students in deciding those rules? If so, how?

27. What is my policy for cell phones in the class?

28. Have I anticipated worst-case management scenarios, and determined what to do in each case?

29. Have I prepared a handout and/or visual chart to display rules/consequences, major class procedures, and course requirements?

30. How will I document interactions with students and parents?

31. Are aides available, and if so, on what schedule?

32. Do I have keys to my classroom or other rooms to which I may need access?

33. Do I have the necessary furniture for my room? To whom should I communicate if I need something?

34. How will I arrange student desks?

35. What is the procedure for the arrival of students in the morning?

36. How do students leave at the end of the day? Do I have any bus riders, and do they leave early?

37. Do I know if any of my students have a disability or a special need that should be accommodated in the room arrangement?

38. How can I ensure that these students are fully included in classroom culture and activities? If they leave my classroom during the day, what are their schedules?

Bright Ideas

Notes

39. What is the daily schedule for music, recess, P.E., lunch, library, and the computer lab?

40. Where are these rooms, and what procedures should I follow to send or take students to them?

41. What is the procedure for late arrivals and early dismissals?

42. Do I have a substitute-teacher folder prepared, in case I am ill? Does it include class procedures and requirements, a seating chart, and emergency lessons?

Assignments

43. Where and how will I post assignments?

44. What will be my standards for form and neatness (pencil, pen, type of paper, heading, due dates, erasures)?

45. How will students who return from being absent know what to make up?

46. Will I post a "Finished Early?" chart? (See Chapter 12, "Lesson Design.")

Monitoring Progress

47. Will I look at students' test scores and reports from previous years? If so, how will I locate them?

48. What will be the consequences of late or incomplete work?

49. What procedures will I use to monitor work in progress?

50. When and how will my students and I monitor projects or longer assignments?

Bright Ideas

Notes

51. How will I collect completed assignments?

52. What records of student work will I retain?

53. Does the school use a specific grading program or am I free to choose my own? If mandated by the school, how and when do I get training to use it?

54. Will I use a computer grading system that has Internet access, so that students and/or parents can type in a password to see their progress online?

55. How will I easily add or delete student names in the first weeks, as enrollment changes?
    Suggestion: if you use a paper gradebook, one way is to use a photocopy of the first two or three weeks of the gradebook, and then transfer the grades to the actual book once the class roster is more stable.

56. Will I assign numbers for my students, to help collate homework and enter grades?

Feedback

57. What are my grading policies? Points? Letter grades? Tests? Homework?

58. Will class participation count toward student grades?

59. What kinds of feedback will I provide, and when? Will I set up regular times to conference with students and their parents?

Bright Ideas

Notes

60. What procedure will I follow to send materials home to parents?
61. Where will I display student work?
62. What records of their own work, if any, will students maintain?
63. How will I handle grading disputes with students? With parents?

Supplies and Materials

64. What are the procedures for obtaining classroom books?
65. How do I check them out to students?
66. Where do I get daily supplies: markers, paper, pencils, staples?
67. Do I get money to spend on supplies for my room? If so, how do I procure it?
68. What digital materials are available? How do I check them out?
69. What technology will be provided? Computers? Projector? Document Reader? SmartBoard? iPads? And whom do I ask for tech support and training?
70. What are the policies and procedures for making copies?

The First Days

71. Have I prepared a letter home to parents to introduce myself and what I teach, offering them ways they can connect with me and support their child's success in my class?
72. What is the required paperwork for the first day of school, including attendance, school announcements, and the lunch program?

Notes

73. Are my lesson plans prepared for the first few days for each class? Am I prepared with extra ones in case things go faster than I planned?

74. What warm-up activities will I use? (Several are described in Chapter 11, "The First Week of School.")

75. Have I prepared short activities — "supplemental lesson ideas"— to use in case my lesson ends early? (These are described in more detail in Chapter 12, "Lesson Design.")

76. What is the special procedure for the arrival of students on the first day of school?

77. How will I welcome students? What will we do as a class to introduce ourselves and get to know one another? (See Chapter 11, "The First Days of School.")

78. What special assemblies or schedules are happening in the first week?

79. How and when will I receive my class roster(s)?

80. Will I use a seating chart? How will I design it for the first day?

Feeling Overwhelmed?

The checklist is not designed to overwhelm you. If you don't look at it until two months into the school year, you'll find that you've already addressed most of the items anyway. It's here in case you have the time, energy, and desire to channel your concerns and anxieties into concrete action in advance of the start of school. If you do choose to use this list, you probably won't be able to address everything up front. Just address what you think is most important first, and leave the rest for various times throughout the first quarter.

Managing Your To-Do List

Another way to make the days before school a little less stressful is to divide your to-do list (a combination of what's on the Before-School Checklist and what's floating around in your head constantly) into two categories:

▲ Things to do before school starts
▲ Things to do in the first two weeks of school

Some of the items on your list will be included in both categories. For example, if you want to include your students in designing rules and consequences, you can determine the lesson plan strategy for this before school starts, and actually implement it in the first few days of school. (See Chapter 13, "Rules and Consequences.") Or, you can determine most of your classroom procedures before the students arrive, and implement/teach them in the first few weeks, once school starts. (See the section called "The First Week of School" later in this chapter, as well as Chapter 8, "Teaching Procedures.") By dividing your tasks into two categories, you can reduce your anxiety by reducing the number of things you need to do right away.

Ask a Veteran

Make a date with a veteran teacher at your school to talk for an hour, sometime before the first day of school. Once the date is set, put all your questions on one document (either paper or smart phone or electronic tablet). You can start with the Before-School Checklist. Keep this document with you all the time, so you can note everything that comes to mind, as it comes up. This includes all of the questions

Mrs. Allgood says

If you don't look at the checklist until two months into the school year, you'll find that you've already addressed most of the items anyway.

A Closer Look

You can determine most of your classroom procedures before the students arrive, and implement/teach them in the first few weeks, once school starts.

that swirl around your head at night. Know that you will have a definite time with that veteran teacher in which your questions will be answered. You'll relax in the interim, and the process will help you to hone your questions and concerns into one list. Include questions ranging from how to use hall passes to the political climate at the school. I suggest, in fact, making dates with two or three veterans at your school, so that you canvass more than one perspective and increase the likelihood of addressing all your questions.

Sometimes veteran teachers need to be reminded why you want to meet with them and how important these meetings can be for you. This is part of the teacher's rite of passage — learning to ask for help. (See Chapter 3, "Ask for Help.") If one veteran doesn't "get it" or can't commit to helping, ask another and another and another. There's no way around it — to learn the culture of your new school, those who have been there a while are the best source of help.

Making Use of Extra Time

It may seem crazy to add things to the list, but with efficient planning, extra time may be available. Try previewing novels, textbooks, movies, and/or software slated for student use. Construct some simple substitute lesson plans and activities. Create assignments and tests, purchase special supplies, decorate the classroom — even update your teacher wardrobe. Don't forget to leave messages for friends explaining that you'll be busy and unavailable until June!

What if You're Hired at the Last Minute?

I got my first job on Thursday afternoon, September 30, a month after school had started. That night I attended Back-to-School Night and introduced myself to the parents of the students I hadn't yet met! A year prior to that, at 8:15 a.m. on a Monday, I was given a two-month, long-term substitute job for a class that had started fifteen minutes earlier. First, I was handed a set of novels I'd neither heard of nor taught; then I was introduced to the class and set loose. Unfortunately, these scenarios are all too common.

Although being tossed directly into the fire is not an ideal way to start, there are strategies that make it easier. Since developing lesson plans is the top priority, limit homework assignments that necessitate grading in the first week or two. This tack also will free up some time for the Before-School Checklist. In this "emergency" situation, the two most critical questions on the checklist are: "Do I have a buddy and/or mentor teacher?" and "Do I have phone numbers of colleagues I can ask for help?"

> I was handed a set of novels I'd neither heard of nor taught; then I was introduced to the class and set loose.

This is barreling down the interstate, holding the wheel with one hand and the driver's instruction manual with the other. The good news is that there are always teachers out there who are willing to help, and that the learning process goes incredibly fast. Questions that cause a swerve on the first day will be easily addressed two weeks later. It's akin to how some young children learn a second language. There is a silent period where they absorb information without speaking, then all of sudden, bam! — full sentences.

Room Arrangement

When setting up a classroom, there's a lot to consider:

▲ How easy is it for the teacher to circulate among her students? Can she easily get within two feet of every student, without having to squeeze around student desks and belongings?

▲ Does the arrangement maximize the physical safety of the students? Are heavy or sharp items secure? Is there ample room for students to move without elbowing one another?

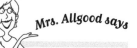

Mrs. Allgood says

> When newly hired and "dropped into the class," limit homework assignments that necessitate grading in the first week or two.

▲ How close are the students to the front of the room? Closer is better for learning content and behavior.

▲ How close are students to one another? Are they close enough to share with a partner, yet far enough apart not to distract?

▲ How easy is it for students to walk to and from the water fountain, pencil sharpener, and front door?

▲ Can students see the teacher, the TV, and the board?

▲ Can all students easily face forward during whole-class instruction?

▲ Are frequently used materials easily accessible? Are they so prominent that they are a distraction?

- ▲ Are there personal touches in the room, such as plants, pets, or photos?
- ▲ Are the walls and bulletin boards decorated with posters, quotations, themes, student work? It helps to keep things simple at the start, adding student work as it is generated.
- ▲ Is technology placed towards the perimeter of the class to allow for some students to work independently during direct instruction? Or is the room "digital-centric," optimizing the use of technology throughout the lesson?
- ▲ Are there places for students to put their coats and lunches (primarily elementary school)?
- ▲ Are there areas for student centers and student collaboration?

Seating arrangements should match the activities you are doing. For direct instruction, there is nothing wrong with rows, even for younger students (see page 120 in Chapter 8, "Procedures," for a visual sample of this). For cooperative learning, group work, classroom community meetings, small group activities, and the like, the seats need to be arranged differently. Seating formation can be changed frequently, as long as the students are taught and retaught the procedures for moving desks. In his book, *Tools for Teaching*, classroom management consultant Fred Jones (www.fredjones. com) maps out and critiques a variety of useful seating arrangements.[2]

> For many new teachers, preparing well in advance is a mythical goal.

There are many applications and programs available to help you design your classroom. Ask others at your school for the best ones, or go online to find one that works for you.

Wise-Apple Advice

A Last Thought About Getting Ready

I've already dragged one secret from my closet: as a new teacher, most of my lesson planning was done the night before I taught. It wasn't until January that it even occurred to me that it was possible to plan whole units in advance of teaching them. Once I figured that out, my stress level dropped, and I was a more resilient teacher.

For many new teachers, preparing well in advance is a mythical goal, but every ounce of effort nets a triple return. In order to maximize preparation, take a look at the big picture. What units are scheduled? What preparation is necessary for each unit? What can be done in advance? What are the expected outcomes for each unit? In addition to the information above, check for several suggestions in Chapter 11, "The First Week of School," and Chapter 12, "Lesson Design."

11

THE FIRST
WEEK OF SCHOOL

*"Faith is taking the first step even
when you don't see the whole staircase."*

— MARTIN LUTHER KING, JR.

Those section offers practical strategies and approaches for your first week in the classroom. It focuses on the students' needs and your needs, and how to address them both right from the start.

Online Toolbox

The information in this chapter is a good start for getting ready for the first five days of teaching, and will be sufficient for some. For everyone else, our online toolbox will "close the deal." It contains a treasure trove of organized, detailed, and easily accessible teacher-created lessons that cover all major areas of focus for the first week.

Questions Students Have on the First Day — Even if They Don't Know They're Asking Them

▲ Am I in the right room?
▲ Where should I sit?
▲ What do I need to do in order to succeed? Will it be easy or hard?
▲ Who is the teacher?
▲ Does the teacher care about me? Will she like me? Will I like her?
▲ Who are the other students in the room?

▲　Is this classroom physically, emotionally, and socially safe?

▲　What are the rules of this class?

▲　What will be expected of me?

Addressing these potential concerns early on maximizes the level of engagement students will have in their new environment. There are four main areas of focus that — when combined in the first week — address these questions and start the year off on the right track: Rapport, Procedures, Rules and Consequences, and Content. They are explained below, followed by sample planning templates for the first week for both elementary and secondary teachers.

Rapport

Connecting positively with kids helps their nervous systems to be less nervous. As they feel safe and comfortable in your class, they are more motivated to learn and participate, and less likely to act out. Rapport is the "oil" in the class "engine," that keeps it cool and running smoothly.

Rapport builds over time. The first week is simply a chance to begin the process. While there are numerous activities you can do to help establish rapport, you don't need to go overboard in the first week. Much of it can happen as you focus on procedures, rules and consequences, and content. Your positive demeanor, enthusiasm, and genuine care for students, all contribute to an overall feeling of warmth and connectedness in the classroom. Also, remember that providing opportunities for your students to feel connected and safe with one another can be just as important as having them connect with you. Refer to Chapter 7, "Positive Connections," for more on the value of rapport and for dozens of easy-to-use strategies. Below are several strategies you can use in the first week.

Interviews

Students pair off and interview each other, then introduce their partners to the class. Please note that this activity might occupy two class periods for a secondary class of thirty students, but it is usually shorter with younger kids. Variation: Students pair off and choose letter A or B. The B's speak for one minute, initiating with "I don't know" statements such as, "I don't know where you live," "I don't know your favorite color," "I don't know what sports you like," "I don't know what you did this summer," "I don't know what your favorite music is," and "I don't know how you feel about being back at school." Then the A's speak for two minutes responding to the B's statements and filling in whatever blanks they want to address in the B's knowledge. The level of risk is lower, because the A's can speak to topics with which they feel most comfortable. The process is then reversed so that both people get "interviewed." Then students can introduce each other or simply say one thing about their partner to the whole class.

The Big Lie

"How did you spend your summer vacation?" The twist to this one is that students have to make up the most outrageous story they can. This frees up their imagination immensely and offers a window into their personalities when they present to the class. Variation: Two truths and a lie. Students write or speak about their summer vacation, including three key things they did. Two of them are true and one false. The process of the other students' guessing which is the lie can become a contest.

> Students have to make up the most outrageous story they can.

Self-Evaluation from the Future

Students can evaluate their upcoming school year as if it just ended, through either filling out an evaluation form or writing a more free-flowing self-evaluation letter. This is a creative way that students can set goals and look at the long term. At the end of the school year, have them evaluate themselves again, and then give back their original evaluations for comparison. Some teachers of high school freshmen do a written goal-setting activity, and then return the papers to their students four years later at graduation.

People Hunt

This is like a treasure hunt, where students seek information about one another. Each student has a list of statements, such as "This summer I read at least two books," or "I speak at least two languages." They try to find students in the class who fit the criteria on their list. This can be done in an "informal party style" where students are free to mingle and meet each other. It can also be done in a more structured way, with two circles: inner and outer. Students in the inner circle face outward toward a partner in the outer circle. Each pair gets a certain amount

Online Toolbox

A sample People Hunt that you can tailor to your students' needs.

of time, perhaps a minute or so per person, to each make four statements from his People Hunt list, guessing which statements will get a "yes" from his partner, and recording that partners name on his paper. The teacher then rings a chime and the inner circle rotates counterclockwise, so that new partnerships are formed. This more structured activity ensures that everyone is included, and exclusive cliques don't get a chance to form.

Action Thermometer

Initially, this can work similarly to the People Hunt, but with a twist. Students move to different sides of the room (or stand in place) if they have done a particular thing, know a particular thing, or like a particular thing. This can be used throughout the school year, with a focus on getting the students to know one another, or with a focus on forming small groups in the classroom. For example, "Please go to this side of the room if you like dogs better than cats, and that side of the room if you like cats better than dogs." Or "Stand up if you flew on a plane this summer." Or "Go to that side of the room if you have a parent who was born in a different country." In Chapter 12, "Lesson Design," using the Action Thermometer for teaching content is explained in detail.

Ally Circle

Students stand in a circle, and move to the center when they match a criterion. For example, the teacher can say "Move to the center if you are wearing blue," or "Move to the center if you played video games yesterday," or "Move to the center if you agree with the latest supreme-court ruling." This allows students to non-verbally express themselves, and see commonality with others. And, depending on the nature of the criteria, those who go to the center can receive support from the presence of one another, while those standing in the outer circle act as silent witnesses.

Non-Competitive Musical Chairs

Chairs are arranged in a circle, facing in. A single chairless person stands in the middle, picks a criterion — such as "If you are wearing green, get up and change seats" — and then he scrambles for a seat with all of the green-wearing people. The one person who can't find a seat then stands in the center and the procedure is repeated with a different criterion. Criteria can be drawn from what students are wearing, where they've lived or traveled, languages they speak, or movies they've seen. Later on in the year, criteria can shift to class content. For example, each student is assigned a letter of the alphabet. A word related to a lesson is announced, and only those students whose letter appears in the word have to get up and switch chairs. Please note: this can get quite competitive. One good rule is: "If any student hits the floor, the game is over."

Mrs. Allgood says

One good rule is: "If any student hits the floor, the game is over.

Teachers Learning Student Names

Learning student names can be daunting, especially for secondary teachers who have five or more classes each day. In the beginning, try using a seating chart with your students' first names in alphabetical order. Or, take pictures of your students (with permission from your administration) and put them on your computer, electronic tablet, or seating chart. Some teachers (particularly in elementary school) gather photos of the students in the previous year, and study the names over the summer. Some place photos of their students on the students' desks on the first day of class, so that everyone knows where to sit. If you don't have images of your students before school starts, you can easily collect them soon after and use student photos to assign seats, groups, and class chores.

Name Games for Students

Most teachers focus diligently on learning students' names. Often, however, teachers mistakenly assume that the students know one another's names. One way to help with this is a name game. Students can compete to see who can say everyone's name in the class. Winners, and there can be more than one, receive a prize. If many of the students know one another from the previous year, but new students have also joined the school, then new students can try to name half of the students.

Mrs. Allgood says

Once the initial procedures are established, let your content determine which procedures are best for you to teach next.

Whether or not students' names become the subject of a game, it helps build a sense of community when students learn one another's names early in the school year. One simple way is to provide students with nametags. Another is to give them an extra-credit, written quiz on one another's names.

Procedures

Below are two lists of procedures that you will need to establish in your classroom(s): The First Day of School, and The First Week of School. Every teacher and teaching situation is different, but the situations listed are often the ones that happen first. Some of these may not need your overt attention right away, and some may need to be taught. You may discover after a day or two which procedures you most need to emphasize explicitly, based on what you're seeing in your classroom. Once the initial procedures are established, let your content determine which procedures are best for you to teach next. For example, if you plan on having students work in groups, then teach group work procedures first. If you plan on the students' doing a lab, then focus on the procedures for setting up and cleaning up the lab, before the students get started.

Please refer to Chapter 8, "Teaching Procedures," for the nitty-gritty on how to teach procedures.

The First Day of School

- ▲ Students entering the classroom
- ▲ Teacher greeting the students
- ▲ Students finding their seats
- ▲ Quiet signal
- ▲ Raising hands to answer or ask questions
- ▲ Handing out materials
- ▲ Collecting materials
- ▲ Bathroom policy
- ▲ Dismissing students at the end of class, the lesson, or the day
- ▲ Lining up and walking in hallways

The First Week of School

- ▲ Headings on papers
- ▲ Moving in and out of pairs
- ▲ Moving in and out of groups
- ▲ Transitioning from tables to carpet and back
- ▲ Active listening or Polite Position
- ▲ Turning in completed work
- ▲ Returning from being absent

▲ Entering the classroom late

▲ Students getting water to drink

Some of these procedures can be taught quickly, and some may require more time and focus. Remember that procedures are the railroad tracks for your students' success. Emphasizing them early and often will keep the train of learning on target.

If you are having challenges in implementing procedures, take a look at Chapter 15, "Making Changes," for guidance.

Online Toolbox

Lesson plans for teaching key procedures in the first day and week of school.

Seating Chart

Consider using a seating chart on the first day when students enter your room. They will thus know where to sit, and won't be exposed to the awkwardness of worrying about being chosen by others. Plus, it will reduce the possibility of groups of friends' sitting together and focusing more on each other than on the lesson.

Establishing Rules and Consequences

There is no one best way to establish rules and consequences with your students. Some teachers share and review with their students a list of five or six rules and their consequences. Others use activities to involve students in helping create the rules. Some blend both modalities, offering students choices only around certain rules and consequences. Please refer to Chapter 13, "Rules and Consequences," for details on how to decide which rules to use, how to word them, and how to introduce them to your class.

If you have a lot of ground to cover regarding rules and consequences — not to mention your syllabus — then consider teaching them in small chunks over several days. However you do this, make sure to check for understanding. Some teachers create a scavenger hunt in the classroom as a form of review. Others quiz their students, and have them study rules and consequences as a homework assignment. One idea is to require a score of 100% on a quiz of class

Online Toolbox

Lesson plans that introduce rules and conse-quences, sample teacher lists of rules and consequences, and step-by-step templates for choos-ing them for your students.

principles, rules, and consequences. Students can take the quiz as often as necessary. The teacher holds onto the perfect quizzes for reference later in the year, if necessary. (This is explained in more detail on page 220 in Chapter 13, "Rules and Consequences.")

Content

Check with others at your school as to how "fluid" your class rosters are in the first week. If it's customary for rosters to change in the first week as the school tries to balance numbers, then consider making your first week of content into a self-contained unit, so that when Mark is transferred into your class in the second week, he doesn't feel a week behind. In anticipation of this, some teachers plan a "review" unit for the first week that is based on high-interest content from the previous year.

Mrs. Allgood says

Require students to score 100% on a quiz of class principles, rules, and consequences. They can take the quiz as often as necessary.

Ideally, the first week will be rigorous and engaging. As students focus on work in the first week, they internalize your expectations for the year. The work itself can help build rapport, as students feel motivated and safe in your classroom. Academic lessons are often more "teacher-led" than "student-centered" the first week, even if the rest of your year will focus on student-centered instruction. It takes some time to set up the routines and procedures that make student-centered instruction possible. Plus, as students settle down to work, their quiet focus can help them internalize that you are indeed safe and structured.

Calendar Templates for the First Week

Below are two calendar templates for the first week of school that integrate rapport, procedures, rules and consequences, and content. By looking at the templates, you can get a better sense of a possible balance between how much each category should be taught in the first week.

Please remember that these are simply templates, and that your first week will likely be quite different from what you see below. Use the templates as jumping-off points to tailor your lessons to the specific needs of your students, and to your particular teaching style. Know also that in many cases, each of the four areas of focus can be taught at the same time. We can certainly build rapport while teaching content, for example. Nonetheless, separating them can help you hone your approaches in designing lessons for the first week.

In the online toolbox, you can view an interactive version of these same calendars, which includes clickable links to lesson plans and activities. Simply go step by step: use the calendar provided, choosing the lessons that you like from the online toolbox, modifying as necessary. This can help take the stress out of the first week, give you more breathing room to connect with your students, and help you to land on your feet.

Online Toolbox

Clickable calendars with links to lesson plans and activities.

The First Week of School — Secondary Template

DAY 1	DAY 2	DAY 3	DAY 4	DAY 5
Meet and Greet Have a first day activity on desks (A, B)	**Greet and Seat** (A,B)	**Reinforce Start of Class Procedure** (B)	**Start of Class Procedure** (B)	**Start of Class Procedure** (B)
Teach Procedure: *Getting Attention/ Quiet Signal* (B)	**Teach Procedure:** *Start of Class* (B)	*Syllabus and Rules Activity* (B, C)	*Syllabus & Rules Quiz* (B, C, D)	**Informal Quiz on Names** or play a *Name Game* (A)
Introductions Introduce yourself and the class, perhaps with *a letter of introduction*. (A, D)	*Appointment Clocks* Create partners using a pre-partnering technique. (A)	**Introduce First Unit of Study** (D)	**Skills Lesson: Questioning** Teach how to *question a piece of text* (D)	**Materials Check** Check to see who has all materials. (B)
Movement Activity Review something using a movement activity and teach *music for transitions* procedure. (B, D or A)	**Model** *Talk to Text* with **Cold Read** (D) **Skills Lesson: Talk to Text** (D) **Teach Procedure:** *Pairs & Groups* (B) *Pair Share* for **Talk to Text** (D)	**Content Lesson** with guided practice. Incorporate various *participation techniques*. (D)	**Teach Procedure:** *Dismissal* (B)	**Teach Procedure:** *Hand Raising* (B) **Content Lesson** (D) *Reflection Activity* Such as an exit slip or quick write or write-pair-share.

A = Building Rapport   B = Teaching Procedures   C = Establishing Rules   D = Teaching Content

The First Week of School — Elementary Template

DAY 1	DAY 2
Meet and Greet students at the door. Have a *Getting to Know You/Welcome Activity* ready on students' desks (A) **GRADES K-1 ONLY:** *School Tour, Lining Up*, and Hallway Procedure (A) Teach Procedure: *Getting Attention.* (B) Teach Procedure: *Transitions T-Chart* *Welcome Activity Mixer* Follow-up to the "Welcome Activity." (B) Teach Procedures: *Bathroom* and Water (B) **Introduce First Content Piece** Reading Response or Narrative Writing (B) Teach Procedure: *Readiness for Recess* including getting snack, lining up and hallway procedure (A)	**Greet Students at the Door** (A) Teach Procedure: *Morning Routine* (B) Teach Procedure: *Pair-Share* (B) **Establish Rules and Expectations** (C) *Introduce Team Task Routine with Cooperation T-chart.* Assign the first Team Task, making class rules (B, C) **Freeze Game** to reinforce attention signal (A, B, D) **Popsicle Stick/Clip Decorating Continued** (A, B) **Review Readiness for Recess** (A, B)
Morning Recess	
Teach Procedure: Entering Classroom (B) **Introduce Daily English Language Arts Routine** (B, C, D) **Reading Instruction Day 1**(D) *Read Aloud and Classroom Activity* (D) *Play Name Game* (A) Teach Procedure: Lunch Routine (B)	Review procedure for entering the classroom (B) Practice Daily Language Arts Routine (B, D) Reading Instruction Day 2 (D) **GRADES K-1 ONLY:** *Guided Discovery* — Using Scissors (B) *Writing Lesson. Stage 1: Planning* (A, D) Review Line Up and Lunch Procedure (B)
Lunch	
Teach Procedure: Entering Class After Lunch (B) *Introduce Math though Graphing* (A, D) **Math Routine and Assessment** (D) **GRADES K-1 ONLY:** *Guided Discovery* — Using Markers (A, B) **Play Freeze Game Again.** To reinforce attention signal (B) *Stick/Clip Decorating* for assigning jobs (A, B) **Play Name Game Again** (A) **Review "How I Get to School" Graph** (B, D) Teach Procedure: *Dismissal/Lining Up* (B) **Homework:** Bring in a "souvenir" that represents what you did over the summer	Math Content Lesson D **GRADES K-1 ONLY:** Guided Discovery — Math Tools (B, D) **Introduce Classroom Jobs** Teach Procedure: *Getting Supplies & Cleaning Up* (B) *Art Activity* (A, B, D) **Review Dismissal Procedure** (B) **Homework:** Bring in a favorite photograph of yourself
A = Building Rapport B = Teaching Procedures C = Establishing Rules D = Teaching Content	

DAY 3	DAY 4	DAY 5
Reinforce Morning Routine (B) *Assign Jobs* using previously decorated sticks/clips (B) *Introduce Student of the Day or Week Routine* (A, B) **Assign Table Presidents** (A, B, D) **Teach Procedure:** *Independent Work Time* (B, D) **Line Up for Recess** with Snack (B)	Reinforce Morning Routine (B) **T Chart: Showing Respect** (A, B, D) **Daily Language Arts** (D) *Reading Instruction Day 4* (B, D) *Read Aloud* (B, D) **Reading Groups** (B, D) Line Up for Recess **with Snack** (B)	**Morning Routine** (B) **Introduce Physical Day.** (A, B) **Morning Meeting/Message** (A, B, C, D) **T Chart: Problem Solving** (A, B, D) **Daily Language Arts** (B, D) **Author's Chair** — half the class presents their first writing orally **Line Up for Recess** with Snack (B)
Morning Recess		
Review procedure for entering the classroom (B) **Practice Daily Language Arts Routine** (B, D) **Reading Instruction Day 3** (D) **Teach Reading Group Routine** (B, D) **Writing Lesson. Stage 2: Rough Drafts** (B, D) **Line-Up for Lunch** (B)	**Writing Lesson Stage 3: Publish** (B, D) **Introduce Science or Social Studies Unit** (D) **Line-Up for Lunch** (B)	**Reading Groups** (B, D) **Science/Social Studies Unit Continued** (D) **Line-Up for Lunch** (B)
Lunch		
Math Content Lesson (D) **Guided Discovery** — Water Colors (A, B, D) **Continue Art Project** (A, D) **Play Name Game Again** (A) *Question of the Day* (A, B) **Reinforce Dismissal Procedure** (B) **Homework:** Bring in your favorite T-shirt. Also take home letter of introduction to parents and list of needed supplies. Have parents sign letter and return with their contact information	**Math Content Lesson** (D) **Finish Art Project** (D) **Hopes and Dreams Individual worksheet** (A) **Reinforce Dismissal Procedure** (B) **Homework:** Bring in a family photograph. Remind students that signed parent letter and supplies are due tomorrow	**Math Games** (A, D) *Highs and Lows* (A, B) **Independent Work** (D) **Dismissal Procedure** (B) **Homework:** Assign as necessary

A = Building Rapport   B = Teaching Procedures   C = Establishing Rules   D = Teaching Content

Setting the Tone in the First Days

Mrs. Allgood and Mrs. Meanswell approach the first week of school quite differently. Below are examples of these differences.

Mrs. Allgood	Mrs. Meanswell
1. Greets students at the door with a smile and welcome.	1. Sits behind her desk, shuffling paper, or prepping materials.
2. Uses a seating chart when kids enter.	2. Lets kids sit wherever they want.
3. Writes her name, grade or subject, and room number on the board.	3. Waits until everyone is seated to verbally tell them her name and grade or subject.
4. Has something interesting or fun for students to do right away without her help.	4. Lets kids chat and wander until she is at the front and asks for their attention.
5. Takes attendance aloud the first day or two to get pronunciation and nicknames down, but from then on uses her seating chart to take roll silently while students are engaged in beginning tasks.	5. Calls roll verbally every day, taking away from instructional time.
6. Introduces herself briefly and gives a concise overview of her goals for the class.	6. Goes on and on about herself or the class, or, alternately, is a closed book.

Mrs. Allgood	*Mrs. Meanswell*
7. Plays a name game or some other activity that helps her kids meet and learn about one another.	7. Doesn't provide an activity to help kids connect with one another.
8. Hands out a syllabus or parent letter and engages students in an activity to review some of it.	8. Reads the entire syllabus or parent letter aloud, or has none.
9. Has students move and talk to one another regularly in class.	9. Lectures for long periods of time or rarely has students talk to one another or move from their seats. Conversely, has students move and talk, but without sufficient structure to keep them focused.
10. Introduces, models, practices, and reinforces key procedures.	10. Presents all procedures verbally and/or in writing without practicing.

Myth vs. Reality

Many teachers, especially new teachers, operate under limiting belief systems that tend to inhibit their ease and quality of teaching. Some of these "myths" are debunked below:

Myth: Your first day and/or week will determine the quality of your year.

Reality: How you start your year does set the tone. But you can always make changes. Each day is an opportunity to reinvent yourself as a teacher, develop your inner authority, and maximize student engagement and learning. (See Chapter 15, "Making Changes," for help.)

Myth: You must demand respect or students take advantage of you.

Reality: Respect isn't received through demands. Rather, student respect is earned through providing safety, structure, and consistency. Students thus perceive you as firm but fair, flexible, and friendly.

Myth: Student misbehavior is a personal attack that needs to be addressed aggressively.

Reality: Students misbehave for many reasons. Among other things, it is a way for students to test the waters to see if you will provide safety and structure consistently while holding them accountable for their choices in a firm but compassionate way. Chapter 14, "When Consequences Don't Work," addresses the myriad reasons why students act out.

Myth: Students who are not taught respect and appropriate behavior at home will never behave appropriately in class.

Reality: While life at home certainly influences life at school, students are able to behave differently in different environments. This outcome is based on what is expected of them and how those expectations are taught and reinforced in the different settings. As an example, many kids with divorced parents will act differently at each parent's home.

Myth: Don't teach content in the first days of school. Focus only on procedures.

Reality: Teaching content right away is a great way to establish an academic and rigorous focus. Just remember to blend your focus on procedures, content, and rapport as well. And plan for students who transfer in late and might miss the first week of content.

Myth: Don't smile until Christmas or students will perceive you as weak.

Reality: Students benefit when they feel that their teacher likes them and is enthusiastic about teaching. Inner authority is a relaxed state that arises as we allow ourselves to be human, rather than trying to override our humanness.

Wise-Apple Advice

Final Thoughts About
the First Week of School

It's great to be as prepared as possible. And, it's also great to prepare for feeling underprepared, no matter how much you prepare! It's the nature of teaching that often gives rise to this feeling of incompletion. No problem: in the midst of everything that happens in the first week, remember to notice what works for you, what you enjoy, and what the students respond to. As the school year unfolds, you can sprinkle those gems into all the corners of your lesson plans.

12

LESSON
DESIGN

*"Student divided by
confusion equals algebra."*
— LAURIE HALSE ANDERSON

CLASSROOM MANAGEMENT doesn't occur in a vacuum; it is intricately tied to what we teach and how we teach it. The ideal classroom is a place where learning is enjoyable — and high-level engagement can happen every time we teach a lesson. It's no surprise, then, that by motivating and engaging students, we can keep management problems at a minimum. More and more in today's most effective classrooms, kids can't wait to get started, and there isn't any issue about "settling them down." They come into the classroom, get into their groups, and begin working without any intervention from the teacher!

While Mrs. Allgood's classes aren't necessarily this seamless, she does appear to consistently provide her students with creative and meaningful activities. When things hit a lull, she simply comes up with a new idea that "wows" the kids, nipping their boredom in the bud. How do we emulate Mrs. Allgood to make our lessons motivate as well as inform? How do we address the nitty-gritty — the daily requirements of organization — while still packing zip into our teaching?

This chapter offers practical structures and strategies for designing your lessons, focusing on four areas: 1) organizing the lesson, 2) starting the lesson, 3) the lesson itself, and 4) closure. You'll notice that throughout the chapter, there are references to the brain and how it learns. In the last decade or so, there has been a huge and increasing focus on the brain, as scientists and educators discover more and more about how our brains function.[1] What exactly is brain-compatible learning? Here's a practical answer: find out what the brain likes, and use it when teaching content. Several "brain-friendly" approaches and strategies are woven throughout this chapter.

Organizing the Lesson

Mrs. Meanswell starts designing her lesson by focusing on what she will teach. Mrs. Allgood starts by focusing on what she wants the students to learn. This is an essential key to standards-based teaching. The steps of any effective lesson trace a natural progression, connecting students' prior knowledge with what the teacher wants them to take away today.[2] Whether you use the traditional five-step lesson plan, "I do, we do, you do," "Into, through, and beyond," or another approach to delivering your lessons, a simple key is to help our students connect the dots: "You are here; we're going there." This helps us focus on what is developmentally appropriate for each student's learning, even as we hone in on the logistics of the lesson.

The Brain's "Closet"

Think about your closet at home. If you throw things in it indiscriminately, pretty soon it will be hard to remember exactly what's in there, and even harder to find the things you need. If your closet is organized, however, with hangers and shelves and drawers, you can put a lot of stuff in it, know exactly where everything is, and find things right away.

A Closer Look

Mrs. Meanswell starts designing her lesson by focusing on what she will teach. Mrs. Allgood starts by focusing on what she wants the students to learn.

The brain is similar. It needs to organize information in order to be able to retrieve it. Instead of using shelves and hangers, it uses several approaches, including metacognition — thinking about and understanding one's own learning.[3] When you go on a trip, it helps to use a map to plot your destination and the stops along the way. By periodically looking at the map, you also can reflect on where you've been and where you're going.

In a similar way, you can organize your lessons by "mapping" your school year. Where have the students been? Where are they going? How does what's happening in class fit into the yearlong map? How does the yearlong map align with the larger PK-12 curriculum map? Not only will you benefit from this metacognitive look at the big picture — your students will also. Build into your lessons periodic "pit stops" where students can be reminded of where they have been, where they are going, and the value of getting there.

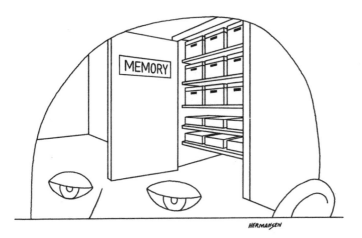

The brain likes to organize its closet.

Starting the Lesson

How a lesson starts can determine how smoothly the class runs and how much the kids learn. The first step sets the tone and direction.

Silent Work to Begin a Lesson or Transition

There are dozens of strategies for silent work, often referred to as "Do-Now's." Beginning a lesson in silence gives students a chance to relax, reorient from whatever they were focusing on before class, and search in their brains' "closets" for the topic at hand. It also gives us a chance to dispense with any individual student issues without having to worry about the "Popcorn Effect," that troublesome tendency of the group to lose focus when we have private conversations in the classroom. (For more on this, see Chapter 9, "Consistency"). These "Do-Now" activities can be anything we normally have students do, as long as they can do it quietly and without having to ask for directions or clarifications.

Mrs. Allgood says

Assign several Do-Now activities so that your "go-getters" have something to do while other students are still focused on the first item. Design at least one open-ended question each time.

A Closer Look

Anticipate
and address
potential student
concerns up front.
"Sell" the lesson.

Ideally, we want to design these activities so that no one will finish before it's time for the next step. One method is to assign several activities, so that your "go-getters" have something valuable to do while other students are still focused on the first item. When everyone is done with the first item, call the class to order. Extra work done by your "go-getters" can be shared in small groups, addressed in class, or collected for extra credit. (More about early finishers is addressed toward the end of this chapter.) Another method is to design at least one open-ended question for each warm-up. For example, ask students to come up with as many words as they can by using two or more letters from the word "cornucopia" or the word "abundance." Since they don't know how many words are possible, they will continue to look for quite a while. There are many sources where teachers can download "Do-Now" activities that contribute to enriching student learning while being engaging and developmentally aligned for independent work.

Refer to the Previous Lesson

Ask students to describe what the class did the day before. Ask key memory and analysis questions about the previous lesson. Look at the big picture of the unit and note how yesterday's lesson fit into the big picture. This can help them to anchor what they are learning into long-term memory.

Give an Overview of Today's Lesson

Post an agenda for the lesson. Describe what's coming and why. Place the day's lesson in the context of the big picture of the unit, and perhaps the big picture of the whole year. Focus as much as possible on the goal — what students should learn during the lesson — not just on what they will be doing.

Connect the Lesson to the Students' Lives and the Real World

Our students are inspired when they care about what they are studying. Our brains are wired for survival, and they are motivated by relevance.[4] If Amaya understands the connection between what she's about to be taught and the potential of succeeding in the debate club or at her dream job or in getting along with her best friend, she's much more likely to focus. If that link isn't happening, then try to get her "into" the lesson. For example, she can relate her own experiences to the experiences of a character in the book she's reading in English class. She can imagine how her life might be different if she were living in the time period she is studying in social studies.

> The three themes of my technology unit were "Chaos, Frustration, and Fun."

The Frame

How we frame a lesson has a huge effect on its success. Relating it to the students, as described above, is one way. Another is to be proactive by anticipating students' potential, legitimate concerns and addressing them up front. This idea is more immediately obvious to middle school and high school teachers who teach the same lesson more than once a day. As the day progresses, clues emerge that can help frame our lesson so students will be more interested. Two examples follow.

One day I showed the first part of the movie *Casablanca* to my high school students. I assumed that they would love the movie, since it is clearly one of the best ever made (no bias here at all), but my first period students hated it! They complained, "It's boring! It's slow!" So, for second period, I introduced the movie by asking the students what a classic movie was. We discussed and brainstormed the differences between a classic movie and music videos, such as black-and-white versus color, and the power of using few camera angles versus many. Then I asked the students to take a deep breath and focus on s-l-o-w-i-n-g d-o-w-n in order to appreciate the subtleties of a truly classic movie. They ended up not only loving it, but even expressing excitement when I was to show the second part the next day. In contrast, without my successful framing, many first-period students complained that they had to watch more of "that dumb movie."

Several years ago, I taught a technology project in which students made personal and historical web-based timelines. Any time students use technology, I anticipate problems, and my students experienced every single possible snafu. There weren't enough computers, some computers froze, and data was lost. Despite the problems, they created spectacular finished projects, but I was one burned-out teacher, having had to contend with student complaints the whole way.

Fool that I was, the next year I decided to do it again. But this time I introduced the unit differently. I wrote the word "chaos" in the upper left corner of the board, and told the students that it would be one of the

Mrs. Allgood says

> Have students compare and contrast D-Day, the invasion of Normandy, to a surprise birthday party.

themes of the unit. I laid out for them all of the things that could go wrong. Then I listed a second theme under "chaos" — "frustration" — an inevitable reaction to the chaos that results when technology breaks down. Finally, I added the word "fun," and said that if the students didn't fight the chaos and the frustration — if they didn't give up when things went wrong, but instead took them in stride — they would arrive at the third theme of the unit.

Sure enough, during the project, things went wrong. But this time, the students were much more tolerant. Somewhere in the middle of the unit, I asked students for a show of hands. "How many are in chaos?" One-third of the hands went up. "How many are in frustration?" Another third. "How many are having fun?" One more third of the hands went up. "Everyone please look at those who are having fun," I said, "and know that this is your future, if you don't get too sidetracked by the chaos and the frustration." At the end of the unit, the projects were again spectacular, but this time I didn't need stitches.

Remember, the frame sells the content of the lesson, and provides an anchor for all of the student learning that's to follow. Make it meaningful. Make it novel. Make it compelling.

Provide a Unifying Metaphor

Sometimes a simple analogy or metaphor can provide a "hook" that wires information into our students' brains. One example later in this chapter is the use of juggling to show the importance of breaking information into parts. An example from social studies class is comparing the planning of D-Day — the invasion of Normandy — to planning something relevant to their lives, such as a surprise birthday party.

▲ ▲ ▲

The Lesson Itself

Variety

I remember teaching an incredibly powerful lesson to my tough ninth-grade class. They were in a circle, taking turns completing sentences such as, "I am proud that…," or "I really care about…." Light bulbs were going off in their heads. They were hungry to express and hungry to appreciate one another's expressions. But after about fifteen minutes, the hunger started to erode. Kids started making side comments and fidgeting in their seats. My comments, formerly on the order of, "Thank you for sharing and listening," began to be replaced by, "Shh!" and "Please stay focused." As fulfilling as the exercise was, they needed variety.

Unless students are working on self-directed projects, try to plan at least three activities per lesson — at least one of which has the teacher off-stage — and switch activities at least three times every fifty minutes. In addition, employ shifts in focus and energy at least every ten to twelve minutes (see "Changing States" later in this chapter). For example, if we have students doing oral reports, every ten minutes they can write a summary or highlight or talk to a neighbor about their highlights. But regardless, try not to spend the whole period on oral reports. Build in other things to do as well, such as an opening warm-up activity, and a closing brain-teaser.

Legal Talking

The brain loves to talk! Just observe your students during their time at recess or between classes. If they aren't texting, surfing the Net, or playing video games, they're probably talking. This is a healthy thing, and can help kids learn — when they take their existing concepts and vocabulary and apply them verbally to new material in your class. For all but a handful of students, it is unrealistic to expect them to sit and listen attentively and absorb everything we say in a fifty-minute lecture (secondary) or a twenty-minute lesson on the carpet (elementary). Their brains want to talk, so let's build this in to our lessons.

When possible, make talking "legal" in the classroom. If students are supposed to be working silently on an assignment at their desks and instead there are islands of conversation or laughter or clucking sounds, then all students perceive that the teacher is not doing her job to address the noise. So she has to constantly put out sparks before they combust into fires. This makes her a fire fighter. And it means that most of her energy is focused on making the room quiet, rather than on addressing student questions about the assignment.

Providing students with opportunities to work together can remove the necessity for absolute quiet while increasing attention, energy, and retention. One solution is to pair off

> **Wise-Apple Advice**
>
> Unless students are working on self-directed projects, try to plan at least three activities per lesson — at least one of which has the teacher off-stage — and switch activities at least three times every fifty minutes.

Mrs. Allgood says

Pair off students and have them do the worksheet together. Then, talking is "legal," and some noise in the room is expected. We are free to put our energy where it belongs — focused on student learning.

students and have them do the assignment together. Then, talking is "legal," and some noise in the room is expected. The teacher is free to put her energy where it belongs — focused on student learning.

In structuring this kind of activity, either the teacher or the students can designate partners, and final papers can be individual or pair submissions. One of my favorite scenarios is to have each student hand in his own paper, stapled to his partner's. I then grade them separately, and choose either the lower grade or one randomly selected as the grade for both partners. While this doesn't guarantee that the students truly work together in a democratic fashion, it does encourage them to participate and focus with each other.

One more variation is to make the assignment into a game. Call it a treasure hunt. Give the teams ten minutes to "find" as many answers as possible. Collect their papers at the end, and return them the next day with recognition for the winners. This competition will ensure that no pairs of people talk with any other pairs, and students will tend to focus the entire time.

Slow Down Delivery

Our students who are identified with special needs often require more time to process information. Our English-language learners may need additional time and support as well. Let's say you are going over questions with the class, you're on question five, and Sally has only processed questions one through three. She probably won't raise her hand and say, "Excuse me teacher, but could you please slow down? I need more time than most of the rest of the students in the class, and I would like a quality education today, so could you please give me a chance to catch up?" More likely, Sally will do one of two things: she'll remain silent and fall through the cracks, or she'll disengage and act out as an unconscious signal of frustration, to let us know that she isn't getting it. We then may address her behavior as inappropriate and never understand that she simply needs a little more time. In addition, when she acts out, our attention goes toward her behavior rather than toward the lesson, slowing the whole class down. Better to build in processing time for her in order to minimize her misbehavior, and thus give the class more time to focus on content. In other words, we can slow down in order to speed up. Here are a few strategies that can help.

Silent Think-Time

In the middle of our lesson, we can simply pause and give students a minute or two to silently reflect on the material that we've been teaching. We can ask students to go over their notes, take a look at the textbook, or simply sit and reflect on what's just been taught or the question that we just asked. Sally can use this time to catch up with the lesson. Then, when we begin the discussion again, she is less likely to act out, and we are thus more likely to cover more ground in the lesson.

Increase Wait-Time

As a new teacher, I remember being so nervous that I would never allow time for students to process my questions. Silence meant that somehow I was doing something wrong or the students were off task. In reality, students often need more time to think than we think. Try silently timing the gaps between when you ask a question and when it appears no one has an answer. Sometimes we need to wait ten or fifteen seconds before students begin to raise their hands with responses — it can seem like an eternity. Certainly, if a transfer of information hasn't occurred in Mark, then waiting longer will not make a difference. In that case, Mark may need a new way for us to teach him the concept. Several diverse strategies and approaches are shared in this chapter. Often, however, students just need a little more patience on our parts to allow the transfer to take place.

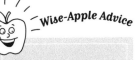

Wise-Apple Advice

We can slow down in order to speed up.

Assume the Best When Students Don't Answer

Silence in response to a question does not necessarily mean that students don't know the answer, nor does it mean that they are being belligerent. They could:

- ▲ be intimidated;
- ▲ be able to answer part, but not all of the question;
- ▲ prefer, for reasons of their own, to remain quiet;

▲ need more time to process the question;

▲ need the question or lesson broken into smaller parts.

One strategy is to give each student three index cards, each drawn with a different traffic signal — red light, yellow light, and green light. To check for understanding in a lesson, simply ask students to hold up one of their cards. Green means they understand the lesson and are ready for more. Yellow means they could use a few examples or illustrations. Red means they are stuck and need help. A quick scan of the room will provide a cue as to what to do next. Alternately, students can also hold a thumb up, sideways, or down to indicate quality of understanding of the lesson.

Increasing Student Participation

When only a few students participate in class discussions and activities, the others are more likely to space out and act out. How do we create total participation?

White Boards

Give each student a small white board. You can create these using laminated pieces of white copy paper or by placing white copy paper into clear plastic protector sleeves. Ask a question and have all students write a possible answer down, and then hold their boards up. You can quickly see right answers, wrong answers, and no answers — and then go from there, either focusing on correct answers or having students dig deeper. **Variation**: have students share what they wrote with a partner first, and then hold up their boards.

Call on Students Randomly

Use a randomization app on your cell phone, or popsicle sticks or playing cards with student names on them. For work in groups of four, give each student in the group a number, 1–4. During class discussions, call on all the 2's or all the 3's, for example, to stand and report out.

Eight Raised Hands

Teachers often call on the first student to raise his hand. This ultimately can mean that the teacher and one or two students have a great lesson, but the rest of the students are left behind. One strategy is to tell the class that no one will be called on until at least eight hands are raised. Each student is only allowed to raise one hand! The go-getters in the room — the ones who walk in the room ready to be called on — will do their best to motivate the other students in the class to raise their hands as well. It will take more time, but more students will use that time to process their answers and raise their hands. Eight is not a magic number, but it tends to work for a class of twenty-five to thirty students.

Say "Thank You," Instead of "Right"

When eight students have their hands raised and the first one is called upon, instead of acknowledging the correctness or incorrectness of his answer, simply say, "Thank you," and call on the next student. After hearing all eight responses, provide the correct answer. This technique accomplishes several things. It increases the number of students who participate in a discussion, it encourages students to speak their ideas aloud because they aren't as intimidated about getting an answer wrong, and it focuses the students more on learning than on getting the answer right or impressing the teacher. Plus, it becomes an instant assessment tool for you, as you can quickly see what a healthy percentage of students in your class are thinking. It doesn't matter if all the students say the same answer. In fact, in many discussions where there is no single "right answer," this technique can create a launching pad for more in-depth dialog. The goal is for the maximum number of students to actively participate.

Class Choral Recital

Every once in a while, ask all the students to say an answer aloud at the same time. It's novel, it gets their attention, and it increases their involvement. It's also safe for those who aren't sure of the answer, especially if they're reciting an answer after we've already given it to them. Many of our reluctant students are right-brain-dominant learners who struggle in the typical left-brain-dominant classroom setting. The choral recital is a right-brain-dominant activity, which can help our reluctant learners to participate and learn.

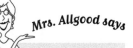

Mrs. Allgood says

One strategy is to tell the class that no one will be called on until at least eight hands are raised.

Breaking Up Direct Instruction

Ideally, our lectures should be short enough that kids can fully pay attention to them — no more than ten to twelve minutes for high school, and even shorter for elementary school. Grace and I teach a workshop called "Fifty Ways to Leave Your Lecture," focusing on numerous things students can do to actively engage their brains in short gaps between these mini-lectures. Three that are easy to implement in your lesson are summary, highlights, and comparison. They can each be done five different ways, with students:

1. speaking in pairs (known as the reciprocal teaching strategy);
2. speaking aloud to the teacher/class;
3. writing;
4. processing through silent think-time;
5. creating images that capture the essence of the task at hand.

Summary

Pause in the middle of your lesson, and ask students to summarize with a partner what you just taught. This can be accomplished through timed and structured monologues back and forth ("Person A: speak for one minute while Person B listens. Then switch."), or in less-structured conversations. Or, ask students to write down in their own words what you just talked about. Ask them to come up with a title about what you just said, because a title is a form of summary. Or, ask them to create a 140-character tweet about the lesson thus far.

By using their words, they efficiently connect their own language and concepts — information they already know — to your language and concepts. This provides a space in the "closets" of their brains to store your information as their own, for easy recognition and retrieval.

Highlights

The following exercises build on the Summary idea and are a little more sophisticated:

▲ Pause in your teaching and ask students to write down two or three key highlights about what you just taught.
▲ Ask them to share highlights aloud with a partner.

- ▲ Ask them to raise their hands and share different highlights aloud to the whole class.
- ▲ Ask them to draw a picture that highlights one or two aspects of the lesson.

Again, this form of active engagement allows students' brains to organize the new information for easy retrieval.

Comparison

Pause in your teaching, and ask your students to compare what you just taught to something they might find in their refrigerator at home or an object or device around the house or in the classroom. For example, ask students to compare photosynthesis to a lawn mower. It's goofy and novel, which helps to keep the information lodged in memory, because "lawn mower" becomes a mnemonic device to aid in retention. In addition, any attempt at comparison means the brain is "working with its hands" to try to find similarities and differences. This effort tends to increase retention dramatically.[5]

PS: In the case of photosynthesis and a lawn mower, one connection is between gasoline and sunlight for fuel. In other examples, if there is no obvious point of comparison, just the attempt to consider one is powerful enough to radically increase learning.

A Closer Look

Building in creative and enjoyable breaks can capture — or recapture — kids' attention, keep them actively involved, and break up the monotony of a lecture or discussion.

Changing States

The brain is wired for survival, and it seeks equilibrium. Any change of state stimulates the brain, causing it to become alert and focused. Building in creative and enjoyable breaks can capture — or recapture — kids' attention, keep them actively involved, and break up the monotony of a lecture or discussion.

Movement

Our brains are very hungry; they "eat" oxygen and glucose for energy. They use about 20 to 25 percent of our energy, yet weigh only about 2.5 percent of our body weight.[6] Indeed, feeding the brain is a full-time job! The one sure-fire way to increase oxygen and glucose to the brain is through movement. In fact, just having your students stand up for a few

A Closer Look

The more stepping stones in the stream, the easier it is to cross it.

seconds and then sit down can cause a significant increase of the flow of oxygen and glucose to their brains. Just imagine what will happen if students move around the room. Elementary students can take a quick break from carpet time to touch heads, shoulders, knees, and toes. Secondary students can take a break from a lecture to stand, find a partner, and share highlights from the lecture. More ideas along these lines appear below.

Vary Tone and Volume

It helps to speak with, not at, students. Sometimes when teachers speak in a monotone, they edit out all indicators of enthusiasm for the subject. Students pick up on this, get bored, feel unappreciated, and begin to act out. In addition, since our brains are wired for survival[7], we continuously scan the environment. Any subtle changes in our tone and volume will tend to keep our students' brains attentive and alert.

Breathing

Ask the students to take a deep breath and then exhale together. They will enjoy watching the teacher model this almost as much as they'll enjoy doing it. For more on the power of breathing for students, see the "Mindfulness" section in Chapter 7, "Positive Connections." For more on the power of breathing for teachers, see the "Mindfulness" section in Chapter 5, "Got Stress?"

Stretching

Students can stretch in their seats with their arms over their heads, or standing up. Try breaking the lesson into "innings," and schedule in a seventh-inning stretch.

Cross-Laterals

Have your students march in place and touch right hand to left knee and then left hand to right knee, or give themselves a pat on the back on the opposite side. This gets blood to the brain and activates both the right and left hemispheres. A minute of this is like pressing "reset" in students' brains.

Action Thermometer

Place four phrases around the room: "Strongly Agree," "Agree," "Disagree," "Strongly Disagree." Ask questions and have students move to the phrase that represents their answers. Debate the issues; as students change their opinions, they can move about the room.

Variations: Have students go to the right or left side of the room, depending on their answers to a variety of questions. Examples: "If you are left-handed, have a pet at home, like Rock-and-Roll, prefer beaches to mountains." Or, make it content related: "If you think the answer is seventeen…if you think the character in the novel should say yes…if you think the main cause was economic…." Assign each student an element of the periodic table, and have him move to various places in the room depending on the number of electrons in the element, or whether it is solid, liquid, or gas. Give younger children objects to hold, and have them sort by shape or texture or color. In history lessons, students can "become" historical figures, and sort around the room according to the field — politics, art, sports, music — in which they became famous.

Ball Toss or Frisbee Throw

After a student catches the (soft) Frisbee, he says one thing he's learned from the lesson. Then he tosses the Frisbee to another student. This can be done with students in a circle, or while they are at their desks in their normal seating arrangement. You can also use the Frisbee or ball as a motivator to call on students in a class discussion. Many times I've seen two or three raised hands become a sea of hands when I bring out my foam Frisbee. Another strategy is for teachers to ask each student to crumple his answer into a ball, and throw it to the teacher at the front of the room.

▲　▲　▲

Principles and Tips for Successful Lessons

Smaller Steps Equal Faster Learning

Mrs. Allgood is quite a juggler. But she knows that if she hands each student three balls, and then performs a slick juggling demonstration, only a few students will catch on. However, it's a different story if she starts with one ball and then builds up from there with regularly scheduled

A Closer Look

If the first step on the escalator is too high, then they'll never get on it.

stops to check for mastery and to offer hints. That way, just about all of her students can learn the basics of juggling in a relatively short period of time. Plus, their motivation will remain high, because they can mark and appreciate their progress as they learn.

Whether it's juggling — or skiing (straight to the double-diamond, or should we start on the bunny slope?), playing an instrument, or learning algebra, smaller steps make the process easier. The more stepping stones in the stream, the easier it is to cross it.

Over the years Mrs. Allgood has learned to appreciate the important art of breaking learning into clear and doable steps. This is true not only with procedures and behavior, but also with content. Mrs. Allgood seems to have handouts, engaging activities, and manipulatives for every step of her lessons, allowing students to progress at whatever pace fits their abilities. Because she molds this strategy over her basic assumption that students want to learn, what seems like complex material is learned more easily in her classroom. This can be a fun, intellectual challenge for her. In fact, if Mrs. Meanswell, who is just learning how to do this, tried to break things into too many steps, she'd be hard pressed to do it.

Student Success

As much as possible, build in success for students, even if the successes seem miniscule at first. Contrary to what some suggest, I believe that we learn more from our successes than from our failures. When students experience success early and often, it helps to build their confidence, which in turn helps them to maintain their focus. It also helps their brains systematically retain new information. A series of positive, low-stress exposures to new knowledge is more likely to increase new learning than a series of negative, higher-stress experiences. When we are under extreme stress, our fight-or-flight instinct kicks in. Our bodies and brains focus instinctually on survival, minimizing our focus on higher order thinking.[8]

It is especially vital to make the initial steps in new learning small enough that students can master them. If the first step on the escalator is too high, then they'll never get on it. As students gain confidence, we can make the steps more challenging. Ideally the steps should be small enough

A Closer Look

Embracing frustration can often act like the irritation in the oyster than yields the pearl.

that students are able to take them, and large enough that students feel a sense of accomplishment as they progress.

Frustration

Sometimes our students get frustrated. This is often a powerful and necessary ingredient for real learning — a process that often seems nonlinear. We grow in leaps, sputters, and spurts in a process that inevitably generates feelings of frustration. When our students push away the frustration, they don't stick around long enough to receive the wisdom that follows. Conversely, embracing frustration can often act like the irritation in the oyster than yields the pearl.

As teachers, we need to foster a positive attitude in our students toward feeling frustration in our classrooms. In his book *Emotional Intelligence*, Daniel Goleman points to various factors as indicators of emotional intelligence.[9] One of them is the ability to delay gratification — which goes hand-in-hand with the ability to experience frustration without acting it out.

This concept can be true for our own experiences. Teaching can be incredibly frustrating at times. If we welcome frustration as an essential part of learning, then we will be less likely to take our stresses home with us, and more likely to grow and blossom as teachers. Plus, we'll model this receptivity to our students, thus encouraging their learning and growth.

> I love it when kids come back after an absence and say, "Did you do anything while I was gone?"

Including All Students

Human beings cannot be separated from their cultures. When we design lessons, we need to include and encourage the celebration of the various cultures of our students. This is discussed more fully in the "Culturally Responsive Instruction" section in Chapter 7, "Positive Connections."

Some Kids Will be Absent

We must plan for this! Otherwise we'll have a sea of questions and complaints at the start of the day or class: "What did I miss?" "Did we do anything important yesterday?" "What should I do today?" "I don't have the homework because I wasn't here yesterday." "Did you do anything while I was gone?"

Ask administrators and other teachers how they address the issue of absent students. Some schools have standard procedures for parents to pick up homework for their children. The following are additional suggestions:

- ▲ Find a place in the room for extra handouts.
- ▲ Use board space or butcher paper to display lessons/homework for each week.
- ▲ Have a para-educator (instructional aide) prepare packets for absent students.
- ▲ Use a student logbook (described below).
- ▲ Use a student buddy system, where students are responsible for contacting each other at home.
- ▲ Coordinate with the office for communicating assignments to parents.
- ▲ Post key ideas, learning resources, homework assignments, or a video of your teaching the lesson online.

Some secondary teachers post the day's lesson online each day before teaching the lesson. Students can access this from home or during independent work time.

Student Logbook

Students can keep track of daily activities and assignments, and then post them in the class logbook and on the classroom website. I employed this with a lot of success, and it was effortless for me. Each day a different student was assigned to take careful notes on what we did in class, including details of the homework assignment. The next day when an absent student returned, he would look in the logbook or online to catch up. If, after looking in the logbook, he had to ask me what he missed because the lesson description was unclear, then the student who wrote the log would not receive credit for doing it.

One variation I developed turned out to be even simpler. I'd allow certain students do the log for extra credit. This helped ensure that good note-takers were the ones who did the work.

There are two side benefits of the logbook. First, at the end of the year I had documentation of everything that had transpired, which I used as an auxiliary lesson-plan book for the next year. Second, early in the term, the book's cover became the subject of a class art contest (this can be done with an online logbook as well). Since all four sides of the notebook cover were designed, four students could win. Thus, the logbook was beautiful, and students took pride in it.

Accepting Late Work

How many days late should we accept student work? Much of the decision depends on the culture of the school. One teacher I know didn't accept work that was more than one week late. Her bulletin board was divided into five sections labeled Monday through Friday, and each day's homework list was posted there. One week after its original due date, the teacher removed each list. For example, on Wednesday the eleventh, she removed the homework assignment that had been due on Wednesday the fourth, and replaced it with the current homework assignment.

Like most teachers, she provided a standard deduction in points for late work. How much to deduct is a personal decision, but please remember that kids often have legitimate reasons for being late. Further, if students are chronically late but produce quality work, a rigid late policy may discourage them from ongoing effort and participation.

> If, after looking in the logbook, he had to ask me what he missed because the lesson description was unclear, then the student who wrote the log would not receive credit for doing it.

Clean Slates

Some students reach a point in the school year or semester where they have so many incomplete assignments that they won't be able to pass the class without having a chance to make up work that is quite late. With an inflexible late policy, those students know that they will fail, no matter how hard they work going forward. As an alternative, consider creating periodic "clean slates," where students can make up work that is long overdue. A second chance can mean the difference between success and giving up from a lack of hope. We need to design clear systems, but allow room for forgiveness and a fresh start.

In addition, in situations where the learning is cumulative and students have done poorly in the first quarter, try giving the second quarter's report card more weight than the first quarter's. Or, be inclusive when creating quizzes. For example, if your mission is to determine if students are keeping up with the assigned reading in a novel, and you have one student who is always a day or two behind, then you know he will fail every quiz if it covers only "today's assignment." But if the quiz includes questions from chapters one through seven — not just chapter seven — then the student will be more likely to feel successful, and to receive a passing grade.

Homework

We've discussed creating a space on the board or wall where homework assignments are always posted. Try going one step further: clarify that students are responsible for posted homework, even *if it isn't discussed in class*. This will create a safety net in case you get sidetracked.

Ideally, spend time before the class ends, focusing on the specifics of the homework and how it relates to what was just studied. Check to see that all students have the assignment written down and are clear about what they need to do that night to be successful. Occasionally, this can include private discussions about what time they will do their homework, and in what rooms or at which desk in their home. Keep in mind that many students don't have support at home. By addressing these homework-related details, we can help them find appropriate environments, or arrange for them to do homework at school before they leave for the day.

Delay Classwork that's Based on Homework

It helps to delay classwork one or two days when it is based on homework, so that late homework assignments can be addressed in class.

As a new teacher, I often had students respond to and edit each other's writing in groups. One day, twelve of my twenty-seven students came to school unprepared. They hadn't written their rough drafts, and thus couldn't really do the activity I had planned. So I gave them a chance to write quietly while the other fifteen students worked in small response groups. This wasn't ideal, because:

▲ Students who didn't do their homework were rewarded with class time in which to do it.
▲ These students were deprived of valuable group response time.
▲ My attention during the class was divided by having to keep the writers quiet when I really ought to have been fully focused on the response groups.
▲ The overall quality of student work suffered.

I then realized I should collect rough drafts on Tuesday, and hand them back on Thursday for the student response groups. This gave late students an extra two days to complete the homework assignment — outside of class. While I held them accountable for being late, they still had a buffer zone before the response groups took over. For Tuesday and Wednesday, I planned other, related activities.

Grading vs. Feedback

Mrs. Meanswell focuses on grading her students' work. Mrs. Allgood focuses on giving her students *feedback*. Grades are for parents and colleges. Feedback is for student learning. Once teachers understand that assessment is an aspect of teaching, they open up to a wide variety of ways to provide feedback to students in addition to grades — including oral critiques, comments by other students, publishing student work, portfolio review, providing rubrics, and reviewing assignments in class.

When Students Finish Early

Always anticipate what to do when some students are finished early with an in-class assignment. Put a permanent activity list on the wall, or write in advance on the board a specific, appropriate task. Ideally, these extra activities should be things early finishers can do in silence, without having to get out of their chairs; otherwise, prepare ahead of time for any potential disruption. For example, if the main activity is silently taking a test, followed by reading an awkward, crackly newspaper, all students should *first* get newspapers, find the article to read, fold the paper, and place it on the floor next to their desk. *Then* they can take the test.

Create a "Finished Early" Poster, and place it in the front of the room. List three or four things students can do if they are finished early. Some of these items should be generic, and doable any day of the school year, and some should be specific to the day's lesson. You can take an arrow and point it to the item that students should do first that day. This can work for students of any age. For young children, make the poster non-verbal. Students can have pre-made packets, in their folders

I then realized I should collect rough drafts on Tuesday, and hand them back on Thursday for the student response groups.

or desks, that they take out and work in when they are finished early. Here are several samples.

The "Finished Early" poster can be written on the board, projected onto a screen, or posted in the front or on the side of the classroom. It's particularly helpful in case you have a surprise visitor or need to have an impromptu one-on-one talk with a student. Suggested activities include starting on their homework, drawing a picture, making up a rhyming poem, doing a puzzle, solving riddles, answering extra credit questions, or reading in their novel, textbook, or the newspaper. Once kids are engaged and on task, you can go about your business.

Supplemental Lesson Ideas

Find lesson ideas that are specific enough to your content that they are relevant and valuable, and generic enough to your content that you can use them at a moment's notice throughout the year. Ideally, fill an emergency file with relevant activities instantaneously available for that last five minutes, ten minutes, twenty minutes, or the whole lesson. When I first student-taught, this file was probably the most valuable thing I had. Ideally, the activities will tie in seamlessly with what you're teaching that day. If not, as long as they are connected and relevant to the broader subject area focus, you're golden.

Earlier in this chapter, in the paragraph on "variety," I referred to a risky creative lesson plan where each of my ninth-grade students took a turn finishing sentences like,

A Closer Look

Mrs. Meanswell focuses on grading her students' work. Mrs. Allgood focuses on giving her students feedback.

"I am proud that…," or "I really care about…." Although engaged for the first fifteen minutes of this activity, noise slowly built up, followed by my voice as I tried to restore focus. Mercifully, the bell finally rang after the activity had continued about ten minutes longer than it should have.

My student-teaching supervisor was observing that day. After class she remarked that I should have ended the activity after fifteen minutes and moved on to something else. I told her I wholeheartedly agreed, that I had been aware of it at the time, but *I couldn't think of anything else the students could do.* Bottled up by my inexperience and my nervousness at creating a safe environment for my students to communicate personally to each other, I just painfully slogged through those last tough minutes. Today I can think of twenty or thirty things I could have used. For example, I could have asked my students to move their desks back, and then take out a piece of paper and write reflectively about the activity for five minutes. Then they could have read their writing aloud to a partner or two. This could have been followed by a brief class discussion of what they wrote.

How do we generate these lesson ideas and activities?

- ▲ Ask colleagues at your school.
- ▲ Go online. There are hundreds of web sites offering lesson ideas for fees or for free.
- ▲ Try slightly varying what you've already done.
- ▲ Ask students to summarize what they've learned, or pick out key highlights.
- ▲ Ask them to generate questions about the learning that they don't know the answers to.
- ▲ Ask them to generate "game-show" questions about the learning that they do know the answers to.

The key is to keep students engaged throughout the lesson in ways that are motivating and relevant, using whatever tools you can muster.

Teacher Down-Time

Ideally, teachers should reserve five minutes at the start of each lesson, and additional time in the middle, when they are "off stage" — not delivering content or circulating and talking with students. While the class is writing, watching a video, working in small groups, or using technology, teachers can focus on individual issues or resolve problems. For example, if Mark disrupts a lesson because he wants to know why he can't turn in his homework late, simply redirect him to ask the same question during the group work that is coming up in four minutes. Talking to him privately during down-time avoids the dreaded "Popcorn Effect" discussed in Chapter 9, "Consistency." This is also addressed in the section "Don't Over-Explain" in Chapter 6, "Holding Our Ground."

For teachers of younger children, off-stage time can often seem like a myth. Nonetheless, there are times during the day that are better than others for addressing student issues. Identify these times in advance, cultivate them as much as possible in lesson plans, and take advantage of them every day.

If a lesson has the teacher "up front" all the time, students are likely to be exhausted at the end of the day. Students' brains love to talk, move, and problem-solve; when they are constantly expected to sit and listen to the teacher, they miss out on many active learning opportunities. Even more significantly, perhaps, is the benefit of teacher down-time for teachers. Just knowing a respite is coming — an oasis in the desert of direct instruction — will provide invaluable peace of mind.

Mindfulness

Mindfulness is an awareness practice that is gaining ground with schools, particularly with at-risk youth and children with special needs. It can be adapted for students of any age and for any subject matter. According to Daniel Rechtschaffen, author of *The Way of Mindful Education*, early research findings suggest that teaching youth how to exercise mindfulness:

- ▲ raises attention and test scores;
- ▲ reduces impulsivity;
- ▲ decreases anxiety and depression; and
- ▲ develops happiness and empathy.[10]

Rechtschaffen says:

> We tell our children to pay attention...but we rarely teach them how. We tell them to be nice to each other, but how often

do we offer them the skills to develop empathy and kindness? We tell our kids not to hit [others], but we don't give them tools to work with their impulse-control. Attention, empathy, emotional-regulation; these are all teachable traits….Mindfulness practices help foster [these and other] invaluable traits for becoming a healthy and successful human being.[11]

How it works is remarkably simple. For example, students (and teachers) start by slowing down internally and paying relaxed attention to their bodies through mindful walking (feeling their feet slowly connecting with the ground with each step), eating (paying attention to chewing and swallowing), or breathing (sitting and noticing their rib cages rising and falling with each breath), among other actions. This attention helps students to feel safe and ready to focus. Once this habit is established, they pay attention to their breath, the sound of a bell, or other sensory phenomena to cultivate their attention. As they feel more relaxed physically and mentally, they then can begin to cultivate emotional intelligence through bringing awareness to their feelings. Mindfulness includes dozens of practices. None of them takes much time, and any can help focus and connect students to one another and to the teacher.

Rechtschaffen suggests that teachers also participate in the practices, not only to reap the benefits personally, but also to model for their students the power of simple attention.[12] (See page 55 in Chapter 5, "Got Stress?", for a sample mindfulness practice for teachers.)

Mindfulness is a practice, but it's also an underlying approach to life that can benefit students in a variety of ways. It's included in this chapter about lesson design because related lessons can help students to learn more and act out less. These concepts could easily be included in Chapter 7, "Positive Connections," or Chapter 13, "When Consequences Don't Work," because they can help connect students to teachers, increase student academic achievement, and reduce student misbehavior.

When the Lesson Design Contributes to Misbehavior

Students might act out because the points on the road map of the lesson are either blurry or aren't ordered to maximize student learning and engagement. Try rearranging elements or reallocating the amount of time for each one.

▲ If students can't focus while working on their own, then they may need the support of a partner, the group, their teacher, or additional modeling and samples.

▲ If you attempt to deliver new learning in the form of worksheets, struggling learners may have a hard time processing the material independently. If they have not first had opportunity to learn the relevant skills or concepts, then they may begin to act out.

▲ If too much time is spent on direct instruction without giving students a chance to actively engage with the new material, then they may get frustrated and/or bored and begin to act out. Sometimes they need minimum direct instruction and maximum group and independent learning and practice — coupled with frequent check-ins and multiple opportunities for movement.

▲ If the lesson doesn't provide closure, then students will tend to remember less, and may come back the next day feeling inadequate or antsy.

Structuring your lessons in an intentionally engaging, organized way, with elements of direct instruction, group and independent work, and formal and informal assessment, will tend to decrease misbehavior and increase student focus and achievement.

Closure

The last three minutes can be the most significant of any lesson, as they can markedly increase student retention. Rather than have kids mill about the room as they put stuff in backpacks or cubbies, actively engage them with closure activities.

A Closer Look

By slowing down, we speed up. Taking time to make connections will increase retention and actually allow us to go faster in the long run.

Mrs. Meanswell's closure often takes the form of looking at her watch and saying, "There's the bell. We'll continue this tomorrow. And don't forget your homework...." Conversely, Mrs. Allgood consistently focuses on closure. She doesn't frame her units as one big lesson that is randomly broken up by bells or other subject area studies. She deliberately designs beginnings and endings to each lesson that allow her students a chance to reflect on their learning and increase the likelihood that information will move from short-term to long-term memory. Much of what has been shared in this chapter will work for active engagement during closure:

▲ Focus on the big picture — where have we been and where are we going next?
▲ Summarize the day's lesson.
▲ Pick key highlights from the day's lesson and connect them to student's present or future real-world experiences.
▲ Compare what you learned today to an aspect of a baseball game, or a crow bar, or a blender.
▲ Come up with a unifying metaphor that captures the essence of the lesson.

Wise-Apple Advice

The Closure on Closure

Whenever possible, have the students actively involved during closure. They can speak aloud to the class, a partner, or a small group. Closure also can involve pictures and role-playing, predictions about what's coming next, a look at the big picture, or a celebration of the day's learning. Even though closure takes away from time spent in teaching new material, by slowing down, we speed up. Taking time to make connections will increase retention and actually allow us to go faster in the long run.

INTERVENTION — What We Do In Response

> **Mrs. Meanswell:** I hope I didn't see you looking at Don's paper.
>
> **Mark:** I hope you didn't either.

13

RULES AND CONSEQUENCES

> *"We ask for strength and the Great Spirit gives us difficulties, which makes us strong."*
>
> — NATIVE AMERICAN PRAYER

ALL TEACHERS, either overtly or subtly, employ rules and consequences. This chapter is about how Mrs. Allgood uses them — both what she does and why she does it. The subject is divided into three main sections: principles, rules, and consequences. Principles are the underlying "big picture" goals for the class. Rules and consequences are specific classroom behavior policies that help support the principles.

Before getting into the details, let's take a look at the big picture, which includes an ongoing philosophical debate in education about the need for and the use of consequences. This issue is discussed at the end of this chapter, in the section called "Intrinsic vs. Extrinsic Motivation."

My stance is twofold. First, in their essence, consequences in life are simply pointers, giving us feedback to help guide our choices. They are the fruits of the choices we make. In that sense, all consequences are actually positive in that they spur us into self-awareness and change. In the classroom, however, they are often perceived as positive or negative, and this affects how and when we use them with our students.

Second, prevention should be the dominant focus of teachers. Ideally, assuming the best about students, thorough preparation, authentic caring, teaching procedures, being consistent, creating positive connections with students, and developing our inner authority are a recipe which makes a true difference in the classroom and in our students' lives.

Yet sometimes kids act out anyway.

All of us, especially when we first start out, need stuff we can use right away. And consequences are often the "stuff" that does the trick. Consequences are the bottom line, the cork in the bottom of the bucket that keeps the water from flowing out. Almost everything up to now in this book is about *prevention* — stopping things before they occur. Consequences are about *intervention* — stopping things from occurring again. And yet in that sense, even consequences are prevention as well, as they are used to curtail future misbehavior. This awareness helps soften our orientation toward our students, even if their behavior rubs us the wrong way.

This chapter has a lot of strategies and approaches in it. I don't try to sell any particular one. Try on some of the strategies and see if they fit. However, even as you use rules and consequences, please don't rely too heavily on them as a mechanical substitute for your genuine and personal enthusiasm for your students and their learning.

Principles

Principles are akin to guidelines. They are more general and often more value-laden than rules. They are not specific or behavioral in nature. However, they are very effective as opening "slogans" that are attached to rules, and they can add a sense of underlying purpose and spirit to a list of rules and consequences. Many teachers include one or two principles as mission statements under which their rules appear. A few common principles are listed below.

- ▲ Treat one another fairly.
- ▲ Cultivate respect and responsibility.
- ▲ This is a safe place to learn.
- ▲ Our classroom is a community.
- ▲ Students have the right to learn and the teacher has the right to teach.
- ▲ Be safe, kind, and productive.

Under any of these umbrella statements are five or six specific rules that close the door on potential misinterpretations from students.

Rules

Rules define what we can and can't live with in our classroom. They are what we would see in the classroom if our principles were being supported.

Wording the Rules

Rules should be specific, clearly stated, and worded behaviorally rather than morally. If we leave the door open for misinterpretation, then some students will leap across the threshold. The more specific, behavioral, and clear our rules are, the "tinier" students will have to be to fit through that doorway. For example, "Listen attentively and silently while other students contribute to a class discussion" is a solid behavioral rule. Mrs. Meanswell often gets tripped up because her rules sound more like principles. She assumes that her rule "respect one another" isn't open to misinterpretation, but her students often have very different ideas than she about what respect looks like.

Limit the Number of Rules to Five or Six at the Most

We can't cover everything with only six rules, but we can address the big stuff. More than six rules will ultimately confuse and/or intimidate our students, at the same time diluting the importance of the key rules that really matter to us.

The following are examples of classroom rules. Some are more appropriate for younger students, and others for older students. Some are very specific, covering only a very particular behavior, like gum chewing, while others are more foundational.

> **A Closer Look**
>
> Consequences are the bottom line, the cork in the bottom of the bucket that keeps the water from flowing out.

> **A Closer Look**
>
> Principles can add a sense of underlying purpose and spirit to a list of rules and consequences.

- ▲ Follow directions quickly and quietly.
- ▲ Don't interrupt others' right to learn or my right to teach.
- ▲ Be at your station or seat when the bell rings.
- ▲ Follow all the school rules.
- ▲ Keep hands, feet, and other objects to yourself.
- ▲ Raise your hand and wait for permission to speak.
- ▲ No put-downs.
- ▲ Bring all books and materials to class everyday.
- ▲ No gum chewing in class.

▲ No cell phones out during class.

▲ Listen quietly when someone else is talking.

▲ The teacher, not the bell, dismisses the class.

▲ Use appropriate language.

▲ Use appropriate volume in class, as indicated by the teacher.

▲ Touch others' belongings only with their permission.

▲ Place all trash in the basket.

▲ There is no "arguing with the ref" during class. If you disagree with my decision, signal me that you want to discuss my decision with me after class. (This is discussed in more detail in Chapter 9, "Consistency.")

Which Rules to Choose?

There is no hard and fast rule about what rules should rule in the classroom — or what rules we should rule out. It helps to avoid some typical miscues, as exemplified by Mrs. Meanswell's gaffes. She has rules that:

▲ She isn't organized enough to enforce — "Late work only accepted for three days, and for gradually reduced points."

▲ She doesn't feel strongly about, and thus doesn't enforce consistently — "No bathroom use during instructional time."

▲ Are too specific and don't cover enough territory — "Sharpen pencils quietly."

▲ She has copied from Mrs. Allgood across the hall, but isn't comfortable with — "No gum chewing."

▲ Aren't clear enough — "Respect one another."

In addition to avoiding the above mistakes, it's most important that our rules cover the main classroom behaviors and coordinate with school and district policies.

Consequences — Five Key Assumptions

Many teachers look to classroom management workshops and books for an exotic new consequence — one that will close the deal on misbehavior. Maybe, they think, it could be an incentive so powerful that Mark is automatically and permanently focused; maybe someone will develop a Velcro® suit to keep him in his seat! As far as I can tell, there aren't any mysterious, foolproof consequences out there. And yet our assumptions about consequences, the ones we choose, and the ways that we use and deliver them, make a big difference.

Below are five key assumptions about consequences, followed by a rather extreme example that illustrates all five.

1. There are no punishments, just consequences.
2. Consequences are used as a pause to get our students' attention.
3. Consequences should be organized in a tiered hierarchy, starting with the mildest first.[1]
4. We have no control over our students.
5. Consequences teach students that they have the power of choice.

Dan and the Flying Hammer

One day I was teaching woodshop as usual. I had already learned that classroom management in a woodshop class is absolutely critical, especially with my alternative high school kids. I had to know that the students could be trusted to take care of themselves and one another during those times when I was absorbed in cutting wood and, for a moment, necessarily oblivious to their actions. Since natural consequences to "spacing out" in woodshop class can be permanent and disabling, such as the loss of a finger, my insistence on keeping kids focused in this class was even greater than in any other classes I taught.

> **Mrs. Allgood says**
>
> Rules should be specific, clearly stated, and worded behaviorally rather than morally.

On this day, I was using the table saw, which requires a high degree of concentration. Out of the corner of my eye I vaguely saw something coming toward me in the air — in surrealistic slow motion. A large "implement of destruction," a rotating hammer, slowly crossed my line of vision and careened onto the floor near my feet. I finished cutting my piece of wood, turned off the saw, looked up in the direction from which the large implement of destruction had come, and immediately saw students scattering in the wind. Sara was suddenly fascinated with the wood planer. Eli had his nose in a book for the first time in his high school career. Dan, however, was caught like a deer in the headlights. It was clear from the position of his body and the guilty look on his face that I had found my source.

> **A Closer Look**
>
> There is no hard and fast rule about what rules should rule in the classroom — or what rules we should rule out.

"Dan," I said in my firm-yet-soft teacher voice, "please come over here and let's talk a minute." All the machinery in

A large "implement of destruction," a rotating hammer, slowly crossed my line of vision and careened onto the floor near my feet.

the shop had stopped. All eyes were on Dan, waiting to see how this drama would play itself out.

He erupted immediately, coming toward me in a hail of defense: "I didn't! It wasn't me! You can't prove it! It wasn't a large hammer! It didn't go very far! No one was hurt! No!"

I remained as calm as I could, and simply said his name several times to calm him down. That didn't work. Whatever was going on with Dan went beyond this simple classroom experience. I asked Dan to take a seat at the back table, so that he could calm down. But he didn't stop. He seemed intent on arguing and escalating the situation. So I told him again that I'd be happy to talk to him in a few minutes, once he had a chance to calm down, by taking a seat at the back table. He still didn't stop. I tried walking away from him, to unplug him from whatever was driving him. But he followed me, arguing the whole way.

My redirecting strategies clearly weren't working. I became aware of an impulse in me to rise up to meet and magnify his anger and upset with my own. But I chose to stay calm, and go under the wave. I decided to give redirection one more try. Out of earshot of others, so he wouldn't feel cornered, I quietly said to Dan, "Neither of us wants to see this escalate any further. Please take a seat and we can talk about it after class." He began to argue again, and I added, "If you don't take a seat, I'm going to have to send you to the office."

I started to walk away, but Dan didn't sit. Instead he followed me, filling the shop with a loud barrage of excuses and defenses. Finally, I said: "Dan, you need to go to the office now. If you don't, then the principal may very well choose to suspend you for your behavior." He stopped in his tracks. It was as if his plane had suddenly landed, or his alarm clock had suddenly gone off.

"But...," he began to implore.

"Please, Dan," I quietly responded, "don't make it any bigger than it has to be. Please go to the office, have a seat and wait for me there until after class. If you want to take the time to write a letter to me explaining what's going on with you, that would be great." Dan finally decided to go. As soon as he did, I looked up and suddenly the machinery was back on, Eli had abandoned his book, and class was back to its usual state of controlled chaos.

After I informed the principal of what happened, Dan was directed to a study hall, instead of woodshop class, for a couple of days. Two days later his father came in and met with the principal, Dan, and me to work things out. Dan seemed his normal, enthusiastic self, rather than his abnormal, ranting self, and we had a relaxed conversation. Dan explained that the hammer had flown out of his hand when he was telling a story and waving it about, and that projecting it toward me was by no means an intentional act (even though he knew that waving a hammer was a very dangerous thing to do). He asked me why I sent him to the office, and why he had missed class for two days. I replied, "I didn't discipline you because of the hammer. It was because of your behavior afterward. I sent you to the office because it was the gentlest way I could find to diffuse the situation and get your attention. Do I have your attention now? Good. Let's talk about the rules of the woodshop...."

> My student had just thanked me for disciplining him!

For five minutes, we had a cordial conversation. Dan convinced me that he could return safely to woodshop class, a class in which he actually excelled. We reviewed the rules, and that was that. As Dan was leaving the principal's office, he said to me, "Thank you, Mr. Smith," and walked out.

Something in that simple sentence set a light bulb off in my head. My student had just thanked me for disciplining him! *He wanted to learn behavior*, he knew he needed to learn it, and he thanked me for it. The consequence was there to provide him with the guidance that he was hungering for. Later on, Dan and I had a private conversation, in which he shared with me some of the personal challenges that he was facing in his life. This valuable conversation, which taught me about what was at the root of Dan's aberrant behavior, would never have taken place if I had over-reacted to his misbehavior.

▲ ▲ ▲

The five key assumptions about consequences are all illustrated in the above story. First, *there are no punishments, just consequences.* I hadn't punished Dan; I had merely connected him with a simple consequence that did him the service of slowing him down. Even the extreme case of referral to the office is still a tool to teach students what they are hungry to learn.

Second, I realized that *consequences are used as a pause to get our students' attention.* It just so happened that in this case, a referral was what it took.

Third, I used a *hierarchy of consequences, starting with the mildest first.*[2] I slowly and calmly increased the consequences for Dan, stopping with the first one that got him to pause in his tracks.

Fourth, during the confrontation with Dan, unless I used handcuffs, rope, or Velcro®, *I had no control over him.* Calming down and ultimately following the rules were up to him. Yes, I had the power of suggestion. Yes, I could influence his decision with my voice, my tone, the redirection strategies I employed, and/or the consequences I doled out, but ultimately the decision was his. The deeper our respect for this, the easier it is for us to remain calm and on our students' side in moments when we wish we had control over them.

A Closer Look

> All choices bear fruit, whether sweet or bitter. It is our job to allow students to gently learn and internalize the sometimes wonderful and sometimes biting nature of responsibility.

Fifth, at the end of the meeting in the principal's office, it was affirmed that *Dan had the power of choice.* He became aware that he made choices that day in the woodshop class — to throw the hammer, to argue with me, eventually to leave the class and calm down. Later, he made a choice to abide by the class's rules in the future. He also became aware of the emotional charge in his life that had influenced his choice to wave the hammer in the first place.

Let's look at this last assumption with a sharper lens. With choice comes responsibility. All choices bear fruit, whether sweet or bitter. It is our job to allow students to gently learn and internalize the sometimes wonderful and sometimes biting nature of responsibility. When we provide consequences for students, we are simply connecting them with the fruits of their choices, and giving them an opportunity to assess those choices. For example, if Mark is talking to his neighbor while Mrs. Allgood is trying to explain something to the class, then she can simply walk over to Mark's desk and stand next to him. In most cases, her proximity — the consequence — reminds him that he is talking out of turn. He reassesses his choices, asking himself:

Am I talking out of turn? Yes.
Do I want Mrs. Allgood to go away? Yes.
Should I stop talking and pay attention?
Yes, I think I will.

Mrs. Allgood's proximity is a consequence that gets Mark to pause and reassess the choice he is making.

To take the scenario one step further, suppose Mark continues to talk when Mrs. Allgood moves away from his desk. She realizes that the consequence of proximity is too mild, so she chooses a different one. She says Mark's name. If that doesn't get him to pause and make a new choice, then she quietly informs him that if he continues to talk, he will have his seat changed. If that doesn't work, then she connects him with the next consequence in her hierarchy.[3] This isn't done because Mark is bad or wrong, but because Mrs. Allgood is honoring her right to teach and her students' right to learn. As Mark quiets down, he learns about choices and personal responsibility. And the class has a greater chance to learn content, because disruptions are kept at a minimum.

> **A Closer Look**
>
> When we assume the best about our students, we see consequences as a way to accelerate their growth.

School is an essential laboratory where students can exercise the muscle of choice at a young age in a relatively safe environment. When compared with "real life," consequences in school — such as changing seats or detentions — may seem artificial. Still, they can provide gentle practice for students who need to realize the value and impact of their own choices. Later, when they get "on the street," they will be less likely to hurt themselves, others, or property, and more likely to make choices that nurture themselves and others.

When we assume the best about our students, we see consequences as a way to accelerate their growth. Rather than coming across as against our students, we increase the likelihood of being seen as on their side. This orientation helps us be firm and soft simultaneously, allowing us to move quickly along the continuum of inner-authority.

The Nuts and Bolts of Consequences

Now that we've looked at underlying assumptions about consequences, let's get to the nitty-gritty of what to do and how to do it. This section is broken into four main parts: a) which consequences to choose; b) implementing consequences; c) documenting consequences; and d) extrinsic versus intrinsic rewards.

A) Which Consequences to Choose

Consequences should be set up in a tiered hierarchy,[4] ranging from a simple reminder to more serious consequences, all of which should:

- ▲ be natural and/or logical;
- ▲ provide some wiggle room for the teacher;
- ▲ stay within the teacher's comfort zone; and
- ▲ be specific and concrete.

Natural/Logical Consequences

Consequences are natural or logical if they are appropriately attached to student behaviors. One of the best natural consequences I have ever heard was when a fourteen-year old girl kept slamming the door to her room at home. Her father warned her to stop, and when she didn't, he removed the door from its hinges for a week! That week without privacy was a sufficient reminder to his daughter not to slam her door again! The following are examples of natural classroom consequences:

- ▲ When a student writes on his desk, he is asked to clean it — and perhaps other desks — after school.
- ▲ When a student is too chatty with his neighbor, he is asked to change his seat.
- ▲ When students save time in class by being extra-focused, they earn time at the end of class to focus on topics of their choice.

Natural/logical consequences allow students to easily make connections between their choices and the consequences that follow. Students can then more readily internalize appropriate behavior, and more easily buy into their teacher's management system.

Fair vs. Equal

Many teachers are concerned about appearing fair to their students. My approach is to let students know that, as the teacher, my job is to do what will most help each student learn. Period. Sometimes that differs from student to student and situation to situation. As teachers, it's our responsibility, and therefore, it's our call. If you are pitching in a baseball game, you know that some batters do better with a curve ball, and some do better with a fastball. In his article "Fair isn't Equal," educator Rick Curwin says, "No one would go to a doctor who treats all headaches the same, since the cause for one may be allergies and the other a tumor."[5] This approach is equally as true

> A fourteen-year old girl kept slamming the door to her room at home. Her father warned her to stop, and when she didn't, he removed the door from its hinges for a week!

when we work with students. Each behavior situation is unique, and each student responds in his own way to any given intervention.

Teacher Wiggle Room — Multiple-Consequence Options

One way to account for these varied responses is to identify several different but equivalent consequences for the same rule violations. If you establish a hierarchy of consequences that has only one option per level, then you are boxed in. For example, if Johnny has earned a call home to parents, but you know that Child Protective Services is investigating possible abuse at his home, you probably won't want to call his home. Knowing that Johnny may be a victim of child abuse should also inform our strategies for supporting him in school. Having several consequences on the same tier allows you to choose something other than calling home, while staying consistently within your framework. An extensive hierarchical list of consequences appears below.

Online Toolbox

Examples of consequence lists, as well as a template to help you create your own.

Private Meeting with the Teacher

If one of our consequences is "student meets privately with teacher after class," then we've created an opportunity in which we can determine what, if anything, has to happen next. If two students break the same rule, but one student has a legitimate reason, this "leeway clause" allows us to enforce consequences for both, while differentiating for specific situations.

Leeway helps especially if we are using certain consequences for the first time and don't want to set ourselves up for failure by "painting ourselves into a corner." Until we have some experience under our belt, we can't predict exactly how things will go with the consequences we choose. Incorporating leeway allows for some flexibility and responsiveness to situations as they arise — along with time to calm down and consider our options, rather than having to blurt out a decision that we may end up regretting later. For example, out of frustration you yell out "Johnny! Your behavior is so out of bounds that you and I are going to meet together every day after school for the next month!" Now, you and Johnny are stuck together after school for a whole month! Better, I suggest, to blurt, "Johnny! You and I are going to meet!" You haven't committed to much, and you can calm down and come into your rational mind before the meeting occurs.

A meeting with the teacher after class allows a student to save face during the moment of conflict. There's time to defuse the tension, get the class on task, and address consequences later — when the student is more likely ready to learn from the situation, rather than to just complain. Finally, when we meet with a student after class, we have the option to give him some choice about what the best consequence should be. If a student complains that your consequence is too severe, then you can, if it makes sense to you, offer to use his suggested consequence instead, with the understanding that if it doesn't work, you'll revert to yours.[6]

Stay Within the Teacher's Comfort Zone — the "Picket-Fence Syndrome"

Mrs. Meanswell might have a great-looking hierarchy of consequences, but she avoids using one or two key consequences because she isn't comfortable with them. For example, one consequence is that she will call parents, yet she never does. Perhaps she is intimidated, she doesn't see the value in it, or it simply takes too much time and energy. It doesn't matter that Mrs. Allgood, down the hall, successfully calls parents. Mrs. Meanswell has to either be willing to call or find and use other consequences that will work better for her. Otherwise, she will experience "the picket-fence syndrome." The "picket fence" of her consequence hierarchy that holds good behavior in the classroom will have missing pickets, allowing misbehavior to pour through the gaps. She'll also send a message of inner-apology to students, as she is consistently inconsistent in following her own hierarchy.

> **Mrs. Allgood says**
>
> Allowing for a range of consequences for the same rule violations will give us the leeway to make judgment calls, while still remaining consistent.

Be Specific and Concrete

Consequences, like rules, should be behavioral in nature, and clearly delineate actions that students need to take.

What are some possibilities? Every teaching situation is different, so there is no menu I can provide that will work for all teachers. What follows, however, is a simple list of some of the more generic consequences that many teachers have used successfully. Make sure that the consequences you choose mesh well with school and district policies.

Bright Ideas

Examples of Consequences: Five Categories

Category I. Gentle Reminders and Warnings

Nonverbal Reminders

▲ Teacher pauses.

▲ Teacher looks at the student.

▲ Teacher gives a "teacher look" to the student.

▲ Teacher turns and faces the student, with arms at her side.

▲ Teacher walks near the student.

▲ Teacher places her hand on the student's desk.

▲ Teacher points to the work that the student is supposed to be doing, and walks away from the student.

▲ Teacher points to the work that the student is supposed to be doing, and stays next to the student until the student is absorbed in the work.

▲ Teacher gives a nearby student a positive-behavior coupon.

Verbal Reminders

▲ Teacher says the name of the student, either privately or in front of the class.

▲ Teacher says the rule to the student, either privately or publicly.

▲ Teacher states the class rule aloud to the class.

▲ Teacher comments on other students who are behaving appropriately.

▲ Teacher asks the student a question about the assignment.

Nonverbal Warnings

▲ Teacher looks at her timer, signaling that she is about to add time to a class consequence or remove time from a class reward.

▲ Teacher removes a Post-it® note or similar sticker from the student's desk — the student starts with three, and removal of the third results in a specific consequence.

Bright Ideas

- ▲ Teacher picks up a clipboard where she keeps track of individual student behavior.
- ▲ Teacher uses a prearranged hand signal to warn the student.

Verbal Warnings

- ▲ Teacher tells the student — either privately or publicly — that, if he continues, a particular consequence will occur.
- ▲ Teacher says to the student, "That's one." At "three," the student knows that a particular consequence will occur.
- ▲ Teacher lets the class know that its group reward is in jeopardy.

Category II.
Mild Consequences Inside the Classroom

This level is one step up from warnings, in that specific and concrete student behaviors result. As above, these consequences can be communicated aloud, in a whisper, or non-verbally, as long as the procedure has been taught in advance.

- ▲ Teacher asks student to change seats temporarily.
- ▲ Student is asked to take a time out from the activity.
- ▲ Teacher has a brief private conversation with student, in the classroom.
- ▲ Student is asked to get a drink of water or take a breath outside, think about his behavior, and then come back in.
- ▲ Student is given a physical task to perform away from other students, such as stapling packets together, sharpening a box of pencils, emptying the recycling, or delivering something to the office or to another teacher.
- ▲ Teacher verbally appreciates the student when she "catches him being good."
- ▲ Student is asked to flip a color card or move a clip on the class behavior chart on the wall. Each student's day starts green, and can go to yellow or red. Each color corresponds to specific rewards or consequences.

Bright Ideas

▲ Student is asked to check a box on his behavior card and then place it in the slot on the wall.

▲ Student is asked to replace his colored card with a different colored card. A white card, for example, means one infraction. A pink card means a second infraction. (For more on card systems, go to "Documenting Misbehavior" on page 238, later in this chapter).

Category III.
Moderate Consequences Inside the Classroom

▲ Teacher asks the student to change seats permanently.

▲ Teacher lowers student's class participation points.

▲ Teacher assigns an after-class, afterschool or lunch detention so as to have a private conversation with the student and/or have him rehearse the expected behavior or routine.

▲ Teacher removes a potential group reward, such as extra time at the end of class to focus on a class game or preferred activity.

▲ Teacher has student complete a behavior reflection sheet.

▲ Teacher removes an individual privilege, such as time spent on the computer.

▲ Teacher lets the student know that his parents will be called.

▲ Teacher places a referral slip on the student's desk, with the understanding that if the student behaves appropriately until class is over, he can tear up the slip.

Category IV.
Firm Consequences Outside the Classroom

Removal is a separate category for three reasons. First, it means that the student will lose instructional time. Second, it involves other school personnel. And third, it guarantees that the student in question will no longer be disrupting class, at least while he's gone. Removal tends to have at least a temporary quieting impact on the rest of the students. See "Sending students to the office" in the "Implementing consequences" section later in this chapter.

Bright Ideas

The main drawbacks to sending a student out of class is that he loses instructional time, tends to fall further behind, and can act out even more as a result. So, check with your administration about the options described in this section, and the criteria for when to use them. And, please use them judiciously. Sending a student out of class due to our frustration is different from sending him out of class due to his behavior. Oftentimes a student's behavior might not warrant removal — if we are approaching the situation in a calm manner, and going under the wave of his resistance. There are certainly times for student removal from class, but they usually occur less frequently than we think.

▲ Student takes a time-out on the school's designated time-out bench or in the school's designated time-out room.

▲ Student completes an assignment in another teacher's classroom or supervised location on campus; if his behavior doesn't improve, then a referral is possible. Please note that some teachers believe that sending a student to a different teacher's class can belittle the student.[7] Please be aware of this opinion when deciding how to proceed.

▲ Student goes to the office to talk with a counselor.

▲ Student goes to a pre-designated mentor or support person on campus.

▲ Student goes to the office to talk to an administrator. At the administrator's discretion, an additional consequence may be given, including:
  ▲ Detention;
  ▲ School community service, such as lunch detail;
  ▲ Loss of schoolwide privilege;
  ▲ Written apology;
  ▲ Short essay on the causes and remedies of student misbehavior;
  ▲ Behavior contract;
  ▲ Parent/guardian conference;
  ▲ Suspension (from class or from school);
  ▲ Expulsion.

Bright Ideas

Category V.
"Behind-the-Scenes" Efforts

Working effectively and invisibly behind the scenes is a key element of successful classroom management. Mrs. Meanswell might not observe Mrs. Allgood's talking privately with or about her student, but these conversations can make all the difference. Personal contact with the student, his parents, counselors, and other teachers can provide the glue to make desired changes stick. As we connect with a student and those who have influence in his life, our relationship skills come into play.[8]

▲ Teacher talks with student privately outside of class time. Often this conversation can take the form of a structured pep talk, although it can also be more focused on the consequences that the student is incurring and the behaviors that need to change. The combination of firm and soft in this meeting can do the trick. Getting to know the student and asking him to volunteer solutions to his behavior problems can also be quite effective. This is explained in more detail in Chapter 14, "When Consequences Don't Work." Keep in mind that even if the student won't respond during this meeting, it doesn't mean that a positive behavior lesson isn't being internalized. Grace once gave a student the choice to speak with her after school for ten minutes about his behavior or spend one hour after school sitting silently. He chose to sit silently! He then proceeded to stare at Grace for an hour while she unsuccessfully tried to grade papers. But the next day, his attitude toward Grace in class softened. Go figure!

▲ Teacher talks with the student's counselor, the principal, and/or other teachers to gain information that may be helpful in addressing the student's behavior and/or emotional needs.

▲ Teacher talks with parent(s) about student's misbehavior. When this works, it works incredibly well, as word spreads and one call affects several kids. Calling parents is often the first thing that the teacher should do when a student is beginning to show signs of being out of control.

Bright Ideas

▲ Teacher talks with parents to commend student behavior — an underutilized strategy that often bears tremendous fruit. Variation: Call the student at home in the evening and let him know how improved his behavior is. Naturally, his parents will be informed of the call. If they don't believe their child and call the teacher to check up, then you've created a golden opportunity to speak with the parents in a positive way about their child — and you can invite them in for a conference.

▲ One or both parents conference at school with the principal, the counselor, and other teachers, with or without the student. This classic model reflects to the student how he is behaving in all his classes, and keeps him from claiming that one particular teacher has it out for him.

▲ Teacher and student draw up an individual behavior contract, ideally focusing on only one behavior at a time. These are described in detail in Chapter 14, "When Consequences Don't Work."

▲ Teacher has positive contact with the student outside of class. This could consist of simply watching him perform in a school play or soccer game or joining in a game of "wall ball" at recess or lunch.

Student Choice

It helps to frame all consequences around the student's choices. For example, "Mark, the rule in this class is that we listen attentively when others are speaking. You have chosen to talk out of turn, and therefore need to meet with me after class." Or, "If you continue to talk out of turn, you will be choosing to meet with me after class."

Student Participation in Rules and/or Consequences

Many teachers give their students some input in designing rules and consequences.[9] When students do participate, they tend to have buy-in, making them more likely to adhere to the rules and less likely to argue

Bobby was sure glad he had downloaded the "Homework Excuse" app.
Now he would never again have to stress over what to say.

with consequences when they receive them. This approach works as long as teachers are comfortable with it; if we don't buy into it, then it won't fly.

Student input can take many forms, ranging from full to quasi-democratic participation. One way I've done it allows me to decide late in the game how much say I want my students to have. Without telling them why, I ask students to brainstorm a list of good teacher characteristics and a list of good student characteristics. They can do this for homework or in class, alone or in groups. Then I collect and type up the characteristics most commonly listed — usually about ten characteristics for both the teacher and the student. These then become the guidelines for the class, which can be used as the basis for generating specific rules and consequences, or not. Part of my decision depends on what they've come up with. It's up to me. And, because I collate the characteristics, I can weed out those I can't live with. One thing to note is that the guidelines students generate for themselves are usually tighter than we could ever get away with. Also, guidelines for the teacher are almost always sensible and valid, and often include, "The teacher will be fair," "The teacher won't yell," or "The teacher will be available after school to help students with their homework."

This technique can be modified to fit our comfort level. For example, we could generate some of the rules, and have the students generate the others. We could generate the rules ourselves, and have the students help generate some of the consequences for specific rule violations. Or we could make

Mrs. Allgood says

Giving students tailored options can help them buy into the process while helping them see us as on their side, even as we enforce the rules.

up the rules and consequences ourselves, but give students consequence options at the point in time when they break the rules. For example, "Sally, you didn't hand in your homework. You now have two choices: you can work on it during recess, or you can work on it after school." Or, "Mark, you were writing on your desk again. You can either stay after school and clean the desks in the room, or pick up trash around the campus for twenty minutes." Giving students tailored options can help them buy into the process while helping them see us as on their side, even as we enforce the rules. When they've made a choice, they tend to complain less and respond more.

Another element in involving students is to have them think and talk meta-cognitively about rules and consequences. We can ask them why societies (and classrooms) have rules, and to identify situations where consequences are needed. This kind of analysis will help them increase their ownership and support of the system that we set up in our classroom.

Quizzing Students on Rules and Consequences

It's not enough to come up with a discipline plan, whether or not students have some say in its design. Just as in teaching content, the plan needs to be taught. Let's discuss our principles, rules, and consequences with our students, breaking each element down and teaching its parts. We can check for understanding in a number of ways, including a quiz or test. Classroom management consultant Rick Curwin suggests making sure that every student takes the test and that every student gets 100% on it. If a student fails, he can take it again until he gets 100%.

Teachers should keep copies of these quizzes. If during the school year a student claims he didn't know the rule, or wasn't aware of the consequences, he can be referred to the quiz that he aced at the beginning of the year. This same quiz can be used when we meet with parents of children who claim that they didn't know the rules when an infraction occurred.

▲ ▲ ▲

B) Implementing Consequences

Students want to feel safe, welcome, and respected in our classrooms. This can be most challenging when they are about to receive a consequence. If a student feels cornered, then he may be motivated to save face — in which case he will most likely do anything he can to get out of the corner, including increasing the level of conflict. How do we implement consequences without cornering him — while ensuring that the student learns the behavior that he needs to learn and the class runs smoothly? Below are many approaches, preceded by a story, to help with the illustration of these approaches.

Christopher and the Cell Phone

Grace shares this story to teachers in some of her "Conscious Classroom Management" workshops.

> It was the fourth week of school. My tenth-grade students were completing a writing assessment. As I circulated around the room, I saw that one student, Christopher, had his cell phone on the edge of his desk. The cell phone policy at this school was strict: "See it, take it." I knew the policy. He knew the policy. I hesitated. Was it worth the confrontation when he wasn't even using it? I summoned my courage. I walked to his desk and quietly said, "Christopher. Please give me the phone." He looked up. His startled eyes went from me to the phone and back again. He quickly grabbed it and stuffed it in his pocket saying in an anxious voice, "Oh! I forgot."
>
> I replied, "Christopher, I love that you now want to follow the school policy, but in this case, right now, I do need you to give me the phone. You can pick it up at the end of class."
>
> He replied, "No. What? No. I wasn't using it. I put it away, okay?" Christopher was, I decided to assume, testing me to see if I would be consistent in providing safety and structure. The safety would be the calm and kind way that I held my ground with him. The structure would be my follow-through.
>
> In a soft voice, I gently said, "Christopher, you have a choice right now. You can choose to give me the cell phone and pick it up after class, and that will be the end of it. Or you can choose for a third time to not give me the cell phone, in which case you are choosing to step outside, have a private conversation with me, and get a phone call home. I hope you'll decide to give me the cell phone now, so things don't have to escalate, and we can get along with the lesson. Really, it's not a big deal. But it is

your choice. I'll come back in a minute for your answer." And I walked away.

I circulated around the room to keep the rest of the students focused and on task, and then returned to Christopher about a minute later. Again, with a soft but firm voice I spoke: "Christopher, may I please have the cell phone."

"No! What? Why are you making such a big deal about this!?" he blurted out.

"All right, please step outside and we can talk about this in the hallway right outside the door."

"What?! Seriously!? I can't believe you," he said as he stormed out the door. I gave him a moment alone then followed him outside.

I kept the classroom door open so I could observe my other students while talking with Christopher in the hall. "Christopher, I don't know why you won't give me the phone. If the reason is that you didn't want anyone else in class to see you give it to me, you can give it to me out here. I will put in my pocket and keep it hidden from view. I'll give it back to you in private at the end of class. If necessary, you can wait until every other student leaves, and I can give you your phone, along with a pass to allow you to be two minutes late to your next class. This way, no one will know about the phone except the two of us, and there won't be any other consequence for your breaking the rule. At this point, you can either give me the cell phone, or you are choosing a thirty-minute lunch detention today in my classroom. So, Christopher, may I please have the cell phone?"

And he replied, "I AM NOT GIVING YOU THE CELL PHONE!!!"

"Okay. Christopher, while I wish you made a different choice, I respect the choice you made. I'll see you at lunch today."

"Whatever!" he muttered, as he stalked back into the classroom.

> "My experience with kids is that when I let them side-step a reasonable request, nine times out of ten I have to have that same conversation with them later in the week."

The Gray Area of Consequences

This story has two parts. The first is about the steps Grace took to address the breaking of a rule in her class. The second has to do with the options Grace had, and the sometimes-murky nature of those options.

Grace now says:

> If I could go back in time I might have just said, "Christopher, put the phone away or I'll have to take it." This would have ended the confrontation before it began. But hindsight is twenty-twenty. At the time, I didn't imagine that Christopher would be so oppositional. It seemed a reasonable and extremely mild consequence to put his phone in my desk and then return it fifty minutes later (and indeed, this is what happens the vast majority of the time). However, once I had "put my flag in the ground" and had clarified Christopher's choices, I felt that it was best if I continued, so that he would learn that I would indeed pass his tests consistently. True enough, over the years, my experience with kids is that when I let them sidestep a reasonable request, nine times out of ten I have to have that same conversation with them later in the week.

As teachers, we have a series of choices all along the consequences pathway. There isn't always a clear "best choice" to make. Grace didn't know and couldn't know the "correct" fork in the road to take — to let Christopher put his cell phone away, or ask him to hand it over. Even in retrospect, we don't always know if the choice we made was the best one. But if we can assume the best about our students and remain calm as we make our consequence choices, then we increase the likelihood that both our students and ourselves will land on our feet.

Grace reports:

> When Christopher came to the lunch detention, he wouldn't speak to me. But after that day, he softened toward me, I never saw his cell phone again, and his overall behavior improved. Over the next few weeks after the incident, I noticed that Christopher's class became my smoothest. While one can never know for sure, I like to think it was because the students in Christopher's class saw me hold my ground with Christopher, and realized that I was indeed willing to honor the invisible contract of providing safety and structure in my classroom.

The choices that Grace made in her interaction with Christopher illustrate key principles of how to implement consequences with students. Many of these principles follow.

Always Implement Consequences

Even if we use only a nonverbal reminder in a given situation, this helps establish the rules as rules, not just whims. When Mrs. Meanswell ignores inappropriate behavior, the students see her "asleep at the wheel." When Mrs. Allgood highlights infractions by giving gentle reminders, her students see her as the "bestower of grace" in the classroom. Consistency in implementing consequences may be difficult at first, but it sends a clear message to students that we are willing to receive the charge of being in charge. This will assure them that they are in the right room for learning, and thus don't have to act out to see if we are the right teacher for them. Our consistency communicates that we aren't clueless — we are caring.

For example, if Mark gets up to sharpen his pencil at a time when students are not supposed to sharpen their pencils, Mrs. Meanswell may ignore him, thinking that it's fine, because in this case she knows it won't disrupt class. This sends a mixed message to all of her students. They aren't sure if she either knows or notices that Mark is breaking the rule. Therefore, they aren't clear whether the rules are rules or just suggestions. In Mrs. Allgood's class, she gives Mark a quick look to let him know that he can't sharpen his pencil. Or, she gives him a look that acknowledges that he's breaking the rule, and points to the sharpener, signaling that it's okay this one time for him to sharpen his pencil. This sends a message that she is consistent, and that the rules are sound, even though exceptions can be made.

In the story of Grace and Christopher and the cell phone, Grace could have initially asked Christopher to put the phone away or face a consequence. In that case, she would have still been issuing a consequence — albeit a reminder, rather than the actual consequence of removing the cell phone.

A Closer Look

When Mrs. Meanswell ignores inappropriate behavior, the students see her "asleep at the wheel." When Mrs. Allgood highlights infractions by giving gentle reminders, her students see her as the "bestower of grace" in the classroom.

Go from Mild to Strict

Mrs. Allgood always starts with the mildest consequence first. If that doesn't work, she increases the impact of the consequence slightly. She doesn't jump from "reminder" to "detention." This is for two reasons: first, it isn't fair to the student, because then the consequence is being used as a punishment rather than as a teaching tool. Second, it isn't fair to her, because the gray area between the two consequences is so extreme, she'll be hesitant to use the second consequence. Many Mrs. Meanswells box themselves in with systems that demand harshness (see "the Picket-Fence Syndrome" earlier in the chapter). We are not here to be punitive, but to provide a pause during which the student can reassess his choices. If he continues to make a choice that disrupts the class or his learning, then we choose another consequence, another pause. A repetition of the first consequence usually won't serve to pause him the second time; we need something slightly more impactful.

> **A Closer Look**
>
> We are not here to be punitive, but to provide a pause during which the student can reassess his choices.

Our job is simply to act as a go-between or liaison, connecting students with the consequences they choose. We deliver the consequences as gently as we can, but we deliver them nonetheless. Ideally, Mark will recognize his responsibility, rather than perceiving the teacher as the one who has made the tough decision. The more we act as a calm liaison, the more likely Mark will be to own his responsibility and not blame us for our decision. When Grace interacted with Christopher, she did exactly this — going from the mild consequence of taking the cell phone for the rest of the period, to stepping outside with Christopher, to giving him a lunch detention.

Consequences in Action

When you are about to give a consequence to Mark, there is a simple progression that will increase his chances of success, while also helping you to remain calm.

1. **Assume the best about Mark.** He is on your side, doing his best to learn the behavior you are seeking. His resistance arises in part from his need for safety and structure. (For more on this, see Chapter 2, "Assume the Best.") As we assume the best, we soften — and our students tend to soften as well. Each time we go under the wave of student resistance, we do a little more to stem its tide.

2. **Soften your eyes.** Consciously soften the muscles around your eyes and between your eyebrows. It will automatically take the frustration out of your voice, and deescalate possible tension. (See page 73 in Chapter 6, "Holding Our Ground.")

3. **Make Mark's choices — and their consequences — clear.** For example, "Mark, you have a choice right now. You can get on task with your group, or you can move to the back and work by yourself for the rest of the lesson. What do you want to do?" Or "Mark, you can take out your materials and begin the assignment now, or you can step outside and have a private conversation with me, with the likelihood that I will call your parents. What do you want to do?"

4. **Respect the choice Mark makes.** If he chooses to escalate the situation, you don't need to take it personally. It might be that he needs to push against the elevated consequences, in order to more deeply internalize the fact that his choices matter. It might be that you are starting to feel safe to him, and he is giving you one last test. In truth, we often don't know why a student chooses escalation. (For a list of possible reasons why students act out, see Chapter 14, "When Consequences Don't Work.") Regardless, it works to assume the best about the student and yourself and respect the choice being made, without trying to force the student to make your preferred choice.

5. **Give Mark the consequence he has chosen.** If he doesn't calm down or end his disruptions, then follow through with the consequence you specified and that he has now chosen. Then repeat steps three and four, with escalated consequences. For example, after Mark has been moved to the back of the room: "Mark, if you work quietly and productively for ten more minutes back here, you can rejoin your group. If you stay off task and disrupt the class, you are choosing to step outside and have a private conversation with me, with the likelihood that I will call your parents. I'll come back in a minute, to give you some time to make a decision."

When following this progression, remember to remind Mark that he is making choices. Grace uses the phrase, "you have a choice right now" because it reminds Mark that he has power — and it reminds Grace that she doesn't need to corner him, just to clarify what his options are. Consistency and follow-through are keys to successfully implementing this approach. Too often, we see teachers offering students the same choice multiple times, without ever providing a consequence. The following scenario, which takes place over several minutes, is an example of this:

"Mark, stop or you will be moved....Mark, I mean it. You are about to be moved....Mark, I told you to stop. Do you want to be moved?...Okay, Mark, this is the last time I am going to tell you to stop...." The message that this sends to Mark and his classmates is that you aren't providing a solid structure, and your follow-through is inconsistent. It's kinder, and more efficient to offer the choice once, rather than multiple times, before you follow through with a consequence. Your follow-through doesn't need to be mean or full of anger. It is simply a matter of connecting Mark with the choices he is making, so he can learn to connect the two and consider making different choices in the future.

Mrs. Allgood says

The "how" of consequences is often more important than the "what" of consequences.

The "How" of Consequences

In referring to a particular situation in their classrooms, many teachers have said "that consequence doesn't work with my student(s)." My experience, however, is that often the reason is not because of the particular consequence itself, but because of *how* it has been delivered.

We can lecture all we want about appropriate behavior. We can reason, appeal to students' sense of morality, whatever. This will work with most students for anywhere from thirty seconds to several minutes. However, by using a consequence, delivered without animosity, we will better hold our students' attention and reinforce what we're talking about. This means that we don't have to raise our voices, threaten, act mean, react, apologize, hide our heads in the sand, or scold. We can simply, gently, kindly, and firmly enforce the consequence, while internally remembering that we're on the same side as the student, and that he wants to learn behavior.

Let's say Mark has been quite disruptive and needs to stay after class. Mrs. Meanswell says, "Mark! I'm sick and tired of your attitude. I have warned you and warned you, and you still don't listen. You need to stay after class today. No ifs, ands, or buts. I'm not going to tolerate your misbehavior anymore!"

What Mark actually hears is: "*Mark!* Blah blah blah blah *after class* blah blah blah," because the consequence has the power. The subtext of what he hears is, "I am so frustrated that I don't have any control here. I'm getting angry and flustered, and I'm going to take it out on you!" In ranting at Mark, Mrs. Meanswell is communicating her own weakness.

The alternative? A more Allgood-like response: "Mark. Let's talk about what is happening here after class." The consequence itself does the work, and Mrs. Allgood communicates her strength rather than her weakness. This is the "how" of delivering consequences. As long as Mark knows that Mrs. Allgood means business, she can communicate the consequence in as mild or matter-of-fact tone as she wants. Also, by letting Mark know that he will have the chance to explain his behavior, Mark is reminded that Mrs. Allgood will be fair, and he is more likely to cooperate in the moment.

A Closer Look

In ranting at Mark, Mrs. Meanswell is communicating her own weakness.

Both Mrs. Meanswell and Mrs. Allgood want their students to learn morals and values. Mrs. Meanswell tends to focus on values in the heat of the moment when her students are caught misbehaving. Mrs. Allgood addresses them when her students are more receptive. She finds opportunities in class lessons before misbehaviors occur and after misbehaving students have had a chance to calm down.

The "When" of Consequences

Here's a common classroom dilemma: Mark's behavior is inappropriate, and everyone in the class knows that he's breaking the rules. Your experience with Mark tells you that giving him a consequence will cause him to go ballistic, throw a monster temper tantrum, and disrupt the entire class for several minutes. Thus, you have two choices. If you give him the consequence, you will communicate your consistency to your students, but you will lose them because of Mark's tantrum. If you don't give him the consequence, then your students stay relatively focused, but receive the underlying message that you aren't consistent, and your class isn't safe and structured, which will lead, down the line, to more and more acting out. What should you do?

Mrs. Meanswell chooses the first option:

Mrs. Meanswell (from across the room):
"Mark. I warned you and you still haven't stopped. You're staying after school today."

Mark:
"What! No way! I wasn't talking! Why do you always pick on me?!..."

Mrs. Allgood chooses the second option:

Mrs. Allgood (walks up to Mark and whispers to him):
"Hi Mark. I see you're having a hard time today. Why don't you see if you can focus for the next ten minutes, and then you and I can talk privately after the activity and see if we can't find a way to make the rest of your day go better."

Mark: "Okay, I'll try…."

Afterward, Mrs. Allgood can let Mark know how much she appreciates his willingness to refocus. She can also ask Mark to stay after school as a consequence for his initial disruption. He's much less likely to argue with her and much more likely to show up after school because:

▲ he's had a chance to calm down;
▲ he wasn't cornered publicly by Mrs. Allgood;
▲ he doesn't have an audience.

Further, word will spread to the students of her class that Mrs. Allgood was consistent, and that Mark did indeed get a consequence for his misbehavior. As a matter of fact, Mrs. Allgood speaks to her students early in the school year to let them know that sometimes she won't give a consequence right away, if she feels that it would benefit the class and the individual student to wait. As long as she comes through later that day or even the next day, her students will know that her class is indeed safe and structured, and they will relax in that knowledge.

Teachers often give students consequences when instead what the students most need is to practice the class rule or procedure. Imagine that you are coaching basketball, and you have a player who missed most of his foul shots during the game. At practice the next day, you don't tell that player, "You did a bad job in the game at making your foul shots. You need to sit on the bench during practice until you figure out how to do it better!" Additionally, if a player made all of his foul shots in the game, you wouldn't say, "You're so good at making foul shots, you don't have to practice again."

Here, the guiding question for the teacher is: "What will most benefit my student — a consequence from my list, or

> **A Closer Look**
>
> Mrs. Meanswell tends to focus on values in the heat of the moment when her students are caught misbehaving. Mrs. Allgood addresses them when her students are more receptive.

having a chance to practice the procedure or rule again?" Sometimes both are necessary. For strategies for individual students to practice behavior, refer to Chapter 14, "When Consequences Don't Work."

The Last Word — Saving Face

There's nothing wrong with giving Mark the last word, if it can help de-escalate tension. One way, as exemplified in the story about Mark and the cell phone, is to walk away as the student thinks about his decision, and then return to him later. This will help us sidestep some confrontations that would inevitably occur if we challenged the student in the heat of the moment.

Indeed, for some of our students in some situations, deep in their limbic brain, is the association that losing face equals death. In a public confrontation with their teacher, they will defend their position at all costs. No matter what. It doesn't matter that we have eyewitnesses and videotape of their behavior; they will deny it, if it means losing face. We need to understand that for these students, in these moments, our arguments become survival issues. It's up to us to provide space for our students to regroup, calm down, and save face. Giving the student the last word, walking away, and taking time for ourselves to calm down, are all ways to address this fundamental limbic response in our students.

A Closer Look

In a public confrontation with their teacher, some students will defend their position at all costs.

Privacy

Whenever possible, communicate with students privately. This helps students to save face in front of their peers, which can go a long way in diffusing tension. It's easy enough to walk up to a student and whisper to him; students even two feet away won't be able to hear you. And, in situations when we do talk with students in front of their peers, it helps to assume the best about them and speak in a calm and respectful voice. When we treat students with dignity, they are more likely to respond in dignified ways.[10]

Justifying Consequence Implementation

If many students are talking out of turn, how do we decide which one to address with consequences? How do we justify our decision to the student? One answer: When all cars are speeding on the same stretch of road, what does the highway patrol officer say when she pulls over only one car for going ten miles over the speed limit? "Take care of your own driving, and you won't have to worry about what does or doesn't happen to the other drivers on the road." Take a look at "Fair vs. Equal" on page 210 earlier in this chapter.

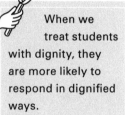

Mrs. Allgood says

Whenever possible, communicate with students privately.

Students are here to learn the value of free will. The more we can connect their behaviors to their choices and provide them with a sense of responsibility, the better off they'll be in the long run.

Yelling

Teachers almost never have to raise their voices. Ultimately, teacher yelling, displeasure, and anger are tiring and tiresome consequences,[11] and they often cause students to bristle. If yelling at our students is habitual, we may "win each battle," but we'll end up creating a war. Students will perceive a lack of safety, which will trigger a tendency to act out. Ultimately, we'll find ourselves coming to work each day readying for battle, rather than anticipating the wonder that can come from teaching and learning. If we find ourselves yelling more than we want to, it's usually a signal that our management system has a loophole that needs addressing. In addition, we might want to look at Chapter 2, "Assume the Best," or the section on teacher anger in Chapter 6, "Holding Our Ground."

A Closer Look

When we treat students with dignity, they are more likely to respond in dignified ways.

▲ ▲ ▲

Strategies for Getting the Class Quiet

For students to learn social skills and fully engage their brains, active learning needs to take place, and this often involves "legal talking." An effective learning environment doesn't need to be "pin-drop quiet."[12] Even so, silence is also a necessary ingredient for successful learning. Below are strategies that help to get students quiet in those "rare" moments when they are clearly talking out of turn.

Proximity

In class discussions, we can go near inattentive students when we are talking. This offers them a gentle reminder to refocus their attention. We can go away from students when they are contributing during a class discussion. By putting distance between the student and ourselves, we compel him to speak louder so we can hear him. Plus, by keeping our distance, we place the whole class in front of us, and we put the majority of the students between the student who is talking and ourselves. This means there is a better chance that more students will pay attention to the speaker, and if paper airplanes begin to fly, at least we can see the source. See Chapter 8, "Procedures," for more on setting up student desks to maximize teacher/student proximity.

Pause

We can stop talking to let students know that they are interrupting. We can pause both our words and our bodies when we are near disruptive students long enough that they don't just pause — they stop.

Eye Contact

This works well when trying to get the attention of the whole class. For some reason, students cannot make eye contact with the teacher and talk to their neighbors at the same time. Asking students to look at the teacher tends to quiet them immediately. One technique for younger students is for the teacher to say, "One, two, three, all eyes on me." The students respond with, "One, two, my eyes on you." Please note: some students are raised to believe that it is disrespectful to look the teacher in the eye. In this case, learn about the customs of students in the class, and if necessary, develop specific, appropriate alternatives.

Mrs. Allgood says

Go near students when we are talking, and away from them when they are contributing aloud.

Hold Up a Hand

When students see our raised hand, they know to stop talking and to raise their hands, thus helping signal others to be quiet as well. A common form of this at the elementary level is called "Quiet Coyote." The teacher holds up her hand making the coyote symbol (middle and ring fingers touching thumb, pinky and pointer fingers straight up —

like ears) with one hand. With the other hand, the teacher counts down silently from 5. Students are required to make the coyote symbol with one hand, and use their other hand to cover their mouths before the teacher gets to zero. There are two advantages to this technique. First, kids have use both hands, so they have to stop what they are working on. Second, kids cover their own mouths, so it's harder for them to talk as they follow the procedure.

Say Students' Names

Addressing individuals is more effective in getting student attention than "class" or "settle down." If Sally is talking to Maria and Mark is talking to Johnny, then saying Mark's name will often quiet Sally, Maria, and Johnny as well.

> **Mrs. Allgood says**
>
> When we "talk over" chattering students, not only do they get the message that they don't need to be completely quiet, but also many students will not hear what we say.

Get Full Silence Before Continuing

When we "talk over" chattering students, not only do they get the message that they don't need to be completely quiet, but also many students will not hear what we say. This will lead to more of the commotion that we're trying to avoid in the first place. Granted, in the beginning it might seem as if we have to wait forever. But by being patient, having students practice, and using other suggestions in this chapter, things will tend to turn around quickly.

Whisper

Many teachers report than when they had laryngitis and could only whisper in class, their students actually got quieter. Try whispering occasionally with your students as a way to calm them down. Going "under the wave" of their noise rather that into it is a great way to deescalate tension in the classroom.

Catch Students Doing Well

Consequences are not just for inappropriate behavior. They are also equally valid for appropriate and/or exemplary behavior. We need to let students know when they are succeeding.[13] Acknowledging Mark for working quietly will help him to appreciate his choices and learn responsibility. Generally speaking, most young students like public praise and appreciation. With older students, it's sometimes better to speak to them privately. One benefit of public appreciation is that other students tend to be motivated as well.

Positive Behavior Coupons

When Mark is working well and on task, silently place a "positive-behavior coupon" on his desk. He knows to take the coupon, write his name on it, and quietly place it in the fish bowl in the front of the room. On Fridays for secondary or at the end of the day for elementary, hold a class raffle where coupons are randomly removed from the fish bowl; give small prizes for the winners. The power of coupons is not only for Mark: when other students see you in "coupon-distributing mode" they immediately become aware of their behavior, and change it for the better, if they haven't been focusing in class.[14]

Let students know that coupons are not given out all the time for every student. They are given out at the teacher's discretion in small, unannounced time windows. And, it won't help a student's case if he argues for a coupon, as arguing is in itself a reason to not receive one.

Count Backward from 10 to 1

Whatever number we have come to when the class is totally quiet equals the number of points (or marbles in a jar) that the class gets toward a group privilege. This can be extra time to focus on their projects or a pre-approved activity of their choice, such as a short video, or the chance to do homework during class. We can also ask for quiet and then count down silently from five to one, showing students what number we are on with our fingers.

Hold Up a Timer

The number of seconds that elapse while we wait can be removed from a pre-set group reward. Or, we can establish a maximum amount of acceptable "settle-down time." If the students "beat the clock" throughout a given time period — twice a day for primary, once a day for upper elementary, twice a week for middle school, once a week for high school — then they receive a class reward. Classroom management consultant Fred Jones (www.fredjones.com) refers to this as PAT: Preferred Activity Time. It's an incentive that students earn by being efficient and productive. If the incentive we give them is an enjoyable, educational activity we want them to do anyway, then everybody wins.

Student Behavior During Independent Work

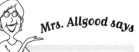

When students are working on their own or in small groups, and we are circulating from student to student, how do we help them stay focused and on task? Try the following three steps, as suggested by Fred Jones[15]:

1. Tell them one thing they are doing that's working.
2. Tell them the next thing they need to do.
3. Move on to the next student.

The strategy backfires if you get hooked into long conversations. We have too many students for that, plus, all of them need to learn independent work skills. Foster this independence with quick spot-checks and reminders.

If a student is not on task, try some nonverbal strategies. Point to his work, which reminds him to get back on track; don't make eye contact; and don't speak to him. If none of these work, then turn to face the student, look at him, and pause. Then look at the work, and if necessary, point to it. Pause again. Make sure to "hang around" for a few extra seconds to see that he is actually working, and not just appearing to work.

If nonverbal strategies don't work, try asking these two questions:

▲ What should you be doing?
▲ What are you going to do now?

We don't need to buy into all the excuses and explanations. We can address the behavior, put the responsibility on to the student, and move on.

Here's yet another strategy. If a student is misbehaving, ask him one or more of these three questions regarding his behavior:

▲ Is it safe?
▲ Is it kind?
▲ Is it productive?

This strategy works best for younger students, but variations can be tailored for older students.

> **Mrs. Allgood says**
>
> We don't need to buy into all the excuses and explanations. We can address the behavior, put the responsibility on to the student, and move on.

Chaos at the End of Class

Ah, that really rowdy moment just before class ends — what teacher hasn't experienced it? Perhaps kids put their backpacks on and gather around the door, waiting for the bell to ring. Certainly a teacher can elbow through the crowd, block the doorway, and command students to return to their desks, while chastising them for charging the door. Inevitably, during the speech, the bell will have rung and the students will quite possibly be complaining that they are missing their break or have to go.

While ideally it's good to "nip such behavior in the bud" (see Chapter 8, "Teaching Procedures"), there's nothing wrong with waiting until we next see students to talk to them about appropriate behavior — and then mete out any necessary consequences. If there's only one minute left and we've already "lost them," we don't necessarily need to reel them in — until next time.

Tailor Kids' Choices

Never give kids choices about anything unless we are willing to follow through with whatever choices they make. When I student-taught my ninth-grade class-from-heck, the one with "Brad the Baiter" (Chapter 2, "Assume the Best"), I remember trying a new management system in the middle of the semester. I introduced a timer to calculate off-task time, and told students that if their behavior improved to a certain point, they would receive a reward in the form of a movie of their choice. When they finally earned their reward, their top movie choice was a horror film and their second choice was X-rated! Needless to say, I couldn't let them watch either, and had to face an uprising of incensed youth who demanded that they get what I had promised them.

Wise-Apple Advice

In some cases, it can ease the teacher's mind if she sets up a meeting with the administrator in advance of sending a student out.

The more we can anticipate worst-case scenarios, the more proactive we can be in successfully — and peacefully — tailoring student options.

Sending Students to the Office

Teachers are often concerned about sending students out of the classroom. They believe that they will be perceived by the administration as weak or incompetent if their students appear in the office. Granted, sending students out is not a good habit, but there are situations where it is a perfectly suitable option. In some cases, it can ease the teacher's mind if she sets up a meeting with the administrator in advance of sending a student out. Let the administrator know that Mark has been particularly off-the-wall lately, and ask, "Would it be okay if I sent him out of class if it happens again?" ("What time would be best for you? Okay, since he's basically always off-the-wall, can I pencil in a meeting with Mark at 10:30....") This places the administrator where she should be — working with the teacher — and removes most of the teacher's anxiety about being judged as weak.

A Closer Look

Sometimes administrators and teachers have different definitions of "support."

This strategy also works well for teachers whose administrators may seem inconsistent in their support. By setting up the meeting between the student and the administrator in advance, the administrator is much more likely to meet with the student effectively.

Sometimes administrators and teachers have different definitions of "support." It helps to clarify exactly what the administrator thinks her role is, and exactly what we think we need, thus narrowing the gap between the two definitions and likely increasing the support we will receive. This clarification can be done directly or through conversations with a mentor teacher, if a new teacher is particularly concerned about how the administration might perceive her.

Often, the administrator and the teacher can and ought to meet halfway. In several schools where Grace has consulted, the staffs created a compromise: teachers agreed to try at least three interventions/consequences of their own choosing in the classroom (unless the student behavior was extreme enough, such as fighting, to warrant immediate dismissal), before sending a student to the office. In exchange, the administration agreed to more fully address the student's behavior during the referral.

Finally, remember that when students leave your room, they miss out on learning opportunities in your class, as well as chances to connect with the class community. Therefore, do your best to minimize this option. And when you do send students out, it's ideal if you can be in on the meeting between the student and the administrator, to help clarify what happened in class and offer support.

A Note of Appreciation for Physical Education Teachers

P.E. is, I believe, one of the hardest types of classes to manage, for several reasons:

- ▲ P.E. teachers have larger classes.
- ▲ They have either no classroom at all (the field) or a room with multiple exit doors (the gymnasium).
- ▲ Students can be far enough away from the teacher that the teacher has to raise her voice. Even though she is yelling to her students and not at them, they don't always recognize the difference.
- ▲ Some students tend to take P.E. less seriously than their other classes.
- ▲ Some use P.E. to go overboard with energy expenditure.
- ▲ Many students find the very nature of P.E. to be a cause for feeling inadequate, and thus act out all the more.

In addition to P.E., classes like family and consumer science, woodshop, music, and autoshop can be quite challenging, especially for beginning teachers. Perhaps the most challenging class to manage is Beginning Band. Sixty kids with noise-makers — whose idea was that!?

▲   ▲   ▲

C) Documenting Misbehavior

Many teachers use check marks on their roll sheets or in their grade books to record inappropriate behavior. The drawback to this is that there are many different types of inappropriate behaviors. If we don't know the details, then we can't recognize patterns, and have less ability to help teach our students to turn things around. Further, documenting the specifics helps when talking with parents, counselors, and other teachers. If students have a section on their report cards for behavior (elementary) or participation (secondary), then having specifics at our fingertips can be quite helpful.

Use an Acronym and a Seating Chart

A simple way to track students behaviors is to use an acronym to describe the particular categories of behaviors we want, and to document and keep track of them on a seating chart. Grace recommends a system she calls DOTS:

D= **Disturbing** Others
O= **Off Task** (without disturbing others)
T= **Talking** Out of Turn (including blurting out)
S= Out of **Seat** (without permission)

This acronym system, and others like it, makes use of a class seating chart for each class we teach. When a student misbehaves, we write on the chart the letter of the acronym that corresponds to the misbehavior. We can later transfer the information to forms that go home to parents and into our computer-grading program. This works best when the seating charts are laminated, so they can be wiped clean each night and used again the next day.

Mrs. Allgood says

Documenting the types of misbehaviors helps when we talk with parents, counselors, and other teachers.

There are also apps for iPads and other tablets that work similarly. With these you can create both positive and negative behavior categories and assign points to individual students with a simple click. You can have parents or other teachers join online, so they can see their students' points and behaviors in real-time. This can be particularly helpful at the elementary level, when your students are with another teacher, such as art, PE, or music. As those teachers also track behavior, you can see exactly how your students are behaving while they are elsewhere in the school.

Using a Card or Clip System

Elementary teachers can set up part of a bulletin board for cards of three to five different colors, depending on the system. Each student has a pocket on the board with a card in it. For example, a green card means that the student is behaving appropriately. Yellow stands for a warning. Peach means the student was warned once, then broke another rule and has earned consequence number one. A blue card stands for two broken rules and consequence number two. Of course, specific consequences are up to you.

A variation of this is the clip system. In this system a long, vertical poster is attached to the wall with four colors, from top to bottom; purple, green, yellow, and red. Each student has a clip (usually a wooden clothespin) with his name on it. All clips start each day clipped to the green part of the poster. Clips are moved up or down (by the teacher or by the student as directed by the teacher) throughout a lesson, similar to the card system described above. Unproductive choices have a student "clip down." When a student clips down to red, a consequence is given, which allows his clip to return to green, for a clean slate. But students can also "clip up" for making productive choices or unprompted actions that are particularly

A Closer Look

Record-keep-
ing systems
are not consequence
systems.

kind and helpful to others. In the elementary school where Grace's sons attended, students could also clip up from purple to the teacher's shirt! If a student's clip made it to the shirt, he was given a plastic gem or shell or other small trinket to glue to his clip as recognition of his achievement.

With both these systems, the students can move their own cards or clips, thus kinesthetically connecting to their behavior, and saving the teacher time and distraction. Another advantage is that both the teacher and all her students can quickly and easily see where students are behaviorally. One drawback is that these systems don't distinguish between types of misbehaviors. That can be done privately via the notebook or iPad, as described above.

Finally, the most effective use of either system allows students to clip up as well as clip down. Otherwise, they can lose motivation when their clip is in the red. In addition, it helps to build in clean slates periodically (such as at recess or lunch), resetting all student clips at green.

Public vs. Private Documentation

Whatever behavior-documentation system you use, keep in mind that public tracking has the potential to cause student embarrassment. This embarrassment might not adversely affect student behavior initially, but over time, it can erode student trust and thus increase student misbehavior.

The card and clip systems mentioned above are public, but take the edge off the embarrassment because they assess everyone. All kids can self-assess their behavior just by looking at their clip or card. However, a system that involves putting the names of misbehaving students on the board, for example, can increase student embarrassment, as chronically misbehaving students feel consistently singled out.

To counter this, there are several ways to "privatize" documentation, while still allowing students to know where they stand. Teachers can use hand signals or verbal cues. One common technique is to whisper, for example, "Joshua, that's a one." (Or say his name and hold up one finger). He knows that if you get to "three" then he will receive a consequence. Similarly, some teachers place Post-it® notes on the desks of misbehaving students, with three notes resulting in a consequence.

Please note: Record-keeping systems are not consequence systems. They may help keep track of trends in student misbehaviors, but for the most part "keeping track" doesn't directly change behaviors. The exception is that every time the teacher goes to click her tablet or write on her clipboard, whiteboard, or seating chart, students tend to temporarily behave better. But if she relies solely on using the threat of clicking or writing to manage student behavior, the effect will wear out very quickly. Concrete consequences still need to be implemented on a consistent basis.

▲ ▲ ▲

D) Extrinsic vs. Intrinsic Rewards

Some people think extrinsic rewards are **training wheels**, temporary motivators that allow students to form positive behavioral habits; once habits are learned, the rewards are discarded from the equation. Others think extrinsic rewards are **crutches** that rely on an external locus of control, one that disables students' natural motivation to participate, learn, and cooperate. The end result of extrinsic rewards, so the crutch-argument goes, is that before engaging in an activity, students increasingly need to know "What's this worth?" or "Does this count?" Many suggest that extrinsic rewards do work for the short term, but eventually lose their power to motivate. Over time, students tend to become numb to them.[16]

> That old adage, "Give a person a fish and she eats for a day, but teach her to fish and she eats for a lifetime," didn't apply to me. When I was a new teacher, I would have starved to death while learning to fish. I needed fish immediately!

Where do I stand in the argument? Somewhere in the middle. I have seen initially motivating rewards slowly lose their luster, and I've watched many Mrs. Allgoods who successfully use reward systems. Overall, I believe it's ideal if teachers can help students to motivate themselves intrinsically — but there are many times, especially in the beginning of their careers or when working with unusually difficult classes, when teachers need to use strategies that work right away, regardless of the long-term issues.

That old adage, "Give a person a fish and she eats for a day, but teach her to fish and she eats for a lifetime," didn't apply to me. When I was a new teacher, I would have starved to death while learning to fish. I needed fish immediately! Therefore, I took whatever I could get. Later on, as I became a better classroom manager, I was able to rely less and less on rewards or consequences to keep my students focused. This can often trip up Mrs. Meanswell, because she watches how Mrs. Allgood does it and tries the exact same style. But Mrs. Allgood has spent years learning and practicing how to intrinsically motivate her students.

When using rewards, I suggest that teachers be conscious of the potential long-term limitations and pitfalls.[17] Counterbalance them with a lot of genuine appreciation of students, as well as individual conversations with them about their behavior and ways they can increase their enjoyment and focus in class. If teachers focus in these conversations on the intrinsic, then students will, too.

Further, some rewards are more natural than others. For example, if students keep class transition times to a minimum, then giving them candy would be an artificial reward. Giving them time at the end of class to do their homework would be more natural, since they saved time to earn time. The more natural the incentive, the more likely students are to internalize their motivation.

How to Introduce a Group Incentive

Students are more likely to work hard for a group incentive, such as a twenty-minute educational game on Friday, if they first have a "free taste" of the incentive. After they've tasted it through a short exposure to the game, they can be required to earn it the next time through appropriate behavior, such as all students' being on time to class, or transition times kept below a certain maximum. An additional approach is to make the criterion for success fairly simple the first couple of times, so the students see the connection between their positive behavior and the incentive they receive. Once they have bought in to trying to earn the incentive, the teacher can make the criteria more challenging. If one or two of your students consistently don't buy in or appear to sabotage your group incentive, you can try "Omission Training," described in Chapter 14, "When Consequences Don't Work."

A Closer Look

The more natural the incentive, the more likely students are to internalize their motivation.

Appreciation vs. Praise

The difference between appreciation and praise, as I define them, is that appreciation is genuine, whereas praise is mechanical. While the impact of genuine appreciation grows with its application, the opposite occurs with praise. Praise might work to motivate students initially, but its value

actually recedes over time. The more specific the appreciation
— "Excellent descriptors in your first paragraph!" rather than
"Good job!" — the more effective it will be long-term.

Praise acts like an addictive drug. Students respond to it
positively at first, but then either become immune to it or need
increasing doses to be affected.

Appreciation, on the other hand, does not fade. As
teachers, if we are genuine in expressing what we appreciate
about our students, then we make and reinforce a personal
connection with them. Like all human beings, they are
hungry for genuine personal connections. Appreciation
addresses that hunger and can positively nurture our
students without ever running out of steam or seeming false.
It is the "gift that keeps on giving."

An example of praise is when an elementary teacher
recites to the class, often in a singsong voice, "I like the way Mark is
sitting at the carpet, I like the way Niyesha has her legs crossed, I like the
way Javiera has her hands in her lap," in order to get all the students to
the carpet in "readiness" position. Many teachers do this, and are quite
successful with it. There is a place in the classroom for praising students,
and in the short run, it generally does work to motivate them. For some,
that "short run" may last the whole school year.

If we are genuine and specific, however, our students will receive a
much more powerful message. An example of this is when the teacher
pulls Mark aside and says, "Mark — I so appreciate your changed
behavior this week. I know that you had your challenges last week, and I
see your efforts. Thank you. It really does make a difference to the class,
and I know that it's making things easier for you." This interaction will
tend to internalize in Mark an appreciation of himself, rather than a need
for external compliments.

Gifts vs. Rewards

Rewards are prizes — food, stuff, activities, extra time — offered
by the teacher as an incentive for students to behave well. The students
know in advance what they can earn with appropriate or exemplary
behavior. Gifts, on the other hand, are spontaneous in nature, coming
as appreciation for positive behavior that has already happened. For

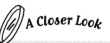

A Closer Look

> Praise acts like an addictive drug. Students respond to it positively at first, but then either become immune to it or need increasing doses to be affected. Appreciation, on the other hand, is the gift that keeps on giving.

example, if Mrs. Allgood uses a timer to track instructional time lost due to student misbehavior, and tells her students they can have a popcorn party on Friday if they stay on task during transitions throughout the week, then she is offering them a reward for their behavior. If, on the other hand, on Friday she announces to the students that they have done so well with transitions throughout the week that she wants to throw them a popcorn party, then she is giving them a gift. The main difference is that rewards are used as extrinsic forms of motivation, whereas gifts are unexpected expressions of appreciation that can highlight students' intrinsic motivations.

Wise-Apple Advice

A Final Reminder about Consequences

Strategies for classroom management, including consequences, are tools for teaching students about behavior and responsibility. All of classroom management is aimed at prevention; consequences are referred to as intervention because they are an attempt at prevention when initial attempts don't work. As with all classroom management, consequences boil down to who and how we are, not just what we do. As we grow in inner authority, make positive connections with our students, and teach procedures well and consistently — and most importantly, as our students grow in personal responsibility and self-direction — our need for consequences will be diminished over time.

14

WHEN CONSEQUENCES DON'T WORK

> *"When the going gets tough,*
> *the tough get supportive."*

S OME OF THE STUDENTS I taught in an alternative high school displayed behaviors that were extreme, such as stealing car sound systems or getting into fights at night with rival gang members. Sometimes they would get arrested, and go to jail for the weekend. They would come back to school on Monday morning, act out in my class, and I would threaten them with detention. Somehow, as compared with the county jail, the idea of school detention didn't have a whole lot of influence over their decisions!

For particularly tough kids and situations (not just kids coming from jail), school consequences don't always change behavior. Nor does employing all the approaches outlined in previous chapters. What then? How do we help our students to make permanent, positive changes? While there are no guaranteed solutions, the most effective approaches arise out of our tried-and-true combination of assuming the best about students and helping them to assume the best about themselves, connecting with them, going under the wave of their resistance, and breaking things into simple steps, as shown in the strategies described below. Keep in mind that all of the strategies in this chapter require commitment, compassion, and patience from the teacher.

Making permanent change can be difficult for anyone — think about examples outside the classroom, such as when adults try to lose weight or quit smoking. Though others can support these efforts, it is up to the individual to do the hard work required for the change to take place. It's no less a challenge when we are working with students, trying to help them to change chronic behaviors. You won't have time to use these strategies with all of your students — just the ones who need them the most.

Addressing the "Why"

To get to the root of student misbehaviors, we may need to address the reasons behind them. This doesn't always seem practical, given the limited time we have. Sometimes we are so busy putting out fires that we don't seem to have the time to find the sources of those fires. But it can make the all the difference.

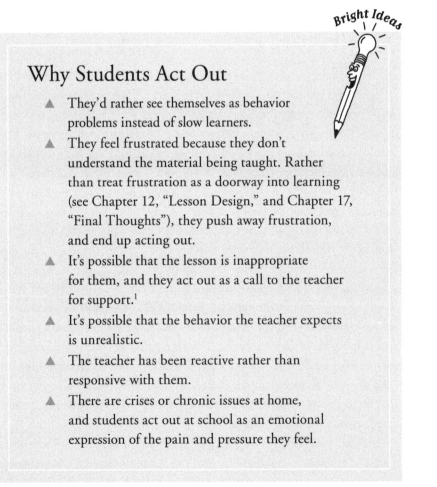

Why Students Act Out

- ▲ They'd rather see themselves as behavior problems instead of slow learners.
- ▲ They feel frustrated because they don't understand the material being taught. Rather than treat frustration as a doorway into learning (see Chapter 12, "Lesson Design," and Chapter 17, "Final Thoughts"), they push away frustration, and end up acting out.
- ▲ It's possible that the lesson is inappropriate for them, and they act out as a call to the teacher for support.[1]
- ▲ It's possible that the behavior the teacher expects is unrealistic.
- ▲ The teacher has been reactive rather than responsive with them.
- ▲ There are crises or chronic issues at home, and students act out at school as an emotional expression of the pain and pressure they feel.

Bright Ideas

▲ They are using drugs. Although drug use is often viewed as a symptom of underlying problems, once done with regularity, the drugs themselves can become the problem. One key symptom of drug use in teens is that they start acting meaner and more standoffish than usual.

▲ Their parents are using drugs, are in trouble with the law, and/or are in crisis.

▲ Students are getting their behavior cues from their parents.

▲ Students are having trouble with prescription medication — not taking it, taking it too much, or not taking it regularly.

▲ They have emotional tension with peers. Many kids are more focused on fitting in and belonging than on succeeding in school.

▲ They are being bullied and/or intimidated by classmates.

▲ They feel isolated.

▲ They feel at odds with their teachers.

▲ They are struggling in other classes.

▲ They are experiencing health challenges.

▲ They aren't eating enough, or well enough, or both.

▲ They don't feel that their culture fits or is welcome in the classroom. (See Chapter 7, "Positive Connections.")

▲ A life of poverty has resulted in chronic stressors, leading to increased acting out, impatience, and impulsivity.[2] (See Chapter 7, "Positive Connections.")

▲ A myriad of other reasons, both in and out of the classroom.

Let's unpack a couple of these reasons below:

Behavior Cues from Parents

Our school had many students whose behavior was so out of bounds that the teachers would turn to one another and ask, "What planet are these kids from?!?" The planets revealed themselves when we met their parents! Once I witnessed a father yelling at his daughter during a parent/teacher meeting, swearing at her that she should never swear in school! Another time I saw a mother model defensiveness perfectly, denying that her son was producing graffiti, even when shown a surveillance video of him caught in the act!

A Closer Look

When a student acts out, it is often a call for help. By addressing these calls directly and honing in on solutions, we provide students with a chance to make real and lasting changes.

Rather than spark derision or cynicism, these incidents can foster our compassion for our students, as we see the messages that they receive in their worlds outside of school. Further, we can have empathy for parents who have their own challenges to address and wade through, as they do their best to raise their children. Finally, we can have compassion and tenderness for ourselves, as we realize the depth of the trials that we sometimes face in serving our students.

Behavior Problems or Struggling Learners?

If Mark tries his hardest in your classroom and doesn't succeed, then he may feel helpless and powerless. Because feeling a sense of power is a key human need,[3] Mark might choose to act out. For example, he may tell himself that he could do the work if he wanted to, but he would rather goof off. He thus feels like he is in the driver's seat and is exercising his personal power to choose to misbehave. In this light, we can see Mark through a lens of compassion, as he struggles to find a positive sense of himself while consistently falling short of academic expectations.

We Know the "Why" — Now What?

Students don't act out because they are bad people. They are looking for ways to establish and maintain a sense of self while navigating through the sometimes-extreme experiences they have. When a student acts out, it is often a call for help. By addressing these calls directly and honing in on solutions, we provide students with a chance to make real and lasting changes. Each "why" for each student is unique, needing a unique approach. Take the time to find the solution or solutions. Read through this chapter. Brainstorm with colleagues. Ask them what has been working in their classes with your students. If you find something, use it. If, however, in your investigations, you discover reasons beyond your control, you can at least gain compassion for your students and yourself, knowing what can and can't be changed. In addition, when students have someone to talk to, just someone who understands the challenges they are facing, they can develop adequate resilience and coping mechanisms — even when they face tough situations for which there are no ready solutions.

Reaching Out to Help a Student

Below is a true story that illustrates one teacher's approach in helping a student who had multiple causes for his misbehavior.

> Eduardo was out of control in the classroom; it was the spring term and he had recently transferred to a large district in northern California. He didn't do his work, he complained, challenged, disrupted, called out constantly, and got out of his seat to distract other students during lessons. His veteran fifth-grade teacher, Mrs. Johnson, tried many strategies, but nothing seemed to work. She was treading water at best, trying to get by with twenty-nine other energetic students.
>
> One day, she decided to take the time to work with Eduardo one-on-one after school. At first, he balked at staying. But after a time, he warmed up to Mrs. Johnson and began to share his feelings.
>
> Mrs. Johnson asked Eduardo, "What do you need in order to make this classroom work for you?"
>
> Tears welled up in his eyes. He whispered his reply. "I need my mother."
>
> Eduardo then revealed that his mother had taken his sisters to Mexico the previous year and had abandoned Eduardo, his brother, and his father, leaving no forwarding address. Eduardo had had no contact with his mother for over a year. He was heartbroken.
>
> Mrs. Johnson had an idea. She asked him, "Would you like to write a letter to your mother? I don't know if it will get to her, but you can try."

Eduardo's eyes brightened. "Yes, please," he paused. "Can I write it in Spanish?"

"Of course," said Mrs. Johnson. She gave him pen and paper, and he proceeded to write a letter to his mother, all the while with his tears falling on the paper.

"As he wrote, you could see his whole body slowly relax and come back to life," Mrs. Johnson recalled as she told me this story.

In this situation, Mrs. Johnson decided to become an active participant with a student in need. Although it took time she didn't think she had, she was willing to take the chance.

As it turned out, she made a wise choice. Following their interaction, Eduardo's demeanor in school radically shifted, and Mrs. Johnson's whole class benefited from the change.

This alone is a great example to illustrate that when consequences don't work, a personal connection can make all the difference. But Mrs. Johnson decided to take a further step.

When she spoke again with Eduardo, she learned that he was living in a trailer with his brothers and his unemployed father one block from the school. They had no plumbing or electricity, and no food. Eduardo and his brothers had been surviving on the free breakfasts and lunches at school. At night and on the weekends, they went hungry.

That day after school, Mrs. Johnson went with Eduardo to the grocery store. She bought two bags of groceries for the family and delivered them to the trailer. She then went to Social Services, and connected Eduardo's family with vitally needed support.

Now retired, Mrs. Johnson says of that experience, "It was one of those special moments in my career. The semester ended, and the next year, Eduardo and his family had moved. I will never know if my kindness made a long-term difference in the life of this young man. I can only hope that it has."

Positive Connections

By connecting with Eduardo, Mrs. Johnson increased his chances of success in school and decreased both his misbehavior and that of the rest of the class. This kind of focus on positive connections can be a lifeline for the "Marks" in our classrooms. Many strategies for this are outlined in Chapter 7, "Positive Connections." The essence of all such strategies is contained within the "Two-by-Ten Strategy" from that chapter. It begins with simply talking with Mark — not about his poor behavior, but about anything he's interested in. Give him a chance to have personal time with us when we are not playing the role of authoritarian.[4] Make this an ongoing commitment. It won't be easy, especially at first. He might be wary of our sudden interest in his life. But if we stick with it, casually and consistently over the course of days — not as a one-time frontal assault — we'll notice that gradually Mark becomes more forthcoming, more involved, and more committed to succeeding in the class. Often our most troublesome students are the ones who most need a positive connection with a caring adult. When we make that connection, students often regain their equilibrium and self-esteem. This alone can result in a switch in their behavior — from negative influence to positive classroom ally.

Wise-Apple Advice

Even though we can't know the lasting results of our kindness, we can still choose to be kind.

"I"-Statements

In moments of conflict with Mark, it can help to make statements about yourself, using the word "I." An example would be, "I feel concerned when I give the class a direction and you come up right afterwards to ask me what it was." In addition, you can repeat back what you heard Mark say. For example, "I hear you saying that you think it's unfair that I singled you out when others were talking as well." Because you are not directly accusing Mark, he will tend to be less defensive.

Mrs. Allgood says

Give students a chance to have personal time with us when we are not playing the role of authoritarian.

Breaking the Cycle of Misbehavior – Five Keys

Sometimes knowing why doesn't help. Other times we can't figure out why. What then? Permanently changing behavior is not easy, for kids or adults. It can take a long time, even with lots of practice and repetition. Nonetheless, in the classroom there are some approaches that do seem to make the difference.

All permanent change involves one or more of the five keys described below, and is more likely if all five keys are used together. (The first three echo consultant Rick Curwin.[5]) In using these keys, it is best to choose one behavior that you'd like to see changed. This can be a challenge, when your student has several misbehaviors, such as swearing, getting out of his seat, interrupting others, and coming late to class. How do you decide which one to choose? Start with the easiest behavior to change, and/or the one that will make the most immediate difference for the student and the class.

To permanently change the cycle of misbehavior, students have to:

1. **want** to change;
2. know **how** to change;
3. have opportunities to **practice** changing;
4. be **conscious** of their choices as they are choosing them;
5. receive ongoing **modeling** and **support** from the teacher.

These keys arise when we assume the best about our students — that they want to behave appropriately and are capable, but are stuck on the details. Below are three examples that help illustrate how these keys can be used to help our students. Each can easily be applied to many individual student misbehaviors in any grade.

Example 1: Elementary School

Mrs. Allgood teaches a second-grade class, and her student Mark has a hard time with transitions. During the long-term art project, he is always the last one to put his materials away and return his chair to where it belongs. She's tried everything to get him to succeed. Once she even offered a group reward if the whole class cleaned up in a given time. But Mark still didn't do it fast enough, and the whole class suffered. What can she do? She assumes the best about Mark — that he does want to learn this behavior. She assumes that, for whatever reason, the way she has taught it is not working for him. All of her pep talks work only for a short time. He gets distracted and loses momentum.

A Closer Look

These keys arise when we assume the best about our students — that they want to behave appropriately and are capable, but are stuck on the details.

Her solution is to break up his required task into smaller pieces. She talks to Mark during lunch about what her expectations are. She gets him to buy in that **he wants to make a change**. She then clarifies how he can succeed. With no one else in the room, she puts the art supplies on his desk and sits him down. She asks him where the supplies need to go when it's time to clean up (**how**).

She shows him (**modeling**), then has him **practice** putting the supplies away. She asks him to talk about the distractions that occur during class, and what he can do to counter them (becoming **conscious of his choices**). **She supports him** by encouraging him to succeed during the next class.

A Closer Look

She gives Mark the minimum amount of support he needs to ensure that he succeeds completely.

The next day, just before the students begin to put their art supplies away, Mrs. Allgood has a brief, private conversation with Mark, reminding him of what they did during lunch the day before. "Mark, remember our talk about cleaning up the art materials? What are you going to do with the scissors? Where does this paper go? How about the markers? Do you think you can do this? You know what, I know you can. I'm going to stand right next to you when the class starts cleaning up, so you can show me how well you can do it. I'm about to ask the class to clean up. Are you ready?" Then she announces to the class that it's time to put the supplies away. She gives Mark the *minimum amount of support* he needs to ensure that he succeeds completely. In Mark's case, it might initially mean that Mrs. Allgood walks him from station to station, handing him the supplies one at a time, and encouraging him as he goes. In content teaching, this is called "guided practice."[6] It's the same in teaching procedures or behavior. When he's completed the task, she lets him know how well he did.

The following day, she does the same thing. On the third day, she pulls back a bit. She tells Mark, "Since you've done so well the last two days in putting your art supplies away, this time when I ask the class to clean up, I'm going to stand in the back of the room and watch how well you do." If this is too big a step for Mark to succeed, she comes up with an intermediary step: "Mark, this time I'm going to stand in the back and watch how well you can put things away. Each time you put an item away, please stop and look at me, and give me a thumbs-up. I'll give you a thumbs-up, and then you can go on to the next station." An alternative intermediate step might be pairing Mark with a student in the class who is consistently successful at cleaning up. Over time, Mrs. Allgood pulls back more and more of Mark's extra support. At some point, Mark will have internalized the appropriate behavior, and will be able to put his supplies away without needing her extra guidance.

The support Mrs. Allgood provides makes a big difference. Her actively assuming the best about him is contagious; he starts to assume the best about himself. He starts admitting that he can change and wants to change, and he is more willing to try. Mrs. Allgood is therefore not only Mark's "imparter of content," but she is also his coach and cheerleader.

Example 2: Middle School

A Closer Look

Mrs. Allgood is therefore not only Mark's "imparter of content," but she is also his coach and cheerleader.

Mark is a seventh-grade student who constantly disrupts class by calling out of turn. Consequences haven't made a difference, because he's essentially unaware that he's doing it. Before consequences have any power, he needs to slow down internally to "the choice point" — the point where is he aware of his choice to call out as he's making it.

His teacher, Mrs. Allgood, has a conversation with Mark during lunch. First, she gets him to agree that it's in his best interest to change his behavior (more on this later). The conversation continues:

Mrs. Allgood:	Mark, if you tried really hard not to call out in class tomorrow, how many times would you call out?
Mark:	None! I promise I'll never do it again!
Mrs. Allgood:	I appreciate your attitude, Mark, but calling out can be a hard habit to break, even if you try really hard. Today in class you probably called out ten or more times. What do you think would be a more realistic number, if you tried really hard?
Mark:	Hmm. Maybe…three times?
Mrs. Allgood:	That seems like a more realistic goal. I'll tell you what. Tomorrow when class starts, I'll put four yellow Post-it® notes on your desk. Each time you call out, I'll give you a private hand signal, by touching my ear like this. When you catch yourself calling out, or when you see my hand signal, your job is to remove one note, crumple it up, and put it in your pocket. Let's see if you can have at least one note remaining by the time class ends.

The next day, Mark does his best to abide by the new policy. He is now kinesthetically monitoring his own progress, slowing down internally, and increasing his awareness of his choice to call out. What happens if he uses up all four Post-it® notes with twenty minutes to go in class? Should Mrs. Allgood give him a consequence? Not initially. Until he's at the choice point — where he's conscious of his choice to call out as he calls out — a consequence will feel more like a punishment than a teaching tool. It would help him more if she simply gave him more notes, and encouraged him to do better the next time. (Kindergarten kids who sit on the floor can put bracelets around their wrists instead of notes on their desks). He is practicing, and his "mess-ups" are part of the learning process. The more practice he gets in a safe environment, the more likely he is to succeed. If Mrs. Allgood finds that he is relying too much on her hand signal, she can create an extra incentive for him to catch himself when he calls out.

In this example, Mark agrees that he **wants** to make a change. Mrs. Allgood shows him **how** to do it, and he gets a chance to **practice** during class. His **awareness** increases, and he receives **ongoing support** from Mrs. Allgood.

For the Post-it® note strategy, Mark removes a negative. An alternative can be to add a positive. Mrs. Allgood gives him a pie chart, with eight slices. Each slice represents six minutes. Mark is told that every time six minutes goes by and he doesn't call out, he can shade in one of the slices. His goal is to have as many shaded slices as he can by the time the forty-eight minute class is over. He can use his watch or the wall clock. Younger kids can use a visual timer, where the red section grows smaller as the time counts down.

These strategies work best if Mrs. Allgood encourages Mark and speaks to him about what happens to him when he calls out. She can work with him one-on-one, modeling the things in class that distract him — which can be a lot of fun. Any way that she can get him to be aware of what he's choosing will help him to speed up the desired changes.

Wise-Apple Advice

Before consequences have any power, he needs to slow down internally to "the choice point" — the point where is he aware of his choice to call out as he's making it.

Example 3: High School

Mark is chronically late to his first-period class. His tardies have piled up and his grade is slipping, but he still comes in late. Mrs. Allgood has a meeting with Mark to discuss his tardies. She asks, "Do you want your grade to keep going down?" As soon as he says, "No," she's accomplished number one — getting him to want to change.

This is the point where many teachers stop. They offer a handshake and a "good luck" to Mark. They reason that the student wants to change, and the proof will be in the pudding. But Mrs. Allgood goes further. She talks with Mark about his pattern in the morning. He tells her that his alarm clock goes off on time, but he keeps hitting the snooze button. She suggests that he put the alarm clock on the other side of the room. She also suggests that Mark's classmate Andrew call him in the morning to make sure he's up. And, she encourages Mark to experiment with going to bed earlier, to see if it helps him in the morning. Mark agrees to try. But Mrs. Allgood doesn't stop there. She knows that Mark is embarrassed about asking Andrew, and may not actually do it. So she asks him when he will talk to him, and what he's going to say to get him to call him. She has Mark repeat the lines he needs to say. She then tells him that she'll check with Andrew the next day to see how the process went. Only then does she end the conversation by encouraging him to succeed the next day.

> **A Closer Look**
>
> He is practicing, and his "mess-ups" are part of the learning process. The more practice he gets in a safe environment, the more likely he is to succeed.

Does Mark show up on time the next day? Maybe. He's certainly more likely to show up, now that he has admitted that he **wants to change**, he's looked at **how** to make that change, he's **practiced** what he needs to say, he's **aware** of his resistance and is willing to make the effort anyway, and he has **support** both from Mrs. Allgood and his friend Andrew.

Here's another high school example, one that can easily be translated to other grade levels. When I taught in an alternative high school, because of the small size of the school and the particular credit needs that students had, sometimes teachers would have students for more than one class per day. One year there was a twelfth-grader named Keith who acted especially surly and demonstrative, and I had him for four classes each day!

Keith was a chronic complainer. He complained about the topic in social studies, the projects in woodshop class, and the computers in computer-prep class. He complained about the fact that he had to go to P.E. at all, the sports activity chosen for each day, and the team he was on, even when his team won! He was a smart kid, but he was lonely, and he kept getting and losing after-school jobs. We got along quite well, but some days it took a lot of effort and wading through frustration on my part.

One day, I took a deep breath, decided to assume the best about him, and pulled him aside. I said, "Keith, did you know that most of what you say each day is in the form of a complaint?" Before he could offer his usual "That's stupid!" I said, "Look Keith, I care about you. You're smart, creative, athletic, and have the capacity to be a positive leader in this school and in your life. The reality, however, is that you're getting in trouble in your classes, and losing jobs and friends. I think it's in part because you complain so much and come across as negative. I want to see you succeed both at school and after you graduate, which is why I'm having this talk with you." Because he knew that I was on his side, he softened. We had a long conversation, in which he revealed some of his self-doubts and emotional challenges. I realized as we spoke that not only did Keith feel isolated, but also he was totally unaware that he was a complainer. He had just adopted a style of talking that felt safe, and he didn't realize how his negativity was affecting his life.

A Closer Look

Many teachers reason that the students say they want to change, and the proof will be in the pudding. But Mrs. Allgood knows not to stop there.

So we came up with a two-part plan. First, we established a private hand signal that I would give him when he complained in my classes (which I used quite often at first!). Second, we agreed to meet regularly to talk about his experience at home and at school, and to review his habitual complaining. While he didn't become a model student, his complaining leveled off to a more acceptable level, and he started feeling more included by others at school.

▲ ▲ ▲

All teachers address one or more of the five keys with their students. Putting them together into a more formal plan helps streamline the process, and it helps fill in the gaps when students are still not changing their behavior. The four behaviors detailed above are: putting things away, speaking out of turn, being late to school, and chronic complaining. Other behaviors that many teachers have successfully addressed with this five-keys approach include student swearing, tantrum-throwing, getting out of their seats, tattling, making off-topic comments, arguing with the teacher, and arguing with other students.

Remember that we need to model appropriate behavior as much as we can to our students. If, for example, we are constantly yelling at students to be quiet, then we send them a mixed message, and they respond with mixed behaviors.

How Do I Use These Strategies with the Limited Time I Have?

This process is labor intensive, and takes a lot of time and energy from the teacher. But it's worth it if we can help kids turn their behaviors around. One strategy is to start with the one student who most adversely affects the rest of the class. Often if one or two key students begin to engage in a positive way, the whole feeling in the class changes for the better.

What if My Student Doesn't Want to Change?

Most students will admit they want to change if we assume the best about them as we speak to them. We may have to wade through the noise in their heads ("I want ice cream and cake for dinner.") to find what their hearts are saying ("I need to eat vegetables.").

In our approach, we can frame the conversation in terms of power. Students want power and control in their lives. Impulsive behavior, for example, is a sign of a lack of power, a lack of self-control. Or, we can frame the conversation in terms of the practical: "Mark, do you really want to keep getting in trouble? I didn't think so...." If a student still won't admit that he wants to change, then we can assume it anyway: "Let's work together as if this does matter to you, and let's see what happens." It can still work.

Mrs. Allgood says

> Start with the one student who most adversely affects the rest of the class.

The key is for us to drop into our hearts, bypassing the noises in our heads of "why bother," and "it won't help," and "it's too much work." We speak directly to our student's heart, bypassing the noises of resistance he might be hearing in his head.

Our aptitude at this type of conversation will grow over time. Our interpersonal skills come sharply into focus, as we wend our way in to our students' hearts, skirting around and under their defenses, and reminding them not only that are they responsible, but also that they are respected and welcome. By itself, this heart-to-heart connection can work wonders. When used with the five keys for permanent change, magic can happen.

Additional Strategies

The Follow-Up Conversation — Three Keys for Temporary Change

The five keys aren't always possible. Time is short, the student is reactive, and/or we are too focused elsewhere. If this is the case, then we can try this simpler approach: have a private conversation with the student after he has experienced his consequence. This conversation should happen after the "dust has settled," and he is receptive. While it is not as thorough as the five keys, it can help to improve student behavior, at least temporarily.

In your conversation, the following three things should happen, in any order:

▲ The student tells the teacher what his misbehavior was.
▲ The student describes what appropriate behavior should look and sound like.
▲ The teacher cleans the slate, creating or reestablishing a positive connection with the student, welcoming him back into the classroom community.

This follow-up conversation can be quick, and while not a guarantee that change will stick, it often can make a huge difference in disarming chronic student misbehavior. It helps the student to look squarely at the choices he was making and the choices he can make in the future, and it helps him to remember that the teacher is on his side. If time is too short for all three steps, the teacher can do the talking in steps one and two, telling the student what his behavior was and what it should be in the future. For example:

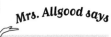

Mrs. Allgood says

"Let's work together as if this does matter to you, and let's see what happens."

"Mark, yesterday you earned a consequence because you disrupted the guest speaker by getting out of your seat and bothering Maria, even after I asked you to stop. We have another guest speaker coming tomorrow. When she's here, please stay in your seat and focus the whole time. I want you to know that I'm glad you're here, and I'm looking forward to working with you on your project later."

The most important of the three steps is number three. The positive connection between student and teacher is often what it takes to short-circuit chronic student misbehavior. A combination of firm (using consequences) and soft (nurturing a positive connection) is often enough to help kids turn their behavior around.

Use Writing

One option is to have students fill out a self-reflection form when they are serving a time-out or a visit to the office. The form can ask them several key questions, such as:

▲ What happened?
▲ How did you feel?
▲ What did you do?
▲ What are you going to do next time?

Another writing option is a student-generated action plan for changing behavior. Questions can include:

▲ What do you need to change?
▲ What's the cause?
▲ What's your solution, and what are the steps involved?
▲ How will you practice those steps?
▲ What type of support do you need?
▲ How will you keep track of your own progress?
▲ How will you know when the problem has been solved?

Online Toolbox

Sample forms you can use.

These forms won't necessarily end conflict, but they will allow the student some reflection time in which he can slow down and be more prepared to squarely and positively address his behavior.

Students with Attention Deficit Hyperactivity Disorder (ADHD)

Although there are several types of ADHD,[7] the ones that teachers deal with the most are ADHD inattentive type and ADHD hyperactive type. They are different, and require different approaches; neither provides a one-size-fits-all approach. My appreciation goes to Maryln Appelbaum, author of *How to Handle the Hard to Handle Student, K-5*,[8] and Rick Curwin, Allen Mendler, and Brian Mendler, authors of *Discipline with Dignity*,[9] for their insightful contributions in this area.

For students who have **inattentive type** ADHD, the approach is to minimize distractions.

Private carrel. If Mark gets distracted during independent work, make a study carrel using two large manila folders. They can be opened, taped together, and placed on his desk to make a screen.[10]

Seating. Seat Mark in a place with minimal distractions. He may be distracted by the noises of the heater, air conditioner, or hallway traffic. He may be distracted by viewing the playground out the window, by the student work that's posted on the side of the room, or the clothing of the students in front of him. Curwin and Mendler suggest that the best placement for Mark is in the wings of the room. Otherwise, if Mark is in the back, he'll be distracted by kids sitting in front of him; if he's in the front, his distractions will be noticed by everyone and grow into their own class distractions.[11]

> **A Closer Look**
>
> The positive connection between student and teacher is often what it takes to short-circuit chronic student misbehavior.

Self-monitoring lists. To help kids stay focused, assist them in organizing their work into small, doable chunks, with lists they can check off or sticky note reminders they can remove when each task is complete.

For students who present with characteristics of **hyperactive** ADHD, there are numerous approaches that can help. The underlying assumption with all of these strategies is that hyperactive kids need to move. The key is to find ways that they can move that don't disrupt the learning environment.

Soft surface. Take an old mouse pad or piece of carpet, and place it on Mark's desk, so that when he taps his pencil, it's quiet, and doesn't disrupt other learners.

Velcro®. Affix a small piece of Velcro® to the side of Mark's desk. It's out of the line of sight, makes no noise, and he can scratch it all day.

Errands. Give Mark a class job that requires him to be physical. It can be organizing the book shelves, setting up lab tables, taking notes to the office, dropping off supplies to another teacher's classroom, or collecting and passing out papers. Though it might seem that Mark can't handle the job, paradoxically, he often can. And when he gets a chance to move, he can focus all the more.

Music Stands. Put a few music stands around the perimeter of the room, so that students like Mark, who prefer standing, can place their materials on the stand. This allows them to be on their feet instead of sitting during lessons, and therefore more likely to be able to pay attention.

Two desks. Allow Mark to use two desks. He can move from one to the other at designated times or when he has completed a certain amount of work. This will help keep his movement in the context of class participation, making it less likely to become a class distraction.

Bungee cords. Safely connect bungee cords or elastic exercise bands around the four legs of Mark's chair, about four or five inches above the floor. Mark can then push to his heart's content against the elastic with his feet. The elastic makes no sound, and can't be seen by other students.

Kick ball. Deflate a kick ball so that it's about 10% filled with air. Have Mark sit on it. Instead of jumping out of his seat, he will slide back and forth on the ball. Similarly, provide a "balance ball" for students, giving them the option of sitting on the ball or in their regular chair, at their discretion.

In addition, refer to Chapter 12, "Lesson Design" for numerous brain-compatible movement strategies for the whole class.

Student Diet and Behavior

Diet is often the elephant in the classroom that people don't talk about. If kids change what they eat, their behavior and academic performance will change as well. Dr. Stephen Schoenthaler, a Professor of Criminal Justice at the California State University in Stanislaus, has researched the link between diet and behavior, IQ, and school performance. He says, "Having a bad diet right now is a better predictor of future violence than past violent behavior."[12]

One research project focused on some 200 schools in Wisconsin, where fried and other less-than-healthy foods were replaced with fresh fruits, vegetables, and healthy meat dishes.[13] A particular school in the study, Central Alternative High School in Appleton, Wisconsin, reported compelling results.

> Grades are up, truancy is no longer a problem, arguments are rare, and teachers are able to spend their time teaching. Principal LuAnn Coenen is amazed at the change she has seen in her school.

Students who previously had been headed for trouble have turned their lives around, according to Dr. Thomas Scullen, Superintendent of the Appleton Area School District.[14]

But food habits seem so intractable. What can teachers do to make a difference? They can start by bringing awareness to the issue.

Teachers can give parents, teachers, and students a copy of a handout describing the above study, or show them the related video. They can talk with students about the relationship between diet, health, and attitude. Ask them what they eat each day, and calculate the amount of sugar that's in each item. In addition, students can research online what studies say about food and behavior, memory, and school performance. They can investigate long-term savings to schools that invest in healthy food, such as reduction in vandalism, security costs, and suspensions. Finally, students can research the connection between government subsidies and the low costs of junk food and fast food, and how that can adversely affect the health and academic performance of children in poverty.

Online Toolbox

Information and video on the Wisconsin diet study.

Behavior Contracts

Teachers can create individual behavior contracts for students that are focused on changing one student behavior at a time.[15] The contracts should be signed by the student, his parents, and the teacher. They can be as detailed and "behavioral" as we want. The focus is to break appropriate behaviors into smaller, doable parts, and to monitor and build upon the successes the student shows. Tying success on the contract to privileges at home and/or school can work well. Tying success to his long-term goals can also be a winner, because the student connects his big-picture desires to the new behavioral skills that he is developing.

Behavior contracts are particularly successful if the students have a hand in designing them, and if they include a timeline and/or rubric for students to monitor their progress.

Online Toolbox

Behavior contract samples.

Omission Training

Omission Training, developed by classroom management consultant Fred Jones,[16] is a strategy that can work well with Mark when he is sabotaging a group-reward system in your class. The strategy can work so well that you may consider setting up a group-reward system for the entire class, just in order to benefit Mark!

Let's say that you have in place a group reward, such as time for an educational game on Fridays (Fred Jones uses "PAT" — known as "Preferred Activity Time"). Throughout the week, students earn extra minutes toward the game by completing transitions efficiently, or behaving well throughout class time. With such a reward system, if Mark is disruptive or doesn't finish the transition, the whole class suffers. Mark then becomes the brunt of student complaints and anger. He also has power — the power to thwart the class group reward.

The difference with Omission Training is that Mark's disruptions cannot hurt the class. If everyone else makes the transition efficiently or behaves attentively for the designated amount of time, then the whole class — including Mark — will earn extra minutes for Friday's activity. What's inventive with Omission Training is that if Mark also succeeds in these (or other) particular behaviors, then the entire class earns even more time on Friday. For example: "Class, you were able to transition from the lab tables to your desks in under forty-five seconds. This earns you two extra minutes for Friday's game. Congratulations. Mark was able to transition in time as well, earning the class an extra minute for Friday. Let's everybody give a round of applause for Mark for helping out the class."

A Closer Look

Behavior contracts ideally should be focused on one behavior at a time.

Note: You may be thinking that this singles out Mark. I agree. But Mark is the kind of student who is already singled out — the rest of the students know he has challenges, and don't question his unique status. Omission Training is designed for this type of student.

This strategy removes Mark's power to hurt the class, and replaces it with a power to help the class. Students soon begin to support and encourage Mark to behave well. He is no longer seen as an outcast, and his good behavior is tied to his positive connections with his peers. Jones says, "If I needed a behavioral program to make an unpopular child popular, I would immediately pick Omission Training. I have seen it bring an outcast child into the middle of the class sociogram in two weeks!"

The details for implementing Omission Training are online at www. educationworld.com/a_curr/columnists/jones/jones018.shtml. They are also in Fred Jones's book, *Tools for Teaching* (www.fredjones.com).

Group Reward for Individual Student Behavior

A related strategy is for the teacher to randomly draw a student's name card, and place that card in an envelope at the beginning of class. At the end of class, the teacher looks at the name on the card. If that student's behavior was exemplary during class, then the teacher reveals his name, and the entire class receives a reward for that one student's behavior.

The benefits of this strategy are that the student only has his name revealed if he has done well. Further, the teacher can, if she wants to, "rig the game" so that when Mark (who chronically misbehaves) has a good day, she can "randomly" reveal his card from the envelope, ensuring that he is connected to his classmates in a positive light.

The Village Intervention

From Grace:

> Kenesha was a student in my tenth-grade world history class. Her mother was in prison and her father was deceased, so she lived in a group home for teenage girls. After threatening another history teacher and intimidating several students, Kenesha was transferred into my class about a month into the school year. On her first day, she walked into my class about ten minutes late and announced "Kenesha here now, b***es! Yah...you know you better watch yourself." When I asked her to step outside to have a private conversation with me, she replied, "Nuh-uh. I'm in this class. So now you got to deal." I again asked her to step out. She replied, "This is bulls**t!" and stormed out; she didn't come back until the next day.
>
> Her behavior didn't improve much over the first few weeks. Each day she would pick a rule to break or an argument to have. When I calmly asked her to follow the rule, such as sitting in her seat or entering class quietly, she would curse and threaten, and eventually storm out of class. I spoke with her social worker, her counselor, the assistant principal, and even tried a behavior plan. But with Kenesha, nothing worked. Not even a little. Not even for a little while.
>
> During this time, I remained calm on the outside. But inside I felt angry, helpless, and close to giving up on Kenesha. I found myself hoping that she would be absent, as I didn't want to have

to face her storm. Ultimately, however, I decided to assume the best about Kenesha. She needed help. Her behaviors came from some unspeakable experiences that no child should ever have to go through. But what kind of help can a public school teacher be to a student who has a history of serious psychological and physical abuse, who is violent and unstable, oppositional and intimidating?

I resolved that Kenesha was reachable and teachable, but that she needed multiple layers of help from multiple adults in and out of school. The staff got together, and we came up with an approach we called "The Village Intervention." Based on a program called "The Lightning Club," created by educator Pete Hall (www. educationhall.com), it made a big, positive impact on Kenesha's outlook and behavior. The steps we created are listed below, followed by a summary of how they helped Kenesha in particular.

▲ ▲ ▲

1. **Assume the best about the student.** Like Kenesha, when Mark misbehaves, he is calling for help. Quite possibly he has suffered severe, traumatic experiences that cause him to attempt to feel safe through aggressive school behaviors. Even so, beneath his bravado, he wants to learn.

2. **Collect and analyze data.** Look at Mark's cumulative file, his test scores, and his record of referrals, suspensions, detentions, and arrests. Talk with his current and past teachers, parents or guardians, counselor(s), social worker(s), group home liaison, probation officer, and anyone else who might have information or insights. Identify common misbehaviors and triggers. And then, identify strengths, personal interests, and possible positive incentives. In Kenesha's case, it turns out that she was interested in fashion design. No matter what your student "Mark" tells you, your team can always come up with incentives to match his interests.

3. **Make an offer.** One adult meets with Mark. This should be an adult who has relatively good rapport with him. She expresses her concern for him as a human being, rather than expressing concern for his performance in school. She shares that a group of adults has been discussing how to find ways to help him have more ease and success at school. Then she asks Mark if he would be willing to meet with the group to help them provide the support that he needs.

4. **Circle the wagons**. Meet with all the stakeholders. This includes teachers, administrators, parents or guardians, counselors and caseworkers, and Mark. Each person gets a chance to express concern and caring for Mark, which stimulates a reality check that not only is he seen, but also everyone cares for him and has not given up on him. Discuss with him what triggers his behavior, what can be done to minimize the triggers, and what in his life interests him. Make sure that someone is present whose primary role is to advocate for Mark — a person who is willing to intervene if the discussion starts to focus on what is "wrong" with Mark instead of how the village can adjust to support Mark's needs.

> When I calmly asked her to follow the rule, such as sitting in her seat or entering class quietly, she would curse and threaten, and eventually storm out of class.

5. **Create a plan**. After Mark leaves the meeting, decide what accommodations can be made, and what incentives can be offered. Create short- and long-term goals. Keep them specific and achievable. Clarify to teachers that it might not be in Mark's best interest to require him to demonstrate appropriate behavior across the board at first. Recognize that he may have multiple behaviors to address, such as:

- ▲ coming to class on time;
- ▲ bringing his materials to class;
- ▲ keeping his comments on task;
- ▲ keeping his language G-rated;
- ▲ not intimidating others in class;
- ▲ remaining in his seat during direct instruction;
- ▲ completing classwork;
- ▲ completing and turning in homework;
- ▲ addressing the teacher with appropriate language;
- ▲ reducing or eliminating arguing, threats, and complaints.

Nonetheless, try limiting your focus to only a few of these behaviors, and let the others go. Choose the problems that he can realistically address — and which if addressed, will immediately tone down his aggressive behavior, thus providing him with a sense of accomplishment. Perhaps, for example, the team might put his focus on coming in quietly to class, sitting in his assigned seat, and raising his hand in order to speak, even if he comes in late and unprepared. Along these lines, identify specific,

> I resolved that Kenesha was reachable and teachable, but that she needed multiple layers of help from multiple adults in and out of school.

observable benchmark behaviors for Mark, so that it will be clear when his goals have been met.

Create tiered, staggered incentives that will encourage Mark to change his behavior. As Mark reaches a goal, provide him with an incentive. The bigger the goal, the bigger the incentive, starting with short-term goals for behavior that last a short time (less than a school day, and often less than a class period).

Make sure that Mark earns an incentive on the first day. Incentives only work if students can taste them and thus begin to internalize the connection between their choices and the fruits that follow.

With Mark's help, identify which adults will be Mark's "go-to" people in and out of school. They should have decent rapport with Mark; he should be told that they will be tracking his progress daily, and that he can go to them for support or a time-out.

6. **Enlist the student.** One or two adults then meet with Mark to describe the plan. In this meeting, allow Mark to offer alternatives to the benchmarks and the incentives. The most important thing is that he buys into the approach, and has a motivation for being successful.

7. **Outside support.** If possible and appropriate, ensure that Mark has access to psychological counseling. Often, students who need The Village Intervention have a very low sense of self-esteem. Counterintuitively, this can get magnified initially, as the team members share their caring and concern. A student might feel unworthy, or experience pain from trauma that can begin to surface. Having a professional on hand with whom Mark can speak on a regular basis can make all the difference.

8. **Implement with consistency.** This is often the hardest part of the intervention. Getting everyone on the same page for a long period of time can be challenging, particularly when teachers have a broad range of approaches and tolerances.

The Village Intervention can tone down student aggression immediately, and set the stage for long-term permanent change. Even if a student doesn't earn his long-term goals, he can experience immediate behavioral and emotional benefits, as he sees a path for easing his school experience.

When faced with a group of caring adults, Kenesha was able to begin to drop her defenses. In the "circle the wagons" meeting, she eventually let on that she was interested in fashion. This helped craft long-term incentives for her improved behavior. She wanted to have a fashion show at school, and imagined what it would be like for a seamstress to create an outfit based on one of her designs. The team suggested that she might like to spend a day at a local fashion design college, sitting in on classes and talking with students and teachers there.

The staff came up with small steps for Kenesha to initially earn small incentives, such as becoming an aide for an art class that she enjoyed. She did "visit" her old behaviors occasionally, and was suspended once during the intervention. However, the staff looked at this as part of her growth process. And indeed, her attitude and conduct markedly improved over time. She felt safer, and was more able to touch a place inside where she did care, did feel cared for, and did want to participate. At the end of the year, she had earned a series of small incentives, and was still in the running for the bigger-ticket goals. What seemed like inevitable expulsion was transformed, as the whole school "village" intervened on her behalf.

Wise-Apple Advice

A Last Word on When Consequences Don't Work

The common threads among all approaches in this chapter are simple:

▲ Make positive connections with students.

▲ Assume the best — the students want to make a change.

▲ Break the change into simpler and simpler steps.

▲ Give students a chance to reflect on their choices.

▲ Provide students the chance to take responsibility for their choices.

▲ Check progress throughout the process.

▲ Provide support along the way.

Not coincidentally, these approaches are the same whether we are teaching content, procedures, or behavior. Once we internalize the pattern of these approaches, there is no limit to the creative solutions we can discover in working with our students.

15

MAKING
CHANGES

"And that is how change happens.
One gesture. One person.
One moment at a time."

— LIBBA BRAY

Ｇ ROWING IN THE TEACHING PROFESSION involves regularly and consistently making changes to improve our craft and better serve our students. This can be challenging for even the best-intentioned teachers. This chapter debunks myths about making changes, and offers simple steps for deciding what changes to make, how and when to make them, and how to stay in inner authority while doing so. Four key questions are addressed and answered:

- ▲ How can I make a change once school has started?
- ▲ What change should I make first?
- ▲ Am I ready to make the change?
- ▲ What are the steps for making the change?

Following this road map can help you feel empowered and relaxed as you make changes efficiently and with the maximum student buy-in and benefit.

How Can I Make a Change Once School Has Started?

Some teachers believe that if they don't start out the school year "on the right track," then they are doomed for the rest of the school year. Not true. Any time we want to make changes in our management system, we

We should give any major policy or procedural shift at least two weeks — ten school days — before deciding if it is working.

can. If we are concerned about what to say to our students, let's tell them the truth: "Class, it's been getting a little noisy lately, so we're going to try something new." When I student-taught my rough-and-tumble ninth-grade English class, it seemed like every two weeks I introduced "Mr. Smith's new classroom management policy!"

If we make changes to our systems in the middle of the school year, it may take longer than we think to see if they are working. If you decide to alter your tennis grip or foul shooting style in order to grow from being a good player to being a great player, then you will most likely have several rough days on the court when you first make the change.

In addition, when you introduce a change to your class, you may also experience a lull, where the novelty of the change works for a day or two, and then student resistance increases in the third or fourth day. This is similar to when a captain wants to turn her moving ship. She first has to slow down, then shift directions, and then regain her original speed. The most vulnerable capsize point is after slowing down — just at the point of turning. And the point when a change in our management system is most likely to elicit chaos is often three or four days after its implementation.

Ten School Days

Teachers make changes just like students learn — one step at a time.

We should give any major policy or procedural shift at least two weeks — ten school days — before deciding whether it is working. Success is more likely if we reinforce our new policy or procedure consistently. Remember, it takes us time to adjust — and our students even more time. By staying focused and patient, you will discover that the benefits to the change will far outweigh any concerns you had about making it.

What Change Should I Make First?

I used to have a hard time making changes in my classroom. I'd leave a staff-development workshop inspired to make seventeen different changes right away. But then I'd hit the wall. "Oh, I can't do it this week because we've got Back to School Night. Next week we've got a special field trip. The week after that, progress reports are due. Then we've got a special assembly, final exams, and parent meetings." After six weeks, I found that I hadn't implemented anything, and it was time for a new staff-development workshop. The old information would be shelved for the new information, which would go through the same process of inspiration and non-implementation.

I finally came up with a formula for making changes that has helped me and other teachers immensely:

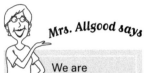

Mrs. Allgood says

We are scientists, and our classroom is our lab. By starting small with one class or situation, we can control the experiment more, and we are more likely to follow through and have success.

1. Make a list of changes you want to see, putting them in priority order.
2. Make sure that number one is doable. If it's too complicated, break it up into smaller steps, assigning a number to each step.
3. Always implement number one only.
4. Start with your favorite class (secondary) or favorite hour of the day (elementary). It's the class that's most forgiving or the time of day that's most calm and relaxed.
5. After the change is working, introduce it to the rest of your classes or the rest of your day.
6. Once it is solid throughout the day, start the process over with a new number one.

Teachers make changes just like students learn — one step at a time. With this formula, number two is never implemented; either it becomes number one, or it doesn't make it to the classroom. This can help reduce teacher stress, knowing that we only have to focus on one thing. By slowing down the agenda for change, teachers find that they actually make more permanent changes more quickly. They are often so busy that making wholesale changes can seem overwhelming and intimidating. That's why one small step at a time works. We are scientists, and our classroom is our lab. By starting small with one class or situation, we can control the experiment more, and we are more likely to follow through and have success. We make our mistakes, learn on the job, and gain confidence in a relatively controlled and safe environment, just like our students. One. Step. At. A. Time.

Am I Ready to Make the Change?

Effective classroom management is as much about who we are as what we do. It's not enough to simply have a plan. Because emotions often drive actions, we frequently need to track and care for how we feel, in order to be able to carry out the plan.

Recognize Where You are in Inner Apology

Once you've chosen a change to make, reflect on your level of inner apology about implementing the change. What are your own doubts and concerns about making the change? Are you concerned that you will feel weak (or students will see you as weak) if you admit that something in the class needs to be changed? Are you concerned that the initial resistance to the change will be overwhelming, because you are already feeling fragile or shaky? Are you concerned that the change will reduce the control you have in the classroom? Make conscious these thoughts and feelings before making the change, and you're already on the path to positive transformation.

Move Toward Inner Authority

If you are concerned that by introducing a change, the students will realize that it's been, for example, too noisy, don't worry — they already know! Assume the best. They want an environment that's more conducive to learning, creativity, and productivity. They are hoping that you'll provide the structure to make that happen. Even if they voice their resistance, you can assume that in their hearts they appreciate what you are offering.

Assume that any student resistance is simply a reflection of your own, and treat resistance and complaining kindly but firmly. Take a deep breath, and speak from your knowing, rather than from your doubts. Hold your ground internally with any noise in your head that says that you can't succeed or shouldn't try. Let what is needed in the classroom be your "true north." As you do this, in most cases, student resistance will soften quickly.

Online Toolbox

Samples of student resistance and teacher responses.

Embrace the worst while assuming the best. Anticipate what types of student resistance you might encounter. Will they complain? If so, what will they say? What "buttons" of yours might they push? Decide in advance what, if anything, you might say or do if the students resist. Focus on the benefits of the change, rather than what didn't work before.

Try practicing what you'll say in front of a mirror or on video. Ask for help. Practice with a colleague or mentor teacher. Or enlist a colleague to try the same thing at the same time in her class. You can support each other to overcome obstacles and brainstorm modifications. Remember that any change is simply a series of small steps. Take them one at a time.

What are the Steps for Making the Change?

You've decided on a change you want to make and a time of day or class in which to do it. You've reflected internally, and are in relative inner authority about making the change. Now what? Below is a road map for how to teach the change to your students.

1. Introduction

Inform your students of the new policy or procedure. As an alternative, (from inner authority) you can include your students in a discussion of the new change, in order to get them on board and possibly elicit their suggestions for alternatives that could work as well. Be sure not to blame your students for why things weren't going well — that will tend to add to their resistance. Simply let them know that you're introducing something new that will help make things better.

Mrs. Allgood says

Let what is needed in the classroom be your "true north." Speak from your knowing, rather than from your doubts.

2. Nonverbal Reinforcement

Describe verbally what needs to happen, and use nonverbals — visuals, hand signals, sound signals, and/or music — to reinforce the change. (See Chapter 8, "Teaching Procedures.")

3. Modeling

Show the students the new behavior by modeling it and/or have a small group of students model it. If you like, have students model both the ideal and not-so-ideal versions. The humor that ensues can be great for getting student buy-in and relieving tension.

4. Practice

Have the entire class practice the procedure. Some procedures that require practice are:

▲ entering the classroom quietly and getting to work right away;
▲ moving desks into and out of groups;
▲ responding efficiently to the "quiet" signal;
▲ lining up;
▲ getting ready for dismissal.

Consider foregoing holding students accountable at first. They are learning and/or practicing, and may need room to make mistakes and try things out. As described in Chapter 13, "Rules and Consequences," an effective basketball coach knows that her players need to practice foul shooting regularly, regardless of their level of success during games. Practice, rather than consequences, is often the key, particularly when you are introducing something new.

After each attempt by the students, de-brief the practice. What worked? What could be improved? Have them practice again. And perhaps again.

5. Accountability

After the first attempts by the class, clarify the group and individual consequences for following or not following the new procedure. You may use your usual consequences. You may choose to use a group reward. Or you may use consequences specific to that practice. For example, if a couple of students aren't "getting it," assess if they need more practice with the group, or if they need to meet with you to practice privately. Consider offering them a choice between the two options.

6. Check for Understanding

Ensure that students understand the procedure and their accountability for it throughout your lesson, from the introduction through the modeling and the practice. Just as you use a variety of ways to check for understanding of content, mix up how you check for understanding of the new procedure. Use a timer if you are asking for smoother transitions. Play soft music if you are asking for quiet, so that the students can hear the music the whole time they are practicing. Assess student knowledge through a class discussion, a journal assignment, or a simple quiz. Ask Sally, for example, to describe the new procedure; then ask Niyesha and Mark if they agree, and if there is anything they want to add to Sally's description.

A Closer Look

Practice, rather than consequences, is often the key, particularly when you are introducing something new.

7. Ten Days

Use and reinforce the procedure for at least ten school days. Apply consequences if necessary. Practice again if necessary. Modify if necessary. Continue to check in with students. Offer genuine praise and appreciation, publicly and privately, to the group and to individuals, when they do it well. In many cases, the fact that you are emphasizing and encouraging the change consistently is enough to make it happen.

8. Reflect

How did the process of implementation work with your one class or one time of day? What can you replicate or do differently when you introduce it to the rest of your day?

9. Make it the New Culture

Once the new change is working well, implement it with all of your classes and/or throughout your day. Thus, what started as a small step with one class or situation has become part of a new culture in your classroom.

Online Toolbox

Reflection tool: "Implementation Trouble-Shooting Checklist" for helping to organize your thinking and plan for future changes. Plus, sample lessons of teachers introducing new procedures."

▲ ▲ ▲

Making Changes Schoolwide

Staff meetings can be used to help all teachers make changes. The goal is for teachers to choose and implement any new idea/strategy/technique they are interested in (or learned from a recent workshop or training).

Staff Meeting 1

Teachers first brainstorm possible changes or improvements they would like to see in their classes. Next, they self-select small groups based on similar goals. All teachers from each group agree to try the chosen technique in their classrooms for one hour a day for five consecutive days.

For example, in an elementary school, one group decides they want to increase the efficiency of students' getting seated quietly and politely on the carpet, such that they are ready to learn. This group decides to try implementing a procedure using a "ready-to-learn " image (from Chapter 8, "Teaching Procedures").

Or in a secondary school, one group of teachers decides that they want to try breaking up their direct instruction into twelve-minute chunks, with engagement strategies utilized in between chunks. They decide to try having students create summaries and/or highlights, both aloud with a partner and in writing, for one minute between these mini-lectures (from Chapter 12, "Lesson Design").

During the next five days, one hour per day for elementary and one class per day in secondary, each teacher tries her group's strategy, making modifications and adjustments as necessary to make it work with her students, and to counter any resistance. She also notes her own resistance to the change, and reflects on the simplest steps she can take to counter that resistance.

Staff Meeting 2

Teachers meet in their small groups to discuss their findings from the first week of implementation. They share successes, challenges, and modifications. Teachers commit to another week of implementation, making use of suggestions from their group.

Staff Meeting 3

Teachers share with the whole staff how the implementation worked, and what they plan to keep and spread to more of their instructional day. For the next week, teachers integrate what they have already begun into their other classes or the rest of their school day.

Staff Meeting 4

The cycle begins again, with new groups and new strategies to implement.

Note: This four-week process also can be organized around one change that the entire staff agrees upon. In this case, the small groups would be based on departments or grade levels, rather than on different changes that various teachers want to implement.

Wise-Apple Advice

The Last Word on Making Changes

Making changes can seem overwhelming. However, we can rapidly improve our teaching and aid student learning, all the while staying centered and relaxed in the process. All we have to do is assume that students want the changes that are needed, and then go step-by-step. One. Step. At. A. Time.

16

STRATEGIES FOR ADMINISTRATORS AND TEACHER LEADERS

> *"The main thing is to keep the main thing the main thing!"*
>
> — STEVEN COVEY

S TUDENT SUCCESS REQUIRES SUPPORT, not only from classroom teachers, but from teacher leaders as well. If you are a school administrator, this chapter is for you. It offers approaches and strategies to help you support your teachers to support their students. It's also valuable for mentors, district-level administrators, and other teacher leaders. The goal is to invigorate teachers to empower and improve student learning, streamline transitions, and increase instructional time, at the same time decreasing referrals and suspensions, and improving the overall classroom and school climate.

Every strategy in *Conscious Classroom Management* can be shared with your teachers. This can be done in casual individual conversations, coaching meetings, staff meetings, follow-up evaluation conferences, and/or faculty bulletins. This chapter highlights a few of those strategies, as well as pointing to other approaches that are unique to your role.

Online Toolbox

An extensive chapter-by-chapter facilitator guide to help with book studies for teachers and student teachers.

As you read, you may find that many of the strategies that assist teachers to support their students also work for you to support your teachers. The parallels between the job descriptions are many. For example, as a school administrator, you have the challenge of being in charge, even as you seek to work collaboratively with your teachers. How do you walk that line and elicit trust, while at the same time knowing that the "buck" stops with you? This is a similar challenge for teachers with their students, and is addressed throughout this book.

Below you will find titles of chapters in the book, followed by strategies and approaches from each that can work for you. Consider this summary as a buffet: if you like an idea, then put it on your plate. If not, then check out the next one. Many of these suggestions stand alone, and others require a closer reading of the chapter to which they are connected.

Assume the Best

▲ Work with teachers to "go under the wave" of student resistance, deescalating tension in the way they interact with their students.

▲ Assume the best about teachers' most resistant students — that their behavior is just a request for support in their learning — and let those assumptions be contagious to your staff.

▲ Understand the need for teachers to sometimes "vent" about their students. And, remind teachers of the struggles their students often face, encouraging teachers to focus on the positive as well. Ask them to follow their hearts so as to connect with the hearts of their students.

▲ Discuss with teachers what drew them to the teaching profession, and invite them to share highlights from their days or weeks that support their visions.

▲ Assume the best about your teacher, even when she seems resistant to change or to feedback. She is doing the best that she knows how. (Like Mrs. Meanswell, she "means well.") From this orientation, you can approach your teacher with kindness, even as you offer specific suggestions to help her provide the best for her students. She will be much more likely to listen, engage, and make the changes she needs to make, as you connect with her heart, as well as her head.

Inner Authority

▲ Make "inner authority" a common phrase in your school, so teachers can talk about and reflect on this (often invisible) quality, and how it changes from situation to situation.

▲ Refer to inner authority when coaching teachers, particularly after you've observed them and noticed that they need support in this area.

▲ In staff meetings, ask teachers to make a list of situations that tend to challenge their inner authority, and then divide the list into two parts: things they can change, and things they can't. Then invite them to focus their efforts on changing what can be changed and accepting what can't. This will inspire reflection and target their energies more productively.

Mrs. Allgood says

Assume the best about your teacher, even when she seems resistant to change or to feedback.

▲ Remind teachers that inner authority is not rigid or harsh. It arises out of assuming the best about students and focusing primarily on what they need, maximizing every interaction into a teachable moment.

Ask for Help

▲ When appropriate, share your own challenges and successes with your teachers.

▲ Encourage them to seek support from you, and from one another.

▲ Infuse a sense of kindness and teamwork into your staff meetings and day-to-day interactions with teachers.

▲ Elicit opinions from teachers early and often, and take advantage of their wisdom and perspectives.

▲ Devote time during each staff meeting for one teacher to share one successful lesson, or for teachers to "show and tell" great lesson ideas with one another. This could be in the form of oral reports or in a "give-one-get-one mixer" during the meeting. When a teacher shares her work with colleagues, her isolation in the classroom is diminished, her self-esteem blossoms, she grows as a professional, and other teachers benefit from her ideas.

▲ When you can, share decision-making power with teachers or teacher committees.

▲ If one of your teachers is having difficulty resolving an issue with a particular student or parent, help her to strategize positive solutions, remind her to document conversations and interactions, and offer to step in if appropriate.

▲ In your conversations with teachers, consider including the question "how do/did you feel in that situation?", rather than asking only "what did you do?" or "what are you going to do?"

▲ When possible, instead of simply telling a teacher what needs to happen, elicit her ideas first and give them full consideration. This helps not only to identify the merit of her ideas, but also to acknowledge the fact that she has ownership of them. She will be more motivated to follow through on whatever action plan is identified.

▲ If you do have suggestions, provide two or three choices for her — as opposed to ten or twenty, or as opposed to none.

▲ Encourage teachers, particularly your beginning teachers, when they feel challenged or overwhelmed.

Got Stress?

▲ Periodically remind teachers of one or two strategies in this chapter in the book.

▲ If you have a faculty bulletin, ask different teachers to write a "stress-reduction strategy of the month."

▲ Routinely express genuine appreciation for your teachers.

▲ Consider asking teachers to share their appreciations of each other with each other.

▲ Map out the times during the school year when teachers have extra workloads, such as back-to-school night, parent-conference week, or when grades are due. Do your best to schedule extra teacher assignments — such as committee meetings or department reports — outside of these dates in the calendar.

▲ Encourage teachers to make the staff room a lively, warm, and inviting place.

▲ Form a committee to offer stress-reducing activities for staff members before and after school, such as yoga, aerobics, or walking/hiking.

▲ During periods of high stress, ask teachers, "When you think about all of the things that we are trying to do, what are you most worried about or concerned about? What kind of support could make this go more smoothly?" Often, you'll find that two minutes of attentive listening is all it takes to help alleviate teacher stress.

▲ Administrators' job descriptions are just as challenging — and as infinite — as teachers'. Many of the strategies in this chapter will work for you as well. Take a few minutes to

Wise-Apple Advice

Offer a mini-lesson in a staff meeting on teacher anger and how to keep it from influencing teacher-student interactions.

find two or three strategies that you can implement on a regular basis to calm and center yourself, and thus remember that you are a human being, not a human doing.

Holding Our Ground

▲ Support teachers by reminding them to focus on what students need, even if it may sometimes ruffle student feathers.

▲ In staff meetings, role-play (or have teachers role-play) different situations where a teacher kindly and firmly holds her ground with a student request, delaying explanations until later. Invite teachers to discuss what feelings arise in those situations, and offer encouragement and guidance, as needed. Remind your teachers that a key to holding their ground lies in going under the wave of student resistance, and calmly asserting what is needed.

▲ In situations where you need to hold your ground with your teachers, do your best to go under the wave yourself in your interactions with them.

▲ When necessary, be willing to hold teachers accountable for their choices and actions.

▲ Teach (or have a teacher teach) a mini-lesson in a staff meeting on teacher anger and how to keep it from influencing teacher-student interaction. Refer to strategies in this chapter.

Positive Connections

▲ Remind teachers to use the Two-by-Ten Strategy with their struggling students.[1]

▲ Use the Two-by-Ten with your teachers. Seek out the teachers in your school with whom you need to build a stronger connection, and try to find common ground outside of pedagogical, administrative, or school or district issues. By engaging in conversations about mutual interests outside of school, and by showing genuine interest and curiosity about another, a deeper connection can be made. This can benefit the connection with one teacher, and affect the entire school culture.

▲ Find occasions to laugh with your teachers. Infuse humor in staff meetings or announcements.

▲ Remember to sincerely appreciate your teachers. Look for the best in them, and acknowledge it often.

▲ Offer to take over teachers' classes and do mini-lessons for students. This can be done as a way to model teaching strategies for teachers or to give teachers a chance to take a needed break. Teaching kids directly can also be rejuvenating for you.

▲ Spend time with teachers outside of the school day and/or off campus.

▲ Give teachers choices whenever possible. Seek to empower them, and watch the magic happen in your school environment.

▲ Smile often.

▲ Listen well.

Teaching Procedures

▲ Challenge your teachers to try to "over-teach" procedures. Most likely, the first thing they'll notice is that things run more smoothly and efficiently in their classes.

▲ Have them report their findings about this in staff meetings.

▲ Form a committee to decide which procedures should be schoolwide, and which should be up to individual teacher discretion. Possibilities for schoolwide procedures include visuals and rubrics for readiness to learn, dismissal, school rules, lining up, walking in the hall, and the wall of readiness. In addition, bathroom use, tardies, sound signals, hand signals, finished-early signs, and music for passing time are often used schoolwide.

▲ With schoolwide procedures, ensure that reminders (visuals and/or rubrics) are posted in appropriate places around the school.

▲ Ask all teachers to have a clear procedure for when students finish early in class.

▲ Ask teachers what their quiet signal is. Remind them to use it consistently.

▲ Ask teachers to consider timing their in-class transitions in order to get a solid sense of the amount of time that transitions actually take.

▲ Do classroom walk-throughs, looking at how the desks are set up. Suggest that teachers create gaps that allow them to easily walk to and teach from the back and sides of the room.

Consistency

▲ Communicate to your teachers that consistency within the classroom is key to making management effective, even if other teachers do things differently in their classes. Consistency throughout the school is a bonus, but not a necessity.

▲ Allow teachers to have some input into the across-the-school procedures and policies.

▲ Give teachers options within schoolwide policies. For example, if teachers are to use a quiet signal, let them each choose the one that works for them.

▲ Be open to teacher-created consequences that are alternatives to the standard school consequences.

▲ Model non-verbal communication (gestures, tone, and volume) when speaking to teachers in staff meetings.

▲ Help teachers to implement a "no-arguing-with-the-ref" policy in their classrooms.

▲ Emphasize hand-raising consistency in classrooms in situations where teachers ask their students to raise their hands. Consider printing up an image of a hand (or other appropriate symbol) and placing in on the back walls of classrooms, to remind teachers to focus on hand-raising consistency that is applied equitably to all students.

▲ Ideally, observe teachers often throughout the school year, both formally and informally.

Wise-Apple Advice

Form a committee to decide which procedures should be schoolwide, and which should be up to individual teacher discretion.

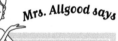

Mrs. Allgood says

Create a document that addresses questions on the "Before-School Checklist" and distribute it to all newly hired teachers.

Getting Ready and the First Week of School

▲ Point teachers new to the school to this chapter in the book as soon as they are hired or transferred.

▲ Create a document that addresses/answers some of the questions on the "Before-School Checklist" and distribute it to all newly hired teachers. Print copies of the "Before-School Checklist" from our website.

▲ Encourage teacher leaders to assign buddies to newly hired or transferred teachers, based on department or grade level.

▲ Create a "bank" of syllabi, parent letters, and lesson plan ideas that teachers in your school use early in each year. Provide new teachers access to the bank so as to assist their own planning.

▲ Offer to review and give feedback about new teachers' lessons for the first week of school.

▲ Offer to review and give feedback about new teachers' rules and consequence plans for the first week of school.

Lesson Design

▲ Model brain-compatible strategies in your staff meetings, including teacher sharing and teacher movement. Debrief the strategies so that teachers can reflect on the benefits.

▲ In staff meetings and staff bulletins, highlight teachers' successes in promoting student empowerment and project-based learning.

▲ Talk to teachers about their plans for addressing make-up work for absent students.

▲ Emphasize teacher sharing of specific and formative feedback with students, not just the recording of grades.

▲ Consider setting aside five minutes in a staff meeting to ask teachers to do a mindfulness practice.

Rules and Consequences

Wise-Apple Advice

Clarify your role in the discipline chain — what it is and is not — and define your expectations. Listen to your teachers as to the type of support they are hoping to receive from you.

▲ Create an environment where teachers feel comfortable talking about classroom management issues with one another and with you. This allows your staff to collectively de-stigmatize the issue, and also invites a sharing of successes and challenges — whether in full staff meetings, small-group staff meetings (by grade level or department, for example), or one-on-one conversations with you.

▲ Involve teachers and students in creating schoolwide rules and consequences. Offer tailored choices for individual teachers within school policies, such as which in-class consequences they prefer.

▲ Meet with individual teachers about their classroom management plans, and ensure that their rules and consequences are aligned with school and district policies and values.

▲ Look for consequences that teachers don't use or aren't comfortable using, even though they are listed in their hierarchy. Encourage teachers either to get comfortable with them or replace them.

▲ Suggest that teachers build flexibility into their consequences so that they have wiggle room and choice as individual situations occur.

▲ Clarify your role in the discipline chain — what it is and is not — and define your expectations. Listen to your teachers as to the type of support they are hoping to receive from you.

▲ ▲ ▲

Office Referrals

Mrs. Allgood says

Ask your excellent teachers to role-play challenging scenarios that are skillfully diffused in the classroom.

Referrals are a last resort, because they eliminate instructional time for students, can bog down office staff, and can send a message to the student that the teacher is less capable than the administrator to handle the situation. Even so, many administrators report that their teachers send students to the office for minor reasons, such as being unprepared or unmotivated. There are several things you can do to both reduce referrals and manage them appropriately when needed.

▲ Define your criteria for appropriate office referrals. You may want to do this with the help of a teacher/administrator committee (which could include parents and students as well).

▲ Once your criteria are clear, inform teachers what they are at various times throughout the school year, using email, private conversations, and staff meetings.

▲ Spend time in staff meetings role-playing — or ask your excellent teachers to role-play — so that the staff can envision scenarios that do not end in referrals and instead are skillfully diffused in the classroom.

▲ Practice redirection in these role-plays, showing how a teacher can respond rather than react to student resistance.

▲ Clarify to your teachers what your role is when students are sent to you. Is there a designated place where he is to sit and wait? Is he sent to a counselor? Are there forms he needs to fill out? Is your goal to calm down the student and send him back to class? Is there a time window before he is allowed to return?

Reducing Power Struggles that Lead to Referrals

Students often get sent to the office when there is a power struggle in the classroom. There are many things you can encourage teachers to do to redirect students, diminish the power struggle, encourage a student to calm down, and keep him focused in class. A teacher can:

▲ Remember to go under the wave, and focus on assuming the best about her student.

▲ Speak to her student privately about consequences, so that he doesn't feel publicly cornered.

▲ Demonstrate her empathy and concern about the student by asking about his well-being. Sometimes gently asking "Are you okay?" — and then listening deeply — can disarm even the angriest student.

▲ Walk away from a student, and let him have the last word.

▲ Delay giving or discussing consequences until he has a chance to calm down.

▲ Offer the student in-class choices, and give him time to reflect on which choice he wants, rather than forcing the issue in the heat of the moment.

▲ Address the student's feelings. For example, "I see that you are quite upset, Mark. Why don't you take a few minutes at your desk to take some deep breaths and calm down? Ask me again in fifteen minutes when the group work has started, and I'll be happy to talk about this with you then."

▲ Focus a student on what is working, rather than what is not working, helping to shift his negative orientation to a positive one.

After a Referral Occurs

When possible, follow up with the teacher after a referral has been given. Referrals often point as much to a frustrated teacher as an unruly student. Consider addressing the teacher's feelings as well as her actions, if you want to help her diminish her referrals. She may be defensive and/or reactive after sending a student to the office. To help diffuse the tension, you can go "under the wave" and model treating teachers in the same calm and respectful manner in which you'd like them to treat their students. Positive connections between administrators and teachers are often born in these stressful situations.

In addition to addressing the teacher's experience and perceptions, clarify if the referral was appropriate, and how the teacher can best handle future, similar situations.

When Consequences Don't Work

▲ In staff meetings, one-on-one conversations, or faculty bulletins, highlight strategies from this book for students who need extra behavior support.

▲ If a teacher complains that her student doesn't care or doesn't want to change, ask her to assume that he does care, and to work with him based on that assumption.
This will allow her to connect more on a heart level.

▲ Help teachers to find out why individual students are acting out.

▲ Direct teachers to focus on what they can do to help students, rather than what they can't.

▲ Model active listening when talking with your teachers, particularly in delicate conversations.

▲ Be the point-person for helping staff help kids. Organize meetings with parents, teachers, and all stakeholders, particularly in implementing the Village Intervention.

▲ Support teachers in interacting with challenging parents. Meet with parents, listen to their concerns, and help form a bridge between parents and their children's teachers.

▲ Help improve the nutritional content of student diets by investigating district guidelines, and/or educating students and their parents.

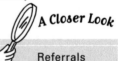

A Closer Look

Referrals often point as much to a frustrated teacher as an unruly student. Consider addressing your teacher's feelings as well as her actions.

Making Changes

▲ Refer to the section in this chapter called "Making Changes Schoolwide" to find a road map for all your teachers to use.

▲ Encourage teachers to list the changes they want to make, and review that list with them.

▲ Remind teachers to go slowly, making changes step-by-step and pausing to appreciate each step they take.

▲ Offer to do "before-and-after" observations of your teachers' classes.

▲ Invite teachers to pair up or form small groups to help one another make changes.

▲ Devote parts of staff meetings and/or faculty bulletins to highlighting the changes that teachers are making.

▲ In your role as coach, focus on how your teacher is feeling about making changes. Validate her feelings, and offer approaches for her to gently make changes that will ultimately help relax her experience and move her into more inner authority.

Final Thoughts and the Big Picture

▲ Optimize teacher success in decisions you make about scheduling. In the past, new teachers were often given the toughest assignments, with veteran teachers' preferences receiving priority. This led to a large number of struggling new teachers, close to fifty percent of whom left teaching in the first five years.[2] This is now changing as districts realize the costs of teacher attrition in personnel, money, and student learning. It's now common for mentor programs to advocate more for their new teachers.

Online Toolbox

▲ Refer to the observation tool in the online toolbox to help teachers with their classroom management skills.

▲ Explore the "Recipe for Learning" with teachers, focusing on fostering students' emotional intelligence about feeling frustrated and lost.[3]

▲ Ask teachers to share with you and one another the experiences and stories in class that lead to a sense of magic in the classroom.

> Refer to the observation tool to help teachers with their classroom management skills.

▲ Ask teachers to discuss with you and one another what drew them to the teaching profession, and to highlight positive experiences that support those reasons.

Finally, seek to expand your teachers' viewpoint. Many see classroom management as a series of problems that need to be solved in order to get to the good stuff called "student learning." From a broader perspective, proactive classroom management is an essential part of the good stuff. When teachers plan ahead and communicate consistent procedures in advance, providing both safety and structure, students learn how to take responsibility and make wise choices. They learn the types of behaviors that are appropriate for success in school and in their lives outside of school.

As we embrace this broader perspective, we see that classroom management affects every aspect of schooling. As struggling teachers become competent, competent teachers become excellent, and excellent teachers use new approaches and strategies to improve their craft, classes run better, students feel more empowered, learning becomes easier, and classrooms become alive with inquiry, esteem, and wonder.

17

PUTTING IT ALL TOGETHER — FINAL THOUGHTS

> *"To learn and never be filled —*
> *is wisdom.*
> *To teach and never be weary —*
> *is love."*
>
> — AUTHOR UNKNOWN

Classroom Management: The Big Picture

We've looked at effective classroom management from a variety of perspectives. By examining Mrs. Meanswell's attempts and Mrs. Allgood's successes, we've illuminated critical ideas and techniques that are often invisible. Below is the same diagram that we started with, showing these keys.

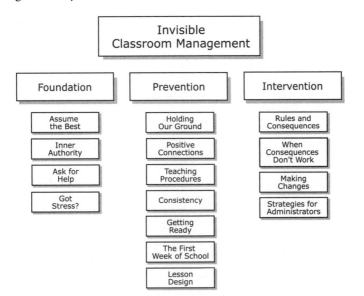

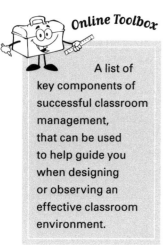

Online Toolbox

A list of key components of successful classroom management, that can be used to help guide you when designing or observing an effective classroom environment.

Effective classroom management isn't simply a matter of doling out consequences. It is profoundly enhanced by connecting positively with students and by designing great lessons. There is no one magic approach, but instead a variety of interactive components. Go to the online toolbox to see a list of these interactive components.

Teaching and Learning: The Big Picture

Several years ago I observed a beginning science teacher teach a fabulous lesson about how students' brains grow and develop. It involved manipulatives, inquiry, teamwork, and video. "Aha's," like light bulbs, were going off in kids' heads all over the classroom. The bell rang to end class, and no one wanted to leave. It was truly inspiring. When I went to document what I saw, I found that the forms I commonly used were inadequate to do justice to what I was seeing in the classroom. I realized then that there is more to student learning than having them jump through the hoops that we're taught in credential school. True learning involves several connected experiences and choices, as described in the "recipe" below.

Bright Ideas

A Recipe for Learning

Start with a **Willingness to Take Risks**.

Add a healthy portion of **Fun**.

Throw in a **Willingness To Be Lost**.

Top it off with a **Willingness To Be Frustrated**.

Blend together and heat until done. The end result is:

Wonder!

Let's "unpack" this recipe one ingredient at a time.

1. A Willingness to Take Risks

Just as in the old "Star Trek" series, we can't beam people onto the ship if our shields are up. Taking risks means lowering our guard, thereby opening ourselves up to new experiences and new learning. This quality of openness is discussed in more detail in Chapter 4, "Ask for Help."

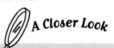

Wise-Apple Advice

True learning is exhilarating, breathtaking, mind expanding, and fun.

2. A Healthy Portion of Fun

True learning is exhilarating, breathtaking, mind expanding, and fun. With all the testing, grades, and homework, we often seem to lose our connection to this in our teaching. For a visceral reminder of learning and fun, try observing a child learning to read or shooting a basket for the first time.

3. A Willingness to be Lost

The moment before we learn something, we don't yet know it. We are lost. If we push away the experience of "lostness," then we won't stick around long enough to receive the knowledge that lies there, waiting.

4. A Willingness to be Frustrated

Several years ago, I designed a lesson where pairs of students shared computers and used a new geography software program to find the answers to a list of questions that I provided. I gave the students only half a minute of instruction as to how to navigate through the program, knowing that it would force them to explore on their own. Sure enough, two types of students emerged. Colin pushed his chair away from the computer in frustration, saying, "This is dumb. I hate doing this." Nyesha, on the other hand, got totally into it, saying, "This is cool. It's like looking for buried treasure, using the computer mouse as a flashlight." Colin felt frustration and pushed it away, while Nyesha embraced frustration and was propelled forward into learning and wonder. As mentioned in Chapter 12, "Lesson Design," frustration can be the irritation in the oyster that yields that pearl.

A Closer Look

There is something fundamental and beautiful — wonder — underlying all of the details of teaching.

By combining these four ingredients, we reveal the magic at the heart of true learning. I include this recipe as a reminder that there is something fundamental and beautiful — wonder — underlying all of the details of teaching. It is one of the reasons many of us got into the profession. By consciously searching for, facilitating, and promoting these four ingredients, we can help increase the moments of wonder in our classrooms.

Further, the two points of view illustrated by Colin and Nyesha are the polarities that we face every day with students in the classroom, and every moment of our own lives. Do we let frustration get the best of us? Or do we step through it and into wonder? Do we buy into the waves of noise in the radio stations in our heads? Or do we honor what we know in our hearts and in our guts? As we facilitate ways for our students to navigate through the waters of learning, we provide ourselves with the same skills. The reverse is also true. As we grow in our own self-appreciation and wonder, we naturally find ways to help our students do the same.

Our Own Lives: The *Really* Big Picture

In Chapter 6, "Holding our Ground," we covered a fundamental concept that has implications reaching far beyond the classroom. An extension of the frustrating-technology example, this concept addressed recognizing our feelings — anger, for instance — without reacting to them. Our ability to be truly happy is, I believe, tied directly to the notion that real happiness is a choice we can make regardless of the transitory experiences we are feeling.

A Closer Look

As we facilitate ways for our students to navigate through the waters of learning, we provide ourselves with the same skills.

As teachers, we choose to take care of business even when we feel angry or guilty. As human beings we can choose to take care of ourselves, our loved ones, and the earth in the same way — by recognizing but not reacting to our inner noises and whims that might otherwise take us off center. The truly visionary leaders in the world are those who can do this on a large scale, receiving and welcoming all their feelings as they stay relaxed and yet passionate about their beliefs. This requires a deep commitment to assuming the best about ourselves and others, even in the light of all the evidence we could use to support the contrary. All human beings have the capacity for goodness. The challenge is to access that goodness in ourselves as we access it in others. The arena of classroom management is overflowing with opportunity to embrace this practice. What more challenging environment can there be in which to continue to assume and remember the best about people?

▲ ▲ ▲

A related concept was discussed in Chapter 3, "Inner Authority," and addressed the continuum of inner apology and inner authority. The internal muscle of inner authority grows over time as we focus on holding our ground, not over-explaining, teaching procedures, being consistent, and delivering consequences in a kind and firm manner. There is, I believe, *no limit* to how much this muscle can grow, and no area in life where this muscle isn't present. Whether it's getting students to put their things away, getting a friend to help us out, holding our ground with our son or daughter, communicating our political agenda in a room full of adversaries, expressing our deep love for a friend or for the earth, or stopping tanks in their tracks — all involve this muscle of inner authority.

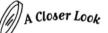

A Closer Look

Real happiness is a choice we can make regardless of the transitory experiences we are feeling.

As we continually reflect on our level of inner-apology, bringing to consciousness our resistances to self-expression, we get a chance to blossom and grow in self-regard, courage, and confidence. The continuum is infinite. It is, I believe, the single defining characteristic of greatness in this world: one's willingness to stand up and hold one's ground with the noise in one's head and the people in one's world, while assuming the best, in ways that invite cooperation. People like Gandhi, Martin Luther King, Jr., and Nelson Mandela come to mind. Even in the face of tremendous resistance, they held firmly to what they believed. They used the power of their convictions — their love of self and other — to ultimately melt much of that resistance. They triumphed because of the strength they had discovered inside themselves, and because of their willingness to assume the best, even about the very people who seemingly stood in their way.

A Closer Look

The muscle that allows us to successfully manage our class-rooms is the same one that allows us to move mountains in the world.

Even though these actions seem so different, the muscle that allows us to successfully manage our classrooms is the same one that allows us to move mountains in the world, whether social, political, scientific, philosophical, or physical. Finding ways to hold our ground in the classroom while still being kind with ourselves and our students is good practice for succeeding and enjoying all aspects of our lives, and for extending our influence beyond the classroom or school into the world at large.

*"There are two things
we must give children:
The first one is roots,
the other, wings."*

— AUTHOR UNKNOWN

ENDNOTES

Preface

1   California Department of Education, "Fingertip Facts."

Chapter 1. Introduction

1   Beaty-O'Ferrall, Green, and Hanna, "Classroom Management Strategies," 4–11.

Chapter 2. Assume the Best

1   Goleman, *Emotional Intelligence*, 1995.
2   Goleman, "Emotional Intelligence," 1996, 49–50.
3   Goleman, *Emotional Intelligence*, 1995, 80–83.

Chapter 3. Inner Authority

1   Dibapile, "A Review of Literature," 79–92.
2   Garrett, "Student-Centered and Teacher-Centered Classroom Management," 34–47; MacSuga and Simonsen, "Increasing Teachers' Use," 4–12; Parsonson, "Evidence-Based Classroom Behaviour," 16–23.
3   Dibapile, "A Review of Literature," 79–92.
4   Simonsen et al., "Evidence-based Practices," 351–380.
5   Irving and Martin, "Withitness," 313–319; Kounin, *Discipline*; Marzano et al., *Classroom Instruction*.
6   O'Neill and Stephenson, "Self-Efficacy," 261–299.
7   Parsonson, "Evidence-Based Classroom Behavior," 16–23.
8   O'Neill and Stephenson, "Self-Efficacy," 261–299.
9   Cavanaugh, "Performance Feedback," 111.
10   Alderman and Green, "Social Powers," 39–44.
11   Wilkins, "The concept," 175–183.
12   Huang, Liu, and Shiomi, "An analysis," 707–715.
13   Beaty-O'Ferrall, Green, and Hanna, "Classroom Management Strategies," 4–11.
14   Milner and Tenore, "Diverse Classrooms," 560–603.
15   Dibapile, "A Review of Literature," 79–92.

16   Simonsen et al., "Evidence-based Practices," 351–380.

17   D'Agostino, Hedges, and Borman, "Title I," 117–136.

Chapter 4. Ask for Help

1   Alderman and Green, "Social Powers," 39–44; Beaty-O'Ferrall, Green, and Hanna, "Classroom Management Strategies," 4–11; Parsonson, "Evidence-Based Classroom Behaviour," 16–23.

2   Dibapile, "A Review of Literature," 79–92; O'Neill and Stephenson, "Self-Efficacy," 261–299.

3   Clunies-Ross, Little, and Kienhuis, "Self-Reported," 693–710; Dibapile, "A Review of Literature," 79–92; O'Neill and Stephenson, "Self-Efficacy," 261–299.

Chapter 5. Got Stress?

1   Day, "New Lives," 7–26; Vesely, Saklofske, and Leschied, "The Vital Resource," 71–89.

2   Rechtschaffen, *Mindful Education.*

3   Mora-Ripoli, "Potential health benefits," 170–177.

4   Otake et al, "Happy People," 361–375.

5   Mendler, *When Teaching Gets Tough*, eBook Location 2131.

6   Seligman, Steen, and Park, "Positive Psychology," 410–421.

7   Mendler, *When Teaching Gets Tough*, eBook Location 1474.

8   Ripski, LoCasale-Crouch, and Decker, "Pre-Service Teachers," 77–96.

9   Markov and Goldman, "Normal sleep," 841–853.

Chapter 6. Holding Our Ground

1   Korb, "Calm Your Face."

Chapter 7. Positive Connections

1   Beaty-O'Ferrall, Green, and Hanna, "Classroom Management Strategies," 4–11.

2   Schreck, *Reach Them.*

3   Sousa, *How the Brain Learns*; Sylwester, *A biological brain*; Tomlinson, *Fulfilling the Promise.*

4   Davis, *How to teach students*, eBook Location 2344.

5   Wlodkowski, "Motivation and Diversity," 7; Wlodkowski, *Motivation.*

6   Wlodkowski, Raymond, personal communication.

7   Ratner, Chiodo, and Covington, "Violence Exposure," 264–287.

8   Beaty-O'Ferrall, Green, and Hanna, "Classroom Management Strategies," 4–11.

9   Kitzmann, "Two by ten."

10   Glasser, "Discipline is not the problem," 36–39; Wlodkowski, "Motivation and Diversity," 7; Wlodkowski, *Motivation*.

11   Milner and Tenore, "Classroom Management," 560–603.

12   Cross et al., *Culturally Competent System*.

13   Gable et al., "Importance," 499–519; Jackson and Wilson, "Overrepresentation."

14   Jensen, *Teaching with Poverty*.

Chapter 8. Teaching Procedures

1   Garrett, "Student-Centered," 34–47; Simonsen et al.,"Evidence-based Practices," 351–380.

2   Bamberger and Cahill, "Teaching Design," 171–185; Rodrigues and Smith, "Linking Pedagogy," 34–36.

3   Gould and Schoonover, "Creative and Critical Thinking," 3–6; Hughes, "Effective Team Player," 22; Marks, Zaccaro, and Mathieu, "Performance implications," 971–986.

4   Wannarka and Rhul, "Seating arrangements," 89–93.

5   Young, "Increase serotonin," 394–399.

6   Wolfe, *Brain Matters*, 83.

Chapter 9. Consistency

1   Gomberg and Gray, "Five Basic Principles," 24–27.

Chapter 10. Getting Ready

1   O'Neill and Stephenson, "Self-Efficacy," 261–299; Simonsen et al., "Evidence-based Practices," 351–380.

2   Jones, *Tools for Teaching*, 29–39.

Chapter 12. Lesson Design

1   Erlauer, *Brain-Compatible Classroom*; Mácajová, "Neuropedagogy," 19–27; Wolfe, "Brain-compatible learning," 10.

2   Bulu and Pedersen, "Supporting problem-solving," 1162–1169; van Loon et al., "Activation," 15–25.

3 Effeney, Carroll, and Bahr, "Self-regulated learning," 773–796; Efklides, "Interactions of metacognition," 6–25.

4 Wolfe, *Brain Matters*, 82, 88.

5 Marzano, *What Works in Schools*, 80.

6 Wolfe, *Brain Matters*, 20.

7 Ibid., 82,88.

8 Cucullo et al., "Shear stress"; Gold et al., "Cerebral blood flow"; Monti et al., "Blood flow and anxiety."

9 Goleman, *Emotional Intelligence*, 80–83.

10 Rechtschaffen, *Mindful Education*.

11 Rechtschaffen, Daniel, oral communication.

12 Ibid.

Chapter 13. Rules and Consequences

1 Simonsen et al., "Evidence-baded Practices," 351–380.

2 Ibid.

3 Ibid.

4 Ibid.

5 Curwin, "Fair Isn't Equal."

6 Ibid.

7 Englehart, "Five Approaches," 103.

8 Beaty-O'Ferrall, Green, and Hanna, "Classroom Management Strategies," 4–11.

9 Wubbels, "International Perspective," 113–131.

10 Doyle, "Situated Practice," 156–159.

11 Englehart, "Five Approaches," 103.

12 Parsonson, "Evidence-Based Classroom Behaviour," 16–23.

13 Cavanaugh, "Performance Feedback," 111.

14 Sexton, "Revelations in the Revolution," 29–40.

15 Jones, *Tools for Teaching*, 58–59.

16 Marzano et al., *Classroom Instruction*.

17 Doyle, "Situated Practice," 156–159.

Chapter 14. When Consequences Don't Work

1 Konings, Brand-Gruwel, and van Merrienboer, "The Match," 439–457.

2 Jensen, *Poverty in Mind*, 18.

3   Glasser, *Control Theory.*

4   Wubbels, "International Perspective," 113–131.

5   Curwin, "Fair isn't Equal."

6   Clark, Kirschner, and Sweller, "Putting Students on the Path," 6–11.

7   American Psychiatric Association, *DSM-5,* Section II, Chapter on Neurodevelopmental Disorders.

8   Appelbaum, *How to handle.*

9   Curwin, Mendler, and Mendler, *Discipline with Dignity.*

10 Appelbaum, *How to handle,* 7.

11 Curwin, Mendler, and Mendler, *Discipline with Dignity,* 194.

12 Schoenthaler, "'Junk' foods," 18.

13 Feingold® Association, "School lunch," 1, 3–4; Keeley, "Case Study."

14 Feingold® Association, "School lunch," 1, 3.

15 Simonsen, et al., "Evidence-based Practices," 351–380.

16 Jones, *Tools for Teaching.*

Chapter 16. Strategies for Administrators

1   Wlodkowski, "Motivation and Diversity," 7.

2   Ingersoll, "Teacher Shortage," 13.

3   Goleman, *Emotional Intelligence,* 1995.

BIBLIOGRAPHY

ABC News. "Students Behave Better With Healthy Lunches." Accessed March 14, 2015. http://abcnews.go.com/GMA/AmericanFamily/story?id=125404.

Alderman, Gary L. and Susan K. Green. "Social Powers and Effective Classroom Management: Enhancing Teacher–Student Relationships." *Intervention in School & Clinic*, 47 (2011), 39–44. Accessed June 18, 2015. doi: 10.1177/1053451211406543.

American Psychiatric Association, *Diagnostic and Statistical Manual of Mental Disorders (DSM-5)*. 5th Ed. Arlington, VA: American Psychiatric Publishing, 2013.

Appelbaum, Maryln S. *How to Handle the Hard-to-Handle Student, K-5*. Thousand Oaks, CA: Corwin Press, 2009.

Bamberger, Yael M. and Clara S. Cahill. "Teaching Design in Middle-School: Instructors' Concerns and Scaffolding Strategies." *Journal of Science Education and Technology*, 22 (2013): 171–185.

Beaty-O'Ferrall, Mary Ellen, Alan Green, and Fred Hanna. "Classroom Management Strategies for Difficult Students: Promoting Change through Relationships." *Middle School Journal*, 41 (2010): 4–11.

Bulu, Saniye Tugba and Susan Pedersen. "Supporting problem-solving performance in a hypermedia learning environment: The role of students' prior knowledge and metacognitive skills." *Computers in Human Behavior*, 28 (2012): 1162–1169. Accessed August 11, 2015. doi: 10.1016/j.chb.2012.01.026.

California Department of Education. "Fingertip Facts on Education in California—CalEdFacts." Accessed November 17, 2015. http://www.cde.ca.gov/ds/sd/cb/ceffingertipfacts.asp.

Cavanaugh, Brian. "Performance Feedback and Teachers' Use of Praise and Opportunities to Respond: A Review of the Literature." *Education & Treatment of Children* (West Virginia University Press), 36 (2013): 111.

Clark, Richard E., Paul A. Kirschner, and John Sweller. "Putting Students on the Path to Learning: The Case for Fully Guided Instruction." *American Educator*, 36 (2012): 6–11.

Clunies-Ross, Penny, Emma Little, and Mandy Kienhuis. "Self-Reported and Actual Use of Proactive and Reactive Classroom Management Strategies and Their Relationship with Teacher Stress and Student Behaviour." *Educational Psychology*, 28 (2008), 693–710.

Cross, Terry L., Barbara J. Bazron, Karl W. Dennis, and Mareasa R. Isaacs. *Towards a Culturally Competent System of Care: A Monograph on Effective Services for Minority Children Who Are Severely Emotionally Disturbed*. Washington, DC: CAASP Technical Assistance Center, Georgetown University Child Development Center, 1989.

Cucullo, Luca, Mohammed Hossain, Vikram Puvenna, Nicola Marchi, and Damir Janigro. "The role of shear stress in Blood-Brain Barrier endothelial physiology." *BMC Neuroscience*, 12 (2011). Accessed November 18, 2015. doi: 10.1186/1471-2202-12-40.

Curwin, Richard. "Fair Isn't Equal: Seven Classroom Tips." Edutopia Blog, October 23, 2012. Accessed November 2, 2015. http://www.edutopia.org/blog/fair-isnt-equal-richard-curwin.

Curwin, Richard L., Allen N. Mendler, and Brian D. Mendler. *Discipline with Dignity: New Challenges, New Solutions*. 3rd Ed. Alexandria, VA: Association for Supervision and Curriculum Development, 2008.

D'Agostino, Jerome V., Larry V. Hedges, Kenneth K. Wong, and Geoffrey D. Borman. "Title I Parent-Involvement programs: Effects on Parenting Practices and Student Achievement." In *Title I: Compensatory Education at the Crossroads: Sociocultural, Political and Historical Studies in Education*, edited by G. D. Borman, S. C. Stringfield & R. E. Slavin, 117–136. Mahwah, NJ: Lawrence Erlbaum Associates, Inc., Publishers, 2001.

Davis, Bonnie M. *How to teach students who don't look like you: Culturally relevant teaching strategies.* 2nd ed. Thousand Oaks, CA: Corwin Press, 2012. https://books.google.com/books?id=QJdyAwAAQBAJ.

Day, Christopher. "New Lives of Teachers." *Teacher Education Quarterly,* 39 (2012), 7–26.

Dibapile, Waitshega Tefo Smitta. "A Review of Literature on Teacher Efficacy and Classroom Management." *Journal of College Teaching & Learning,* 9 (2012): 79–92.

Doyle, Walter. "Situated Practice: A Reflection on Person-Centered Classroom Management." *Theory Into Practice,* 48 (2009): 156–159. Accessed October 22, 2015. doi: 10.1080/00405840902776525.

Effeney, Gerard, Annemaree Carroll, and Nan Bahr. (2013). "Self-regulated learning and executive function: Exploring the relationships in a sample of adolescent males." *Educational Psychology,* 33 (2013): 773–796. Accessed September 8, 2015. doi: 10.1080/01443410.2013.785054.

Efklides, Anastasia. "Interactions of metacognition with motivation and affect in self-regulated learning: The MASRL model." *Educational Psychologist,* 46 (2011): 6–25. Accessed November 23, 2015. doi: 10.1080/00461520.2011.538645.

Englehart, Joshua M. "Five Approaches to Avoid When Managing the Middle School Classroom." *Clearing House,* 86 (2013), 103. Accessed July 6, 2015. doi: 10.1080/00098655.2013.772500.

Erlauer, Laura. *The Brain-Compatible Classroom: Using What We Know about Learning To Improve Teaching.* Alexandria VA: Association for Supervision and Curriculum Development, 2003.

Feingold® Association of the United States. "A different kind of school lunch." Pure Facts: Newsletter of the Feingold® Association of the United States, 26 (2002): 1, 3–4.

Flavell, John H. "Metacognition and Cognitive Monitoring: A New Area of Cognitive-Developmental Inquiry." *American Psychologist,* 34 (1979): 906–911.

Florence, Michelle D., Mark Asbridge, and Paul J. Veugelers. "Diet quality and academic performance." *The Journal Of School Health,* 78 (2008): 209–215. Accessed August 27, 2015. doi: 10.1111/j.1746-1561.2008.00288.x.

Gable, Robert A., Stephen W. Tonelson, Manasi Sheth, Corinne Wilson, and Kristy Lee Park. "Importance, Usage, and Preparedness to Implement Evidence-Based Practices for Students with Emotional Disabilities: A Comparison of Knowledge and Skills of Special Education and General Education Teachers." *Education and Treatment of Children,* 35 (2012): 499–519.

Garrett, Tracey. "Student-Centered and Teacher-Centered Classroom Management: A Case Study of Three Elementary Teachers." *Journal of Classroom Interaction,* 43 (2008): 34–47.

Glasser, William. *Control Theory in the Classroom.* New York: Perennial Library / Harper & Row Publishers, 1986.

Glasser, William. "Discipline is not the problem: control theory in the classroom." *Education Digest,* 51 (1986): 36–39.

Gold, A. L., L. M. Shin, S. P. Orr, M. A. Carson, S. L. Rauch, M. L. Macklin, M. L., . . . and R. K. Pitman. "Decreased regional cerebral blood flow in medial prefrontal cortex during trauma-unrelated stressful imagery in Vietnam veterans with post-traumatic stress disorder." *Psychological Medicine: A Journal of Research in Psychiatry and the Allied Sciences,* 41 (2011): 2563–2572. Accessed July 15, 2015. doi: 10.1017/S0033291711000730.

Goleman, Daniel. *Emotional intelligence: Why It Can Matter More Than IQ.* New York: Bantam, 1995.

Goleman, Daniel. "Emotional Intelligence. Why It Can Matter More than IQ." *Learning,* 24 (1996): 49–50.

Gomberg, Leslie E. and Susan W. Gray. "Five Basic Principles for Effectively Managing the Classroom." *Adult Learning,* 11 (1999): 24–27.

Gould, J. Christine and Patricia F. Schoonover. "Creative and Critical Thinking, Teamwork, and Tomorrow's Workplace." *Understanding Our Gifted,* 22 (2009): 3–6.

Hyerle, David. A Field Guide to Using Visual Tools. Alexandria, VA: Association for Supervision & Curriculum Development, 2000.

Huang, Xishan, Ming Liu, and Kunio Shiomi. "An analysis of the relationships between teacher efficacy, teacher self-esteem and orientations to seeking help." *Social Behavior and Personality*, 35 (2007): 707–715. Accessed June 9, 2015. doi: 10.2224/sbp.2007.35.5.707.

Hughes, Liz. "How to be an Effective Team Player." *Women in Business*, 55 (2003): 22.

Hunter, M. "Knowing, teaching and supervising." In *Using what we know about reading*, edited by P. Hosford, 169–203. Alexandria, VA: Association for Supervision and Curriculum Development, 1984.

Hunter, Madeline. "Generic Lesson Design: The Case For." *Science Teacher*, 58 (1991): 26–28.

Ingersoll, Richard M. "Is There Really a Teacher Shortage?" Research Report, University of Washington, Center for the Study of Teaching and Policy, September 2003: 1–28.

Irving, Olwyn, and Jack Martin. "Withitness: The confusing variable." *American Educational Research Journal*, 19 (1982), 313–319. Accessed August 19, 2015. doi: 10.2307/1162573.

Jackson, Clarence H. and Carolyn H. Wilson. "The Overrepresentation of African Americans in Special Education Programs: A Literature Review." Education Resources Information Center, Institute of Education Sciences, Non-Journal Online Submission, December 2006: 1–35. ERIC Number: ED524464. Accessed September 15, 2015. http://eric.ed.gov/?q=overrepresentation+of+african+americans+in+special+education+programs%3a+a+literature+review&id=ED524464

Jensen, Eric. *Teaching with Poverty in Mind: What Being Poor Does to Kids' Brains and What Schools Can Do about It*. Alexandria, VA: Association for Supervision and Curriculum Development, 2009.

Johnson, Andrew P. "It's time for Madeline Hunter to go: a new look at lesson plan design." *Action in Teacher Education*, 22 (2000): 72–78.

Jones, Fredric. *Tools for Teaching: Discipline, Instruction, Motivation*. 2nd ed. Santa Cruz, CA: Fredric H. Jones & Assoc., Inc., 2007.

Keeley, J. "Case Study: Appleton Central Alternative Charter High School's Nutrition and Wellness Program." *Better Food, Better Behavior*. East Troy, WI: Michael Fields Agricultural Institute, 2004. http://www.thewholeplate.yihs.net/wp-content/uploads/2010/02/Appleton-school-food-study.pdf.

Kitzmann, Lisa. "Two by ten: A strategy used to improve disruptive behavior in the classroom." Action research project toward Master of Arts in Teaching Leadership, Kalmanovitz School of Education, Saint Mary's College of California, Moraga, CA, 2011.

Konings, Karen D., Saskia Brand-Gruwel, and Jeroen J. G. van Merrienboer. "The Match between Students' Lesson Perceptions and Preferences: Relations with Student Characteristics and the Importance of Motivation." *Educational Research*, 53 (2011): 439–457.

Korb, Alex. "Calm Your Face, Calm Your Mind: A quick tip for improving tranquility." PreFrontal Nudity Blog, August 21, 2012. *Psychology Today* website: http://www.psychologytoday.com/blog/prefrontal-nudity/201208/calm-your-face-calm-your-mind.

Kounin, Jacob S. *Discipline and group management in classrooms*. New York: Holt, Rinehart and Winston, 1970.

Mácajová, Monika. "Neuropedagogy and Brain Compatible Learning — Ideas for Education in the 21st Century." *Technológia Vzdelávania* (Technology of Education, Professional Journal on Pedagogy), 21 (2013): 19–27.

MacSuga, Ashley S. and Brandi Simonsen. "Increasing Teachers' Use of Evidence-Based Classroom Management Strategies through Consultation: Overview and Case Studies." *Beyond Behavior*, 20 (2011): 4–12.

Markov, Dimitri, and Marina Goldman. (2006). "Normal sleep and circadian rhythms: Neurobiologic mechanisms underlying sleep and wakefulness." *Psychiatric Clinics of North America*, 29 (2006): 841–853.

Marks, Michelle A., Stephen J. Zaccaro, and John E. Mathieu. "Performance implications of leader briefings and team-interaction training for team adaptation to novel environments." *Journal of Applied Psychology*, 85 (2000): 971–986. Accessed September 7, 2015. doi: 10.1037/0021-9010.85.6.971.

Marzano, Robert J. *What Works in Schools: Translating Research into Action.* Alexandria VA: Association for Supervision & Curriculum Development, 2003.

Marzano, Robert J., Debra J. Pickering, and Jane E. Pollock. *Classroom Instruction That Works: Research-Based Strategies for Increasing Student Achievement.* Alexandria, VA: Association for Supervision & Curriculum Development, 2001.

Mendler, Allen N. *When Teaching Gets Tough: Smart Ways to Reclaim Your Game.* Alexandria, VA: Association for Supervision and Curriculum Development, 2012. http://shop.ascd.org/Default.aspx?TabID=55&ProductId=53991604.

Milner, H. Richard IV and F. Blake Tenore. "Classroom Management in Diverse Classrooms." *Urban Education*, 45 (2010): 560–603.

Monti, Daniel A., Kathryn M. Kash, Elisabeth J. S. Kunkel, George Brainard, Nancy Wintering, Aleezé S. Moss,. . . and Andrew B. Newberg. "Changes in cerebral blood flow and anxiety associated with an 8 week mindfulness programme in women with breast cancer." *Stress and Health: Journal of the International Society for the Investigation of Stress*, 28 (2012): 397–407. Accessed October 14, 2015. doi: 10.1002/smi.2470.

Mora-Ripoli, Ramon. "Potential health benefits of simulated laughter: a narrative review of the literature and recommendations for future research." *Complementary Therapies in Medicine*, 19 (2011): 170–177. doi: 10.1016/j.ctim.2011.05.003. In PubMed.gov (US National Library of Medicine, National Institutes of Health). Accessed August 3, 2015. www.ncbi.nlm.nih.gov/pubmed/21641524.

Morris, Rick. *New Management Handbook.* 3rd ed. San Diego, CA: New Management, 2000.

Morris, Rick. *Tools & Toys (Fifty Fun Ways to Love Your Class).* 3rd ed. San Diego, CA: New Management, 1995.

O'Neill, Sue Catherine and Jennifer Stephenson. "The Measurement of Classroom Management Self-Efficacy: A Review of Measurement Instrument Development and Influences." *Educational Psychology*, 31 (2011): 261–299.

Otake, Keiko, Satoshi Shimai, Junko Tanaka-Matsumi, Kanako Otsui, and Barbara L. Fredrickson. "Happy People Become Happier Through Kindness: A Counting Kindnesses Intervention." *Journal Of Happiness Studies*, 7 (2006): 361–375.

Parsonson, Barry S. "Evidence-Based Classroom Behaviour Management Strategies." *Kairaranga*, 13 (2012): 16–23.

Ratner, Hilary Horn, Lisa Chiodo, and Chandice Covington. "Violence Exposure, IQ, Academic Performance, and Children's Perception of Safety: Evidence of Protective Effects." *Merrill-Palmer Quarterly*, 52 (2006): 264–287. Accessed May 18, 2015. doi: 10.1353/mpq.2006.0017.

Rechtschaffen, Daniel. *The Way of Mindful Education.* New York: W.W. Norton & Company Inc, 2014.

Ripski, Michael B., Jennifer LoCasale-Crouch, and Lauren Decker. "Pre-Service Teachers: Dispositional Traits, Emotional States, and Quality of Teacher-Student Interactions." *Teacher Education Quarterly*, 38 (2011): 77–96.

Rodrigues, Laurel and B. E. C. Smith. "Linking Pedagogy: Scaffolding Literacy and First Steps." *Practically Primary*, 19 (2014): 34–36.

Schreck, Mary Kim. *You've Got to Reach Them to Teach Them: Hard Facts About the Soft Skills of Student Engagement.* Bloomington, IN: Solution Tree Press, 2010.

Seligman, Martin E. P., Tracy A. Steen, and Nansook Park. "Positive Psychology Progress: Empirical Validation of Interventions." *American Psychologist*, 60 (2005): 410–421. Accessed May 28, 2015. doi: 10.1037/0003-066X.60.5.410.

Sexton, Steven S. "Revelations in the Revolution of Relevance: Learning in a Meaningful Context." *International Journal of Science in Society*, 2 (2011): 29–40.

Simonsen, Brandi, Sarah Fairbanks, Amy Briesch, Diane Myers, and George Sugai. "Evidence-based Practices in Classroom Management: Considerations for Research to Practice." *Education & Treatment of Children* (West Virginia University Press), 31 (2008): 351–380.

Smith, Rick. *Conscious Classroom Management*. Fairfax, CA: Conscious Teaching Publications, 2004.

Smith, Rick, Grace Dearborn, and Mary Lambert. Picture This! Visuals and Rubrics to Teach Procedures, Save Your Voice, and Love Your Students. Fairfax, CA: Conscious Teaching, 2011.

Sousa, David A. *How the brain learns: A classroom teacher's guide.* 2nd ed. Thousand Oaks, CA: Corwin Press, 2001.

Stallings, Jane. "A study of implementation of Madeline Hunter's model and its effects on students." *The Journal of Educational Research*, 78 (1985): 325–337.

Swaminathan, Nikhil. (2010). "Do Healthier School Lunches Curb Bad Behavior?", July 30, 2010. *Good: A magazine for the global citizen.* Accessed March 14, 2016. http://magazine. good.is/articles/do-healthier-school-lunches-curb-bad-behavior.

Sylwester, Robert. *A biological brain in a cultural classroom: Applying biological research to classroom management.* Thousand Oaks, CA: Corwin Press, 2000.

Tomlinson, Carol A. *Fulfilling the Promise of the Differentiated Classroom: Strategies and Tools for Responsive Teaching.* Alexandria, VA: Association for Supervision & Curriculum Development, 2004.

van Loon, Mariette H., Anique B. H. de Bruin, Tamara van Gog, and Jeroen J. G. van Merrienboer. "Activation of Inaccurate Prior Knowledge Affects Primary-School Students' Metacognitive Judgments and Calibration." *Learning and Instruction*, 24 (2013): 15–25.

Vesely, Ashley K., Donald H. Saklofske, and Alan D. W. Leschied. "Teachers—The Vital Resource: The Contribution of Emotional Intelligence to Teacher Efficacy and Well-Being." *Canadian Journal of School Psychology*, 28 (2013): 71–89.

Wannarka, Rachel and Kathy Ruhl. "Seating arrangements that promote positive academic and behavioural outcomes: A review of empirical research." *Support for Learning*, 23 (2008): 89–93. Accessed July 14, 2015. doi: 10.1111/j.1467-9604.2008.00375.x.

Wiggins, Grant and Jay McTighe. The Understanding by Design Guide to Creating High-Quality Units. Alexandria, VA: Association for Supervision & Curriculum Development, 2011.

Wikinews. "Junk" foods may affect aggressive behaviour and school performance, October 4, 2005. Accessed March 14, 2016. http://en.wikinews.org/wiki/%22Junk%22_foods_ may_affect_aggressive_behaviour_and_school_performance.

Wilkins, William E. "The concept of a self-fulfilling prophesy." *Sociology of Education*, 49 (1976): 175–183. Accessed September 17, 2015. doi: 10.2307/2112523.

Wlodkowski, Raymond J. "Motivation and Diversity: A Framework for Teaching." *New Directions for Teaching & Learning*, 78 (1999), 7.

Wlodkowski, Raymond J. *Motivation (What Research Says to the Teacher).* Washington, DC: National Education Association, 1977.

Wlodkowski, Raymond J. *Motivational Opportunities for Successful Teaching.* Leader's Guide. Phoenix: Universal Dimensions, 1983.

Wolfe, Pat. "Brain-Compatible Learning: Fad or Foundation?" *School Administrator*, 63 (2006): 10.

Wolfe, Pat. *Brain Matters: Translating Research Into Classroom Practice.* 2nd ed. Alexandria, VA: Association for Supervision and Curriculum Development, 2001.

Wubbels, Theo. "An International Perspective on Classroom Management: What Should Prospective Teachers Learn?" *Teaching Education*, 22 (2011): 113–131.

Young, S. N. "How to increase serotonin in the human brain without drugs." *Journal of Psychiatry & Neuroscience*, 32 (2007): 394–399.

ABOUT THE AUTHORS

Rick Smith

Rick Smith is an award-winning teacher, education consultant, and international presenter. He has shared practical teaching strategies to more than a hundred thousand teachers and teacher-trainers in more than forty U.S. states and fourteen countries, including two years' training American Peace Corps Volunteer Teachers in Ghana, West Africa. A classroom teacher for more than fourteen years, Rick focused primarily on students-at-risk. He's been a mentor teacher and mentor coordinator for many years, and has taught in both Elementary and Secondary Credential programs in northern California.

Attendees of Rick's more than one thousand keynotes and workshops consistently praise his sense of humor, his attention to the details of teaching, and the compassion and deep love he holds for teachers and students. These qualities are evident in the numerous articles he has published in education journals — including "Mentoring New Teachers: Strategies, Structures, and Successes," in *Teacher Education Quarterly*, and "Assume the Best" in ASCD's *Classroom Leadership*.

Rick's goal is to bring out the best in students and teachers by offering nurturing ways to discover both fun and challenge in education, and by giving teachers tools for surfing the challenging waves of the classroom experience.

Grace Dearborn

Grace Dearborn's warm, funny, and engaging style has earned her international recognition as a workshop presenter, instructional coach, and consultant to K-12 schools and districts. Her goal is to help teachers improve their craft through reflecting on what they do, how they do it, and who they are. In this way, her trainings and mentoring are both practical and inspirational, leaving a positive emotional footprint on the teachers with whom she works.

Grace taught at multiple grade levels for more than a decade in the San Francisco Bay Area, and authored curriculum for both elementary and secondary schools. Her year-long literacy intervention social studies course for incoming ninth graders in an urban, low-performing high school in Oakland, California, resulted in a dramatic increase in the school's state test scores over the three years that followed.

In the twenty-plus years that Grace has worked in education, she also has held positions as a New Teacher Mentor Coordinator, Professional Development Director, Literacy Coach, Curriculum Specialist, and Mentor Teacher. Her skill at managing young and adolescent learners is daily put to its truest test, however, by her two sons, Mason and Owen.

Workshops by Conscious Teaching

Rick, Grace, and their team of Conscious Teaching presenters offer several workshops, including:

- ▲ "Conscious Classroom Management: Bringing Out The Best in Students and Teachers"
- ▲ "Rebels With Applause: Brain-Compatible Approaches for Motivating Reluctant Learners"
- ▲ "Fifty Ways to Leave Your Lecture: Brain-Compatible Strategies for Breaking Up Direct Instruction"
- ▲ "Nuts and Bolts for Mentor Teachers: Strategies that Make a Difference"
- ▲ When Consequences Don't Work: Succeeding with Difficult Students
- ▲ "Brain-Compatible Presentation Skills for Teachers and Teacher-Trainers"
- ▲ "Growing Into Inner Authority: Practical Approaches for Bringing Confidence and Presence Into Everything You Do"

For more details about who we are and what we offer, please check our website at www.consciousteaching.com.

INDEX

Notes

Notes

Bright Ideas

PRAISE FOR WORKSHOPS AND KEYNOTES BY CONSCIOUS TEACHING PRESENTERS

"Wow! Wow! Wow! This was the best workshop I've ever attended! Not only was it full of information, but it was also entertaining. I have so many new ideas that I can't wait to implement. I wish I had this workshop years ago. Thank you!"
— Jackie S., 1st Grade, 7th year

"I've been teaching for almost ten years in very tough environments. You instructed us for two hours. Ten years of fuzzy processes crystallized into order and serenity. Class was as quiet as a university library. Total focus. And joy — they were so happy, happier than in my most zany, but ready-to-explode, classes of yore. This is HUGE!!! I don't have words adequate to my gratitude."
— Martin P., Middle School

"You gave me some wonderful, helpful ideas I can share immediately, and over time. After 27 years you've helped me learn more!"
— Cara K., Elementary Principal

"No other workshop has given me as many tools to take back to the classroom and implement instantly. Thank you!!"
— Samantha A., 1st Grade

"Rick has super energy and has so much to share. Please have Rick talk to all the teachers in our district!!! You give inspiration to our profession."
— Laura T., Mentor Teacher

"This was probably the best workshop I have ever participated in. Informative, useful, and based on research. The presenter is knowledgeable and entertaining — a very powerful combination."

— Barbara C., Mentor Teacher

"An exceptional workshop taught by a warm, confident, entertaining, and very wise presenter. Grace is passionate and powerful!"

— Matthew R.,
High School Music, 11th year

"I am saying this in all honesty: this is the best workshop I have been to! I will use so many things. I really enjoy your approach with the music, Frisbees, and juggling. You were fantastic. Thank you!"

— Jennifer G., 3rd Grade

"As a mentor and teacher I was beyond impressed and inspired by your session. I am excited to take what you presented in the session back into our classrooms."

— Amy P.,
High School Mentor Teacher

"Rick put into action what he was teaching us. Fabulous role model! Great workshop!"

— Karen W., 5th Grade

"Grace Dearborn has provided THE BEST instructional in-service I've ever attended."

— Tony D.,
High School English, 28th year

"I feel more equipped to have a happier, more productive classroom and year… I found the workshop to be great."

— Laura M., Middle School Spanish

"Best workshop I have attended! I've probably been to 10–12 in the past several years, on a wide range of topics, and this workshop was superior!"

— Paul K., High School English

"Wow! How can I even begin to thank you for such a wonderful workshop/ day?! I can't wait to try so many effective new teaching strategies! This was the most helpful and wonderful in-service ever!"

— Lisa G., Kindergarten, 17th year

"Grace was great! Never have I been so engaged in a workshop! Innovative and fun strategies that I will certainly use!"

— Susan S.,
High School Math/Science, 4th year

"Such a fast paced workshop — virtually no wasted time — wonderful, practical ideas."

— Kathy A., 4th grade

"As a 'teacher with no behavior issues in her classroom' I was reticent to come today, but I am very pleased that I did. I leave with a 'full plate' of strategies and the realization that I do have some behavior problems to address. Excellent presentation!"

— Annie W., High School Art,
11th year

"Realistic scenarios, timely injections of humor; sensitivity to various levels/ grades. Very valuable/useful presentation!!"

— Kevin T., Middle School

"Grace is bright. She is fun. She is hilarious. She knows the material. I love her! Its useful and this seminar was a great use of time."

— Matt S., Middle School
Math/Science, 1st year

"Rick is a wonder. I am taking so much back with me to share. This is the best I've heard in many years."

— Maria V.,
Elementary Mentor Teacher

To contact Rick or Grace about workshops and keynotes,
or to purchase books, videos, online courses, or other materials, find us at:

Conscious Teaching
21 Crest Road
Fairfax, CA 94930
mail@consciousteaching.com
www.consciousteaching.com
1.800.667.6062